A Guide to Computer
Applications in the Humanities

SUSAN HOCKEY

The Johns Hopkins University Press
Baltimore and London

First published in 1980 by
Gerald Duckworth & Co. Ltd
The Old Piano Factory
43 Gloucester Crescent, London NW1

First published in the United States of America in 1980 by
The Johns Hopkins University Press, Baltimore,
Maryland 21218
Johns Hopkins Paperbacks edition, 1983

Library of Congress Catalog Card Number 79-3378
ISBN 0-8018-2346-3 (hardcover)
ISBN 0-8018-2891-0 (paperback)

Contents

Preface   7

1. Introducing Computers   9
2. Input and Output   18
3. Word Indexes, Concordances and Dictionaries   41
4. Vocabulary Studies, Collocations and Dialectology   79
5. Morphological and Syntactic Analysis, Machine Translation   101
6. Stylistic Analysis and Authorship Studies   122
7. Textual Criticism   144
8. Sound Patterns   168
9. Indexing, Cataloguing and Information Retrieval   189
10. How to Start a Project   220

    Bibliography   230
    Glossary of computer terms   232
    Acronyms, abbreviations and program names   238
    Useful addresses   241
    Index   243

Preface

In recent years there has been considerable growth in the use of computers in arts research, but as yet there exists no introductory guide to the subject. This book is intended to fill such a need. It is based on a series of lectures given in Oxford, lectures which are mostly attended by those doing research in arts subjects. Chapters One and Two introduce many of the mysteries of the computer and may be skipped by those who are already familiar with the machine. The major areas of computer applications in literary research are covered in subsequent chapters, together with a general view of indexing, cataloguing and information retrieval for historical and bibliographical data. For those whose interest is awakened, the final chapter gives a brief guide on how to start a computer project in the academic world.

The examples of computer printout were produced on the ICL 1906A computer at Oxford University Computing Service, whose help I acknowledge. Kind permission has been granted by Professor A. Parpola to reproduce illustrations from *Materials for the Study of the Indus Valley Script*; by Professor J. Raben and Queen's College, Flushing, New York from the paper by Rubin in *Computer and the Humanities* Volume 4; by Edinburgh University Press from papers by de Tollenaere, Berry-Rogghe, Ott, Waite, Kiss, Armstrong, Milroy and Piper in *The Computer and Literary Studies*; by Edinburgh University Press and Minnesota University Press from papers by Berry-Rogghe and Wright in *Computers in the Humanities*; by the University of Wales Press from papers by Fortier and McConnell, Crawford, Shibayev and Raben and Lieberman in *The Computer in Literary and Linguistic Studies (Proceedings of the Third International Symposium)*; by the University of Waterloo Press from the paper by Joyce in *Computing in the Humanities*; by Mouton from papers by Cabaniss and Hirschmann in *Computer Studies in the Humanities and Verbal Behavior* Volume 3; by Terence D. Crawford and Glyn E. Jones from the *Bulletin of the Board of Celtic Studies*, Volume 3; by the American Philological Association from the paper by Packard in *Transactions of the American Philological Association* Volume 104; by Harvest House, from *It's Greek to the Computer* by Andrew Q. Morton and Alban D. Winspear; and by Cambridge University Press from R.L.

Widmann, 'The Computer in Historical Collation: Use of the IBM 360/75 in Collating Multiple Editions of *A Midsummer Night's Dream*' in *The Computer in Literary and Linguistic Research,* ed. R.A. Wisbey. The page from T.H. Howard-Hill (ed.), *The Merchant of Venice* (Oxford Shakespeare Concordance), appears by permission of the Oxford University Press. Illustrations by Shaw, Chisholm, Lance and Slemons are reprinted from *Computers and the Humanities* Volume 8 (1974) and 10 (1976) from the articles 'Statistical Analysis of Dialectal Boundaries', 'Phonological Patterning in German Verse' and 'The Use of the Computer in Plotting the Geographical Distribution of Dialect Items', copyright Pergamon Press Ltd. I acknowledge the assistance of the Association for Literary and Linguistic Computing from whose *Bulletin* several illustrations are reproduced.

Finally, I would like to thank Richard Newnham who first suggested the idea of this book to me after attending my lectures, Paul Griffiths and Lou Burnard of Oxford University Computing Service who commented on sections of the manuscript, T.H. Aston of the History of the University who provided some material and suggestions for Chapter Nine, Ewa Kus who assisted greatly with the typing of the manuscript, Marc Wentworth who provided the illustration of a Chinese character (Figure 2.7), and, above all, Alan Jones and my husband Martin who both read the entire manuscript and provided many valuable comments and suggestions.

Oxford, 1979   S.H.

1. Introducing Computers

The earliest computers were designed for scientific work and were created in such a way that numerical operations were the easiest to perform. Soon computers began to be used more in commerce and industry, when it was realised that a machine could handle large files of data, such as ledgers and payrolls, much faster than the human brain. Computer applications in the humanities have some similarities to those in industry. Both involve large amounts of information compared with scientific or mathematical data. Commercial and humanities applications are characterised by relatively simple procedures such as searching, sorting and counting, whereas the scientific applications, though often using much less data, frequently involve calculations which are much more complicated. In the sciences the growth of computer usage has enabled much more research to be done, as the computer has taken over the time-consuming tasks of performing long and complex calculations. This is no less true in the humanities, where the computer is now used to perform purely mechanical operations for which cards or slips of paper were previously used. However, it must never be forgotten that the computer is only a machine. It can only do what it is told to do, nothing more. Computers rarely, if ever, go wrong and produce erroneous results through malfunction. That, of course, is not to say that erroneous results never come out of a computer. Frequently they do, but they are the fault of the person who is using the computer who has given it incorrect instructions, not of the machine itself. In no way can the computer be blamed for errors; the designer of the computer system or the person using it is always the one at fault.

Instructions are presented to the computer in the form of a computer *program* (always spelt 'program'). The computer will then follow these instructions in logical sequence, performing them one by one. Therefore any problem which is to be solved by using a computer must be described in the form of a program. This involves breaking the problem down into very simple and completely unambiguous steps. At various stages in the problem a decision may need to be taken which depends on what is contained in the information to be processed. In such a case, the computer program will be so constructed that some parts of it will be executed if the answer to the decision is 'yes' and others if the answer is 'no'. The program may contain many such decisions. All must be worked out beforehand in logical sequence, a process which is known as constructing an *algorithm*. The same set of instructions may be executed many times over when a program is running. They are given only once in the program, together with an indication of how many times they are to be done.

A computer program may be compared to a cooking recipe, which includes a series of steps which must be followed in the correct order, but in minute detail, like:

Take some flour
Pour some flour on to the weighing scales until 4oz is registered
Put the flour in a bowl
Add a pinch of salt to the bowl
Take an egg
Break the egg into the bowl
Take some milk
Measure out the milk
If it is less than ½ pint add some more milk
Repeat the last instruction until there is ½ pint
Add the milk to the bowl
Mix thoroughly

The instructions are given in logical sequence. The repeated sequence of getting more milk or measuring the flour on the scales is exactly what might be found in a computer program.

Let us now consider the instructions for counting all the times the word 'and' occurs in a text. They would be something like:

Take the next word
Is it 'and'?
If it is not 'and' go back to get the next word
If it is 'and', add 1 to a counter and go back to get the next word
When all words have been processed, print out the number of 'and's.

The computer program is written in a symbolic form using a computer programming language, a highly artificial 'language' which is totally unambiguous. The computer operates with a very basic series of instructions, such as comparing characters or adding and subtracting numbers. To add up two numbers may require three or four of these basic instructions. Obviously writing programs in the basic instructions will take a long time, as so many are required. Therefore a series of what are called *high-level programming languages* were developed which require much less human programming effort to write. One instruction in a high-level language may be equivalent to five or more in the machine's basic instruction set. Other computer programs are used to translate from these high-level languages into the machine's basic instructions. This process is called *compilation* and the special programs to do this are called *compilers*. The most frequently used computer languages are FORTRAN and ALGOL for scientific work, and COBOL for commercial applications. Any of these three may be used in humanities work, or perhaps some of the more recently developed languages like PL/1, ALGOL68 or SNOBOL. Of these SNOBOL is particularly suitable for analysing information which is textual rather than numerical. Written in SNOBOL, the program given above would become

```
        &TRIM = 1
        & ANCHOR = 1
        LETTERS = 'ABCDEFGHIJKLMNOPQRSTUVWXYZ'
        WORDPAT = BREAK(LETTERS) SPAN(LETTERS) . WORD
MORE    CARD = INPUT              :F(PRINT)
AGAIN   CARD WORDPAT =            :F(MORE)
        IDENT(WORD,'AND')         :F(AGAIN)
        COUNT = COUNT + 1         :(AGAIN)
PRINT   OUTPUT = COUNT
END
```

Learning to program a computer is not at all difficult. On the contrary, it can be an amusing intellectual exercise, though one that demands the discipline of accurate logic. If the logic of a program is wrong, the computer will execute the program exactly as it is and do what it was actually asked to do, not what the programmer intended to ask it to do. 'Garbage in, garbage out' is a saying in computing which is always true, for the machine has no power of thought.

However, it is not always necessary to learn to program a computer in order to make use of it. In the early days of computing, it was soon realised that many people were writing what was essentially the same program and that effort was being duplicated. Instead they collaborated, and the result was a number of general-purpose computer programs called *packages*. Each will perform a variety of related functions, and the user has only to present his data and a few simple instructions specifying which of the functions he would like to perform on the data. More and more packages have been written in recent years. For humanities applications, one such package, called COCOA, makes word counts and concordances of texts. There are others like FAMULUS and INFOL which sort and catalogue the kind of information that is traditionally held on file cards, and others again which deal with some aspects of literary analysis. Each package has its own series of instructions, and it takes only a matter of an hour or so to learn to use them successfully.

There are a number of different kinds of computers. Each computer manufacturer has its own series of machines, such as IBM 370 and ICL 2900. The size and power of the computers in each series or range of machines may vary considerably. Within one machine range, computers are mostly compatible with one another. That is, a program written for a small computer in the range will also work on a larger one. Programs can usually be moved from one range of computer to another if they are written in a high-level programming language, for they can be recompiled into the basic instruction set of the second machine. The most common compilers are those for FORTRAN and COBOL. Except for the small or mini computers, there are very few machines which do not support at least one of these. Some of the other programming languages are not always available on every kind of computer. For this reason, computer packages – at least those used in the academic world – are usually written in FORTRAN, which is the most widely used academic language. The packages are not compiled every time they are used: that would be a waste of computer time. Instead they are kept in a form which is already compiled, known as *binary*.

Large computers, such as those found in university computer centres, can perform several different programs at the same time and can also organise queues of programs waiting to run. To do this, the operation of the computer is controlled by a large program called an *operating system*. This in effect organises the work flow through the machine, the aim being to utilise its resources efficiently. The faster the machine can be made to work, the more programs it can process. Some computer centres may employ two or three programmers whose job is just to look after the operating system and ensure that it is working smoothly. At the other end of the scale, there has been much growth recently in the use of *minicomputers*. These are much smaller computers and are usually dedicated to performing one task only. Such machines, if they are serving only one purpose, do not need an operating system to control them, and are frequently programmed in their basic instructions, not in a high-level language. Smaller still are *microprocessors*, computer memory which can be programmed to perform simple functions, rather like powerful programmable calculators.

The popular image of a computer, as seen in films and on the television, is one of metal cabinets, tapes whizzing round and a very clinical atmosphere of polished floors and a few human operators looking somewhat out of place. A computer is not just one machine, but a collection of machines which are all linked together to perform the various functions necessary to computing. In fact, most of the equipment visible in a computer room is concerned with getting information into and out of the computer rather than actually processing it. These are various devices for computer *input* and *output* and will be described in more detail in the next chapter. Information which is being processed is held in the computer's main memory, one or more of the metal cabinets. The processing itself is done in the arithmetic or logical unit and the results transferred back to the main memory before being printed. Collectively, the machinery in a computer room is called the *hardware*. The programs which operate in the machinery are called the *software*.

Most people who use computers have no knowledge at all of the electronics which make them work. This is the domain of the engineers and hardware experts whose job it is to ensure that the machinery itself is functioning as it should. If it is miswired it will give wrong answers, but this is very unlikely to happen, as a number of special test programs are run after any changes to the hardware and to ensure that it is working correctly. The ordinary user may be curious enough to discover that all information is held in the computer as patterns of binary digits which are called *bits*. Conventionally they are represented by 1s and 0s, but they are really electronic pulses. The computer's memory is divided up into a large number of cells. The number of bits per cell is always constant on one machine, but it may vary from machine to machine. The cells are always called *words* in computer terminology, which is confusing for those who want to analyse text with real words on the computer. Computer storage is measured in units of 1024 words, one unit of which is called a *K*. The actual amount of storage, of course, depends on the number of bits per word. For example a computer of 96K 24-bit words would be a medium-sized machine.

Some ranges of computers, such as ICL 2900s or IBM 360s and 370s, use a different measurement of storage, which is called a *byte*. One byte has eight bits and can be used to represent one character. There are 256 possible combinations of 1s and 0s in eight bits, and so these 'byte' machines can use up to 256 different characters. In practice this number is usually lower, because the machinery used to input material to the computer may not permit so many different characters. Computers whose storage is measured in words tend to use only six bits to represent characters. This means that their character set has only 64 different symbols, as there are 64 possible combinations of six bits. These would normally include upper case letters, digits and a few punctuation and mathematical symbols. By using special symbols and an ingenious program, it is possible to retain the distinction between upper and lower case letters on these machines. On the other hand, because their character set is larger, byte machines have upper and lower case letters as normal characters.

Computer people are fond of jargon. They have names for every part of the computer, whether it is hardware or software. We have already seen that programming languages and packages have names which will not have been encountered elsewhere. Most of these are acronyms such as:

FORTRAN   for FORmula TRANslation

COBOL   for COmmon Business Oriented Language

SNOBOL   for StriNg Oriented symBOlic Language

COCOA   for word COunt and COncordance generation on Atlas

Others are even more naive. PL/1 is merely Programming Language 1, although it was by no means the first to be designed. The computer user must unfortunately acquire some of this jargon. Terms like 'input' and 'output' soon become commonplace to him. If he moves to work on another kind of computer he will find that a different set of terminology is in use for what are essentially the same features. The names of the programming languages and other packages do not change, but many other terms do. Computer people often call their computer 'the machine' and refer to it and its programs as 'the system'. 'The system' has come to be used also to refer to any other set of programs and is a common and ambiguous term in computing. 'The system is down' means that for some reason the computer is not working. It may be hardware problems – that is, something wrong with the physical machinery – or it may be software – that is, a user or operator has given some instructions to the operating system which it cannot understand and cannot detect as an error. When the computer stops working in this way, it is frequently said to 'crash'. This does not mean that any machinery has literally crashed to the floor, merely that it has come to a sudden halt. It may take from a few minutes to a few hours to start it again, depending on the nature of the fault.

The physical environment which is required for computers helps to maintain their aura of mystique. A large computer generates a lot of heat and would soon burn up if it was not kept in an air-conditioned atmosphere. It also requires a constant relative humidity, so that excess moisture does not damage the circuitry. Dust can obviously do a lot of harm to such delicate electronics, and therefore computer rooms must be very clean. Computer room floors always consist of a series of tiles, as many cables are required to connect the various pieces of machinery. These are usually laid under the floor, which needs to be easily accessible for maintenance. When several million pounds worth of equipment is at stake, it is essential to take such precautions. In contrast, minicomputers can often work without the need for the air-conditioned environment. In fact some are even used on North Sea oil rigs.

Early computers had splendid names like ENIAC, EDSAC, ORION, MERCURY and ATLAS. The current fashion is for merely a series of numbers after the manufacturers name or initials. The early computers were much less powerful than our present-day ones, but they were physically much bigger in relation to their power. Modern technology has reduced the physical size of computer storage to a fraction of what it was in the days even of ATLAS, which was in use until 1973.

To conclude our introduction to computers, we can briefly survey the beginnings of computing in the humanities. When Father Roberto Busa began to make plans for the first computer-aided project in the humanities in 1949, the possibilities must have seemed very different from now. Busa set out to compile a complete word index and concordance to the works of Thomas Aquinas, some eight million words in all. He also planned to include material from related authors, bringing the total number of words to over ten million. Initially he had thought of using file cards for what was to be his life's work. In 1951 he began to direct the transfer of texts to punched cards, which were then virtually the only means of computer input. In 1973 the first volume of his massive work appeared. Further volumes of the series have appeared in quick succession, and the 60-odd volumes are now almost complete. It may seem a long time before publication, but it would not have been possible to attempt such a mammoth undertaking without substantial mechanical help.

Busa's project illustrates the oldest and still the most widely used and reliable computer application in literary research, the simple mechanical function of compiling a word index or concordance of a text. Such concordances were of course made many years before computers were invented. Many researchers devoted their lives to producing what is essentially a tool for others to use. Busa led the way, but he was soon followed by a number of scholars, who also investigated the possibility of using a computer to compile indexes of texts. One of the earliest workers in Britain was Professor R.A. Wisbey who, when he was at Cambridge, produced word indexes to a number of Early Middle High German texts in the early 1960s. Wisbey has continued his work since moving to King's College, London, and although his early work was published in book form his latest computer concordance is published on microfiche.

Across the Atlantic a number of scholars in the field of English studies began to make concordances which were published in a series by Cornell University. In Holland, Felicien de Tollenaere also made plans in the early 1960s for a word index to the Gothic Bible, which was published in 1976. In

France, Bernard Quémada and a group of others started work on the Trésor de la Langue Française, an enormous undertaking which would not be possible without the help of a computer. There was also much early interest in word indexing in Pisa. By the middle 60s, the lone pioneer of Busa had been followed by a number of other scholars, who found that the computer was not just a tool for the scientist but could provide much of the mechanical assistance they too needed in their work.

Other applications of computers were soon realised and exploited. Cataloguing and indexing are again mechanical functions. Once it has been decided into which category an item should be placed, the sorting and merging of files is purely mechanical. One of the earliest computer applications was the recataloguing of the pre-1920 material in the Bodleian Library, Oxford. The introduction of modern methods in archaeology has included the use of computers for cataloguing and classification of artefacts, as well as statistical calculations of frequencies of objects found. Some lawyers were early computer users too. As early as 1962, they realised the possibility of using a computer to search large files of legal material to find the documents relevant to a specific case.

The examination of features of an author's style, provided that those features can be defined unambiguously, was seen to be a further application. The Swede, Ellegard, in his study of the *Junius Letters* was the first to use a computer for stylistic analysis; but in 1960, when he was working, machines could not cope with the large quantity of text he wanted to analyse and he used the computer only to do the calculations. Mosteller and Wallace soon followed his lead in their study of the *Federalist Papers* and they used a computer to count the words as well. Meanwhile in Britain a Scottish clergyman named Andrew Morton had publicised the use of computers in authorship studies in several books and articles on Paul's epistles, and had attracted the attention of the newspapers. Everyone knew, or thought that they knew, that the computer could be used to solve problems of disputed authorship. In many authorship studies we shall see that the computer can be used to find much more evidence than could be done manually. Once the programs have been written, they can be run many times on different material for comparative purposes.

From these early beginnings there has been a large growth in the use of computers in the humanities in the last ten years. Many more applications have now been developed in the fields of textual criticism and poetic analysis, as well as concordancing, cataloguing and stylistic analysis. Some are being performed by standard packages, such as COCOA, which are simple to use and readily available in university computer centres. In other cases the researchers have learnt to program the computer themselves. This has allowed them much more flexibility and in addition has involved them in new disciplines which many have found stimulating. In all cases the results are much more comprehensive than could ever have been obtained by hand.

REFERENCES

1. Roberto Busa, Complete Index Verborum of the Works of St Thomas. *Speculum* 25 (1950) 424-5

2. Murray Laver, *An Introduction to the Uses of Computers*. Cambridge Computer Science Texts 5. Cambridge: Cambridge University Press (1976)

3. Ben Ross Schneider, *Travels in Computerland: Or Incompatibilities and Interfaces*. Reading, Mass: Addison-Wesley (1974)

2. Input and Output

Before any information can be analysed by computer, it must first be transcribed into a form which the computer can read, and this almost invariably means that it has to be typed out on one of the computer's input devices. These devices, like the computer itself, have only a limited character set. As we have seen on some computers, and particularly on older machines, the character set consists of only 64 graphic symbols. This is the case on ICL 1900 and CDC 6600/7600 computers. IBM 360/370 and ICL 2900 computers are byte machines and allow a total of 256 different characters. But however many characters any particular computer has, the graphic symbols it uses to read and print these characters are not ideally suited to representing literary material.

Special computer input devices do exist for representing literary material and for languages which are not written in the Roman alphabet, but these are not widely available and so we must consider the situation where only standard equipment can be used. Input is the most time-consuming part of handling a text by computer. Great care must be taken to ensure that the text is adequately represented so that the effort involved in preparing a text for the computer analysis is not wasted because insufficient information has been included.

It is highly unlikely that a computer whose character set includes French accents, German umlaut or Spanish tilde will be available; but if any of these characters appear in the text, they should also appear in the computer transcription of the text. If they are omitted, the computer will be unable to distinguish words which should be distinguished. It would, for example, treat the French preposition *à* as identical with the verb *a*, part of *avoir*. Therefore some of the mathematical symbols must be used to denote such diacritical marks. In French an asterisk * could perhaps be used for an acute accent and a number sign # for a grave accent. A circumflex could be represented by an *at* symbol @ and a cedilla by a £ or $ sign, provided these symbols exist on the computer to be used. The French word *à* would then appear to the computer as A#. The accent may, if desired, be typed before the letter, giving #A. It does not matter which of these is chosen, provided the same conventions are used all the way through the text. Once A# has been chosen to represent *à*, A# must always be given, never #A.

Special symbols must also be used to denote a change from upper to lower case if the computer only possesses a character set of 64 symbols. Preserving the distinction between upper and lower case has been considered unnecessary by some people, and indeed many texts have been prepared for computer use without it; but it may be essential in some languages, for example, to distinguish proper names. It is often advisable to use one symbol to indicate a capital letter at the start of a sentence and another to indicate a capital at the start of a proper name. Both symbols would be given when a sentence begins with a proper name. If $ was used for a proper name and % for a capital at the start of a sentence, 'Jack and Jill went up the hill' would be coded for a 64 character set computer as follows:

%$JACK AND $JILL WENT UP THE HILL

and 'The cat sat on the mat' would appear as

%THE CAT SAT ON THE MAT

where letters which have no preceding symbol represent lower case. On a computer with 256 characters, which therefore distinguishes lower case letters, it may still be advisable to identify proper names with some special symbol. The computer could then distinguish the town Reading from the verbal form 'reading' in the following sentence

Reading is boring.

Four lines of poetry coded for an upper case only computer would appear as

%YES. %I REMEMBER $ADLESTROP £
%THE NAME, BECAUSE ONE AFTERNOON
%OF HEAT THE EXPRESS–TRAIN DREW UP THERE
%UNWONTEDLY. %IT WAS LATE $JUNE.

Here we are using % to represent a capital at the beginning of a line or sentence, $ at the beginning of a proper name and £ for a long dash, another symbol which the computer does not have.

Coding texts which are written in the Roman alphabet therefore involves upper case letters, proper names, diacritics and unusual punctuation; but it is not too difficult to deal with these. More problems arise with languages which are not written in the Roman alphabet. They must first be transliterated into the computer's character set. In Greek, for example, the letter *a* is usually denoted by A, *β* by B, *γ* by G etc. The Greek letter *θ* is conventionally transliterated as 'th' as that is the sound it represents, but in transcribing for computer input, it would be more sensible to choose a single symbol to represent each Greek letter. Q could be used for *θ*, Y for *ψ*, F for *φ*, etc. A Greek word such as *θεος* would then appear in computer Greek as QEOS. Many Greek texts prepared for computer analysis have included symbols to mark accents, breathings and capitals, in fact all the possible diacritical marks. This may well lead to a text which appears cluttered with non-alphabetical characters, but no information will have been discarded. It is a very simple operation to ask the computer to delete all the instances of a particular character, but it takes much longer to insert them afterwards. The first four lines of the *Iliad* are given below with the coding for every diacritic

$M5HNIN 24AEIDE, QE4A, $PHLH7I2ADEW 2$ACIL5HOS
O2ULOM4ENHN, 36H MUR4I' 2$ACAIO5IS 24ALGE' 24EQHKE,
POLL6AS D' 2IFQ4IMOUS YUC6AS 24$A7IDI PRO47IAYEN
3HR4WWN, A2UTO6US D6E 3EL4WRIA TE5UCE K4UNESSIN

With many of the diacritics removed, the text becomes clearer to read

$MHNIN AEIDE, QEA, $PHLHIADEW $ACILHOS
OULOMENHN, 3H MURI' $ACAIOIS ALGE' EQHKE,
POLLAS D' IFQIMOUS YUCAS $AIDI PROIAYEN
3HRWWN, AUTOUS DE 3ELWRIA TEUCE KUNESSIN

but in this form some of the information is lost. It takes a classical scholar only a matter of a few minutes to learn the computer transcription of Greek.

The Russian alphabet has thirty-three letters in the modern script and is really too long for only one computer character to be used for each Russian letter. Characters must be reserved for the ten digits and all possible punctuation symbols and there are then very few characters left to identify such features as capital letters and foreign words. It might just be possible to fit them in, but it is quite feasible to use more than one computer character to represent a single character within the text, provided the computer is programmed to recognise this. The Russian letter ц could then be transliterated as TS and я as YA.

Semitic languages such as Arabic and Hebrew are written from right to left, but in transliteration they are typed into the computer from left to right. There would be no sense in typing the text backwards, as special programming would then be necessary to read it backwards. The vocalisation is normally omitted from Hebrew and Arabic texts, and it can usually be omitted from the computer text. Neither of these languages has capital letters as we know them in European scripts. Hebrew is therefore a simple case because the alphabet is short, only twenty-two letters. The five letters which have different form at the end of a word could be coded in the same way as the normal form, as they have no semantic significance. If ever it were required to print out the material in Hebrew script, the computer could be programmed to recognise that, for example, a letter N at the end of a word is always a final form.

The Arabic alphabet and its derivatives have more letters, and each of these has four different forms, depending on where it occurs within a word, whether it is the first letter, last letter, one in the middle or one standing on its own. The total number of characters then required is somewhere in the region of 130 plus numerals. Fortunately there is no punctuation in classical Arabic and it is of only doubtful validity in the modern language, and so it can be ignored for computer coding. Though for some computers it would be theoretically possible to code all these letter forms as different computer symbols, the normal method adopted has been to use the same computer character to denote each of the four forms of the same letter. The rules for writing Arabic script are so rigid that the computer can be programmed to transcribe it back into the original script if necessary.

Most alphabetic scripts can be dealt with in the ways that have been described. Devanagari has some forty-eight symbols, but a two-character code has been devised without much difficulty. Chinese and Japanese present more problems. One possibility for Japanese is to use the syllabic form of katakana, but this loses the visual representation of the text completely. In coding Chinese, the most sensible procedure is to allocate a number to each Chinese character and record the text digitally. The number could perhaps be accompanied by a transliteration. More than one computer project on Chinese has used the Standard Chinese Telegraph Codes.

When preparing a text for the computer, it is always important to include as much information as possible. Even if it is not all required at once, it may be needed in the future, by other people as well as by the one who originally prepared the text. A small pilot study should always be carried out first. Even a few lines of text prepared in the chosen format should suffice to experiment with particular programs before a large batch is prepared. Foreign words or quotations should be considered with care, particularly if a word index or concordance is to be made. For example, the word *his* in the Latin phrase *in his moribus* which appeared as a quotation in a text should not be listed in a word index under the English word *his*. This would happen unless the computer were told by some identifying symbol that the Latin was a quotation. Similarly if there are lacunae or other omissions in a text, they should be indicated in some way. Otherwise, for example, in Latin the letters 'in' followed by a lacuna would be listed with all the occurrences of *in,* whereas they may be the beginning of a totally different word. It may also be necessary to include information about changes of type faces, for example in a study of printing.

A text must contain reference identifiers in some form so that any features which the computer may find can be located in the original text. This may be done either by giving the line number and other identifiers on each line of text or by using special symbols to enclose reference identifiers within the text. Each identifier would then refer to all the text which follows it until another identifier is encountered. When the latter method is used, the computer can also be programmed to keep track of the line numbers in the text.

Transcribing the material into the computer's character set is only the first part of preparing a text in computer readable form. The transcribed or transliterated text must then be typed on to a suitable computer input medium.

The traditional input media of punched cards and paper tape are not now as universally used as they once were, but we should begin by describing these. A punched card is simply a piece of card $3\frac{1}{4}$ inches high by $7\frac{3}{8}$ inches wide, which is divided into eighty columns vertically and twelve rows horizontally. Special keyboard devices, called *card punches*, are used to make patterns of rectangular holes in the columns. Each column is used to represent one character and normally holes are punched in up to three of the rows for each character. The example in Figure 2.1 shows the letters of the alphabet and numerals represented on a punched card. Different kinds of computers use different patterns of holes to represent each character. These are known as card codes and have names like BCD and EBCDIC. The letters and numerals normally have the same card code on all computers, but some of the punctuation and mathematical symbols ('special characters') may have different codes. If information is to be transferred from one computer to another on punched cards, it is advisable to enquire about card codes before starting. Most computer installations have utility programs to translate from 'foreign' card codes.

Only upper case letters can be represented with any ease on punched cards. The card-punching machines usually print the characters which the holes represent along the top of each card, as you can see from the reproduction of a card in Figure 2.1. This is only for visual recognition: the input device only reads the holes. It is possible to make a copy of a deck of cards on a machine called a card *reproducer*. Only the holes will be copied. If the printing is also required, the cards must then be fed through another machine called an *interpreter* which reads the holes and interprets them into characters which it prints along the top.

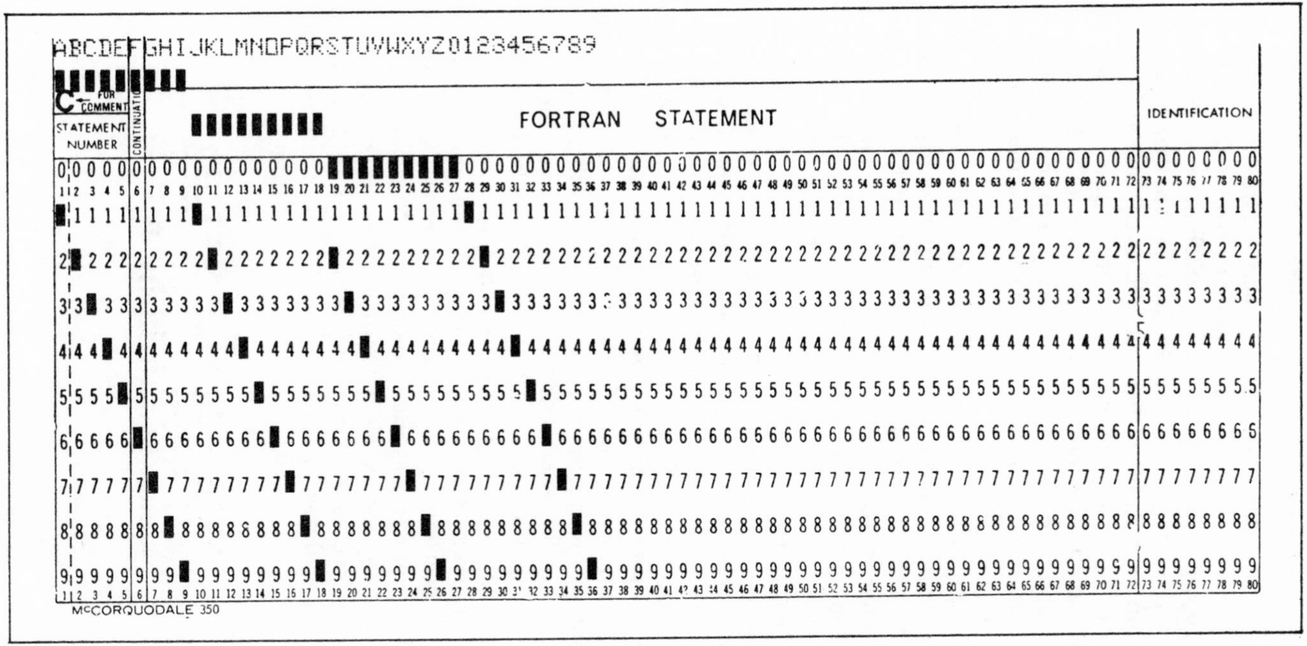

Figure 2.1. A punched card showing the letters and numerals.

Accuracy is of vital importance when typing any material for the computer. One way of checking punched cards is for a second typist to retype them using a card *verifier*. Cards which have already been punched are fed into the verifier, which looks like another card punch. The information on each card is then retyped over the card, and if identical characters are typed a small incision is made into the side of the card. Those cards which have no incision can be checked manually and any discrepancy noted and corrected if necessary. This method is quite effective when two different typists are used, but if the same mistake is made twice it goes unnoticed.

The chief disadvantage of punched cards is that they occupy a lot of room for storage. One card holds a maximum of eighty characters; but it is usually much less, as information is rarely typed to the end of a card. Unused columns on the right are read as blanks, and a program can be instructed to ignore them. One box of 2000 cards is 14 inches long and it would take over forty boxes to hold the complete works of Shakespeare. Error correction is however fairly simple, as usually only one card needs to be repunched and the offending card can be thrown away.

Paper tape has two advantages over punched cards: it occupies less room for storage, and it can represent lower case letters as well as upper case. Most paper tape now in use is 1 inch wide. It has a maximum of eight possible holes across the tape and is therefore known as 8-hole tape or 8-track tape. A row of tiny holes between the fifth and sixth track simply holds the tape in the tape-punching or tape-reading machine. These are known as the sprocket holes. The tape punching machine is a special kind of typewriter, sometimes called a *flexowriter*. It can be used either to punch new tape or to read what is already on a tape, which it does by interpreting the pattern of holes and typing the corresponding characters on a sheet or roll of paper inserted in it. Figure 2.2 shows a piece of paper tape containing the capital letters and numerals.

Only seven of the tracks are actually used to represent each character. The eighth is known as the *parity track*, which is a kind of checking device. The piece of tape shown here is even parity, i.e. there is always an even

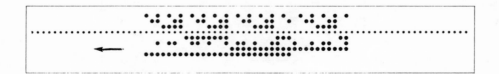

Figure 2.2. A strip of paper tape showing the capital letters and numerals. The arrow indicates the direction of reading the tape.

number of holes for each character. A hole is punched in the eighth track when necessary to make an even number. If the tape reader is working in even parity and encounters a character with an odd number of holes, it has detected an error and stops. It is normally necessary to leave a foot or so of blank tape with only the sprocket holes punched at either end of a paper tape so that it can easily be fed into a reader. This blank tape is called *runout*, and it is always advisable to be generous with it. Like cards, there are many different paper tape codes, each using a different pattern of holes to represent the characters. There are also other widths of paper tape, usually either 5- or 7-track.

The chief disadvantage of paper tape is error correction. Using a flexowriter, the tape must be copied on to a new tape. When an error is reached, the flexowriter is stopped, the correction typed on to the new tape and the old tape repositioned at the start of the next correct section. Alternatively sections of corrected tape can be spliced or glued into the original. These tasks are very laborious and frequently lead to more errors, but they must be undertaken in order to obtain a clean error-free tape. It is for this reason that paper tape is now little used in this manner. If it is used at all, the tape complete with errors is fed into the computer and the errors are corrected, by use of a terminal, as will be described later.

Cards and paper tape are read into the computer via peripheral devices, known as *card readers* and *tape readers*. Card readers can process up to one thousand cards per minute, and the speed of tape readers is in the order of one thousand characters per second. The computer stores up the information for later use, and after being read the cards or tape pile up in a hopper or bin and can be retrieved for further use.

The most common means of obtaining information from a computer is by printing it on what is called a *lineprinter*, so called because it prints one whole line at a time. An example of lineprinter output is shown in Figure 2.3. The reason why this printing appears somewhat ugly is that the machine normally prints at well over a thousand lines per minute. The type face varies from one computer to another, but all have rather inelegant characters. Most lineprinters have only a limited character set, frequently only upper case letters, numerals and punctuation symbols. The size of the paper used for printing varies from one installation to another. The width is usually 120, 132 or 160 characters across the page and there are ten characters to an inch. At the normal spacing of six lines per inch, 66 lines can be accommodated on the most frequently used size of paper page. At eight lines per inch the printing becomes very squashed, as seen in Figure 2.4; but some centres now print at this spacing to save paper consumption. The holes down the side of the paper are there merely to hold it in the lineprinter. Computer paper is always folded in a concertina fashion and the folds are perforated so that each separate document or piece of output

```
REMEMBER ME WHEN I AM GONE AWAY,
GONE FAR AWAY INTO THE SILENT LAND:
WHEN YOU CAN NO MORE HOLD.ME BY THE HAND,
NOR I HALF TURN TO GO YET TURNING STAY.
REMEMBER ME WHEN NO MORE DAY BY DAY
YOU TELL ME OF OUR FUTURE THAT YOU PLANNED:
ONLY REMEMBER ME; YOU UNDERSTAND
IT WILL BE LATE TO COUNSEL THEN OR PRAY.
YET IF YOU SHOULD FORGET ME FOR A WHILE
AND AFTERWARDS REMEMBER, DO NOT GRIEVE:
FOR IF THE DARKNESS AND CORRUPTION LEAVE
A VESTIGE OF THE THOUGHTS THAT I ONCE HAD,
BETTER BY FAR YOU SHOULD FORGET AND SMILE
THAN THAT YOU SHOULD REMEMBER AND BE SAD.
```

Figure 2.3. Upper case lineprinter printing at the normal spacing of six lines per inch.

```
REMEMBER ME WHEN I AM GONE AWAY,
GONE FAR AWAY INTO THE SILENT LAND:
WHEN YOU CAN NO MORE HOLD ME BY THE HAND,
NOR I HALF TURN TO GO YET TURNING STAY.
REMEMBER ME WHEN NO MORE DAY BY DAY
YOU TELL ME OF OUR FUTURE THAT YOU PLANNED:
ONLY REMEMBER ME; YOU UNDERSTAND
IT WILL BE LATE TO COUNSEL THEN OR PRAY.
YET IF YOU SHOULD FORGET ME FOR A WHILE
AND AFTERWARDS REMEMBER, DO NOT GRIEVE:
FOR IF THE DARKNESS AND CORRUPTION LEAVE
A VESTIGE OF THE THOUGHTS THAT I ONCE HAD,
BETTER BY FAR YOU SHOULD FORGET AND SMILE
THAN THAT YOU SHOULD REMEMBER AND BE SAD.
```

Figure 2.4. Lineprinter printing at eight lines per inch.

can be torn off. Many installations use paper which is striped across the page. The stripes are to assist the reader. When, for example, rows of numbers are printed in columns across the page, the stripes guide the reader to see which numbers are in the same row. They are not necessary for the computer, and plain paper can be used just as well. Gas bills, electricity bills and bank statements are now printed by computer, and special pre-printed stationery is used on the lineprinter. If several copies of some printout are required, special stationery can be used which is carbon-backed to make two, three or even four copies at one printing.

Some lineprinters have upper and lower case letters and can give a more pleasing appearance to the printout than an upper case only machine; but even so the quality of the printout they produce is barely suitable for publication. The characters which they print will still not include accents and diacritics which are necessary to reproduce some textual material. Neither will they cater for any change of type fount – into bold or italic, perhaps. It is possible to have special characters made for a lineprinter so that it will print accents, but these are very expensive. It will be seen later that there are other, much better, means of producing output direct from a computer when a final copy suitable for publication is required, but the lineprinter is the normal method of computer output and will certainly need to be used to obtain results at an intermediate stage.

Output can also be obtained from a computer on punched cards or paper tape. This could perhaps be necessary if information is to be transferred to another computer, but it would only be feasible for small amounts of data. There are much better ways of transferring larger quantities of information.

Magnetic tape and *disc* provide the means for storing large amounts of information inside a computer and, in the case of magnetic tape, for transferring information from one computer to another. Suppose that a researcher had laboriously prepared the whole of the plays of Shakespeare on to punched cards and then wanted to perform several different analyses on this material. It would be nonsensical to attempt to feed all those boxes of cards into the computer for each analysis. The obvious solution would be to feed them in once and then store the text on some magnetic media, such as tape or disc. The computer can then access the information on the tape or disc much faster than it can from cards, and the operator is relieved of the cumbersome chore of handling cards.

Magnetic tape looks very much like tape-recorder tape and behaves in a similar manner. It is normally half-an-inch wide and is wound on reels which hold up to 2400 feet of tape. A computer installation may possess many thousands of tapes, but only a few would be in use at any one time. When they are being used, the tapes are mounted on a tape deck which has special heads, which either read the information recorded on the tape, i.e. transfer it to the core store or memory of the computer, or write new information on to the tape from the store. When new information is written to a tape, it overwrites and consequently erases what was there before, just as a tape-recorder does. Therefore care must be taken not to erase or overwrite information which is required. One way of ensuring that this does not happen is to use what is called a *write permit ring*, a plastic ring which can be inserted in the back of a tape reel. Information can only be written to the tape when this ring is in place.

The information is recorded on the tape in a series of rows of magnetised spots across the tape. Each magnetised spot represents a bit and tapes can have seven bits across the tape or more frequently nine bits. The seven bits, or 7-track tape as it is called, can be used to represent one 6-bit character per row, with the extra spot being used to check parity, just as in the case of paper tape. In the case of 9-track tape, eight spots or bits are used to represent data (e.g. one byte) and the ninth track is a parity track. Information is transferred to and from the tape in sections known as blocks. Between each block there is a gap of $\frac{1}{2}$ or $\frac{3}{4}$ inch. It is therefore more economical to write large-size blocks of, say, 4000 or 8000 characters rather than to write blocks of individual 80-character *card images*, as they are called.

The amount of information which can be stored on a magnetic tape depends on the block size used when the material is written. It also depends on the density at which the information is recorded. On 7-track tape the information can be recorded at 200, 556 or 800 rows per inch, commonly known as bits per inch, abbreviated to *bpi*. On 9-track tape the recording density is 800bpi or 1600 or it can now be even higher. Different tape decks are usually required to read 7- and 9-track tapes, and some tape decks may not be able to read certain densities. It is therefore essential to obtain some technical information about magnetic tape formats before attempting to transfer information from one computer to another on magnetic tape. The technical details may be difficult for the new user to understand; but before attempting to copy the material on to the tape, he should always remember to ask the people at the computer centre which is going to read the information what format of magnetic tape it can read. If a user turns up at the computer centre carrying a magnetic tape which has no technical specifications – these are normally written on a sticky label on the outside of the reel – the centre will not be very helpful until more information is supplied about the format of the tape.

Magnetic tapes are easily damaged. They must be kept in the air-conditioned atmosphere of the computer room and will deteriorate if left in the hot atmosphere of a study or office. However, they will withstand being in the post for some time, for example crossing the Atlantic by surface mail. If a tape becomes scratched, the tape deck will be unable to read the section which is scratched and in many cases will stop dead so that the information which comes after the scratch is also inaccessible. Tapes can also deteriorate over a long period of time. It is therefore essential for at least two copies to be kept of material which is stored on magnetic tape. If one becomes damaged, or 'fails', as the technical term is, the information is preserved on the copy and can then be restored to another tape. It is advisable to keep at least three copies of material, such as a text archive, which has taken a long time to prepare. Most computer centres have a utility program which makes copies of magnetic tapes. It is sensible to run this program every time more data has been added to a tape.

Tapes are normally identified by a serial number or name. The computer centre will allocate some tapes to a user, who will know their numbers or names, so that his program may request the correct tape; but he will probably never see his tapes. The computer operators will be instructed by the computer to load the tape on to a tape deck when a program requests it. They will then take the tape out of the rack, mount it on the appropriate deck and return it to the rack when the program has finished. Loading and unloading tapes are in fact the chief occupations of operators in modern computer centres.

If magnetic tape can be compared with tape-recorder tape, magnetic disc could perhaps be said to resemble gramophone records. A magnetic disc is really a series of discs stacked one on top of another with a gap of about an inch between each. They are all mounted together on a vertical spindle. Exchangeable discs can be removed from the spindle or replaced as required and they are sometimes called disc packs. Typical sizes of exchangeable discs hold thirty million, sixty million, one hundred million or two hundred million characters. The speed of access of information from magnetic disc is much faster than that from a tape. Information on a magnetic tape must be read and written serially; i.e. to read from or write to any part of the tape, all the preceding information on the tape must first be read. It takes up to five minutes for a reel of tape to be wound from one end to the other. On the other hand, it is quite feasible to access information randomly on disc. Each disc spins rapidly and a read head is positioned wherever it is required. Normally a disc would contain several or many sets of information, and these are called *files*. Each file may have been written serially, as if it were a tape; or it could have been set up in such a way that any part of it could be accessed without all the preceding information having to be read.

Discs have many advantages over magnetic tape, but unfortunately they are not cheap. The computer centre may have what appears to be a large number of discs and disc drives, but the user will find that they are in constant use, as all the files which are most frequently used by the computer itself are kept on disc. There will not be very much space left for the user to store large quantities of text. He may well be allocated some disc space for small files of data; but once this gets large or full, he will be requested to use magnetic tapes instead.

Fixed discs and drums may also be used as storage devices. The average access times for these is even faster than for exchangeable disc, but there is usually much less space available, particularly on drums. These are not usually available to users at all, but are employed to store files which are constantly in use by the operating system.

Another means of transferring information in and out of computers is by *teletype* terminal. These are being used more and more frequently and are the basis of *on-line* or *interactive* working, where the user communicates directly with the computer from his own keyboard and it responds to him immediately, thus creating a dialogue between the two. A teletype resembles a typewriter and holds paper which allows up to eighty characters across the page. Some teletypes have upper and lower case letters and look like electric typewriters; others have a more restricted character set, like a card punch, and operate only in upper case letters. If necessary, teletypes can be equipped with a special keyboard and character set for typing foreign languages, thus solving some of the problems of transliteration or transcription of input. Although the teletype may have a non-standard character set, what is transmitted to the computer consists of only a pattern of bits. If this pattern of bits is sent to another device for output, such as the lineprinter, it may well appear as a completely different graphic symbol.

The teletype is a somewhat noisy device, though it does have the advantage of providing the user with a piece of paper recording his dialogue with the computer. Another kind of computer terminal is a *visual display unit*, or VDU. A VDU is a small video screen with a keyboard attached. The characters which the user or the computer types appear on the screen, which will hold about twenty lines of text. Some VDUs have a tiny computer memory inside them which allows corrections to be made to a screenful of data before it is transmitted to the computer. Others simply roll the text up the screen as more information is typed at the bottom, so that what is typed gradually disappears from view, though the computer will not have forgotten it. The VDU is quiet – uncannily so in some respects. Like the teletype it can be fitted with a special keyboard. The shapes of the characters it displays are stored on a small electronic chip, and a chip containing any one of many alphabets could be used to display Russian or Greek letters on the screen. Combined with an appropriate keyboard, this makes input of non-Roman alphabets much simpler.

Teletype terminals or VDUs can be situated many miles away from the computer, being linked to it via a telephone line. They can be used in the home if there is another piece of equipment, called a *modem*, which links the telephone to the terminal. The user dials the computer's telephone number and when it replies – automatically, of course – he puts the telephone handset into the modem box, presses a button and is ready to start a computer session. High-speed telephone lines are being used more and more to link one computer to another. A card reader and lineprinter, say in Cambridge, could be used as what is called a *remote job entry* station (RJE terminal) to a computer in Edinburgh. The cards would be fed through a reader in Cambridge, the program run in Edinburgh and the results printed back in Cambridge. In the UK, at least, the university computer centres are linked up in this way in order to pool their resources and give extra benefit to their users. Such a linking of computers is called a *network*.

Using a teletype or VDU terminal is the best way of making corrections to information which is already in computer-readable form, usually stored as files on disc. The computer can be instructed to make changes to files by using a special program, called the *editor*. The places where the corrections are to be made are identified within a file either by the line number or by locating a unique sequence of characters. The actual instructions to be given to the editor vary from computer to computer, but all work in a similar way. Instructions like

T#32
R/AND/BUT/

would be interpreted as

move to line number 32
replace the first occurrence of the characters AND in that line by BUT

The slashes (/) are called delimiters and serve to separate the error from the correction in the editing instruction. In this example the editor has been told to find the place to be corrected by line number. If the line number was not known, it could be requested to find the place with an instruction such as

TC/CAT AND/

which would be interpreted as look for the first line containing CAT AND. Enough text must be given to identify the line uniquely. There may be many ANDs in a file, but the particular one we want is preceded by CAT. There are special instructions for inserting and deleting complete lines, and it is usually also possible to specify an editing instruction which is to be repeated until the end of the file or some other condition is reached. The computer makes a new version of the file with the corrections incorporated into it. The old version can then be erased by supplying the relevant instruction to the operating system. Some computer editing programs work by making one pass through the file. If the user has passed the place where a correction is to be made, that particular dialogue with the editor must be terminated and another begun which puts him back to the beginning of the file. This can be done in the same session. More sophisticated editors allow the user to jump about the file making corrections at random.

The correction of data is much easier using an editor than repunching cards or tape. Many editors display the corrected line on the terminal, so that the user can ensure that it is correct before sending it to the computer. If the information was originally typed on punched cards or paper tape, it can be fed into files in stages and each stage corrected before being copied on to magnetic tape for long-term storage.

People frequently ask whether there are machines which can read material from a printed book and transfer it to magnetic tape or disc. This would eliminate the most laborious part of any computer-aided analysis of text. The answer is that there are machines which can read, but they cannot read directly from a book. They can however read typescript. This is because on a typewriter each letter occupies the same amount of space, whereas in a book the spacing is variable because of the right-hand justification.

Machines which can read are called *optical character readers* (OCR). They can only read certain type founts and they are very expensive to buy. The information must first be typed on special paper using an electric typewriter fitted with a special ribbon and OCR golf ball head. The tpewriter often needs adjustment for OCR work, which renders it unsatisfactory for normal typing. Two type faces which are commonly used for OCR typing are OCR A and OCR B, as shown in Figures 2.5 and 2.6. The former is not very pleasant for the human eye and is frequently typed only in upper case. The latter is much easier on the eye, but has been found

```
R7352VON L{VDWIG} BLAV; L?"LES HVIT CHAPITRES
R7354DE MAIMONIDE OV INTRODVCTION A LA MISCHNA
R735bD'ABOTH..." PAR JVLES WOLF; "DAS WASSEROPFER
R7358VND DIE DAMIT VERBVNDENEN ZEREMONIEN"
R736bVON D{AVID} FEVCHTWANG+Y
```

Figure 2.5. The type face OCR A.

```
Four sets of data are shown here.  In each case the data file is
printed in full and the control cards listed again before the output
from each individual program.
```

Figure 2.6. The type face OCR B.

to be prone to error in reading, particularly in the confusion of lower case *h* and *b*.

Some other manufacturers of OCR equipment have designed their own type faces to suit their reader. One in particular has little strokes or bars underneath the characters. These are read by the machine and incorporate a parity check in the same way as magnetic or paper tape to test for errors or misreads. An experiment with this machine found that the total height of each character, including the strokes underneath, was too great for an electric typewriter ribbon and thus did not register complete characters on the page.

Optical reading has had some success in the area of mark sensing, where pencil marks on a preprinted form are detected by another kind of scanning device and are transmitted to the computer's storage devices. This method is used for the Open University's computer marked assignments and may be a possible method of input for archaeological or historical data.

As far as textual material is concerned, optical character reading has not been very successful. The information still has to be typed. A trained typist types faster than a key punch operator, but now VDUs and teletypes are being used more frequently for input, and these can be operated much faster than a card punch. For OCR work errors can be introduced at the typing stage. They cannot be corrected using correcting fluid, as this changes the surface of the paper. Instead the whole page must be retyped or a special delete character (a question mark ? in Figure 2.5) used to instruct the OCR machine to ignore the previous character. Once the typing is complete, errors can be introduced again at the reading stage. Characters which are misread go completely undetected until the data is proof-read. Characters which are rejected because the machine is unable to identify them are dealt with in one of two ways. Either a special character such as an @ is substituted for them, or the reader stops and displays the shape it has seen on a VDU screen. The operator can then key in the unrecognised character.

We have now dealt with all the major methods of computer input, and have seen how textual material must either be transcribed into the computer's character set or typed on to a special purpose keyboard. We can now consider how output of a publishable quality can be produced by a computer. It is clear that the standard upper-case-only lineprinter output, such as we saw on page 26, is of such a poor quality that it is unsuitable for publication purposes. An upper and lower case lineprinter produces slightly better printout, but it is not really suitable for high quality printing. Another method adopted by Wisbey at Cambridge was to produce paper tape from the computer and then feed it through a flexowriter, which was fitted with a special type face for medieval German diacritics. Paper tape can also be used to drive a terminal which resembles an electric typewriter, and can have any golf ball head inserted in it. Again, this produces output which looks like typescript, not like printing. At a speed of 10 characters a second, it would take some time to print even a fairly short text or concordance on a flexowriter. Paper tape is also prone to tear easily or become entangled, and it is not easy to handle in large quantities.

What is really needed to produce high-quality output is a photocomposing or computer-typesetting device. These machines contain a cathode ray tube (CRT) which is photographed by a camera facing it. They are driven by a magnetic or paper tape containing instructions to display characters on the CRT which are recorded by the camera. The images are then reproduced on film or photorecording paper. The more expensive machines can display any shape on the CRT, whether characters or pictures. The shapes are made up entirely of straight lines. A curve is drawn by a number of very tiny straight lines joined together at the required angles. Any shape can be drawn by the computer, if the relevant instructions are programmed.

Each character is first designed on an enlarged grid and is made up entirely of straight lines. The coordinates of the set of lines for each character are then stored inside the computer. Thick and thin lines, an italic effect, can be created by drawing a series of lines parallel to each other, When the character is drawn at the small size required for printing, the parallel lines appear to be joined up, thus giving a single thicker line. Every time the computer is required, for example, to print an A, it calls up the coordinates for the letter A and instructs the photocomposing machine to draw the letter at the appropriate position on the cathode ray tube.

As the characters are drawn rather than printed, it is theoretically possible to draw or print any character of any alphabet. The designs must first be established and the coordinates for each character stored once. By this method it is possible to print even Chinese using the computer. An example of a Chinese character drawn on a grid of 26 x 26 is shown in Figure 2.7. Some photocomposing machines which work in this way draw their characters only from vertical lines, and for this a very fine definition is required. Others draw straight lines in all directions like the Chinese character shown. More recently much cheaper computer typesetters have become available, which use metal grids containing the shapes of ready-formed characters which can be projected on to an image and photographed. The number of characters available is much lower than on a typesetter which constructs shapes out of straight lines, but several founts can be used on one page and they are available in many different type sizes.

If sufficient special codes have been inserted in the input to indicate change of fount, change of type size, etc, on either kind of typesetter the

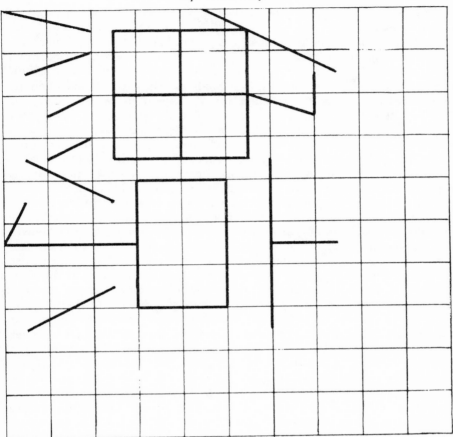

Figure 2.7. A Chinese character drawn on a grid of 26 x 26 by computer.

output can resemble a printed book. All that is needed is a computer program to interpret the typesetting codes and instruct the photocomposer to generate the required characters. The program can include the necessary instructions to make up a page of print correctly with page numbers, titles, footnotes, etc. As any character can be displayed anywhere on the page, the program can also introduce variable-width spacing and thus justify the text to the right-hand as well as to the left-hand margin. Such a program would also interpret codes for capitalisation (if the text was all in upper case) and deal with accents and diacritics. The example shown in Figure 2.8 was typeset by computer and shows the range of possibilities.

One obvious advantage of using a computer typesetting device for printing is that the material does not have to be retyped if it is already in computer-readable form. Suppose a complete text had been prepared for computer analysis and was now error-free. The text would then be processed by the computer in some way, perhaps to make a concordance. The resulting output could then be printed directly on to a computer typesetter without any further need for proof-reading. Once the material which goes into the computer is accurate, the output is also accurate, even if it is in a much expanded form like a concordance. The chance of further error, which would inevitably creep in during conventional typesetting, is eliminated and with it the requirement for extensive proof-reading.

The output from photocomposing machines is usually in the form of photorecording paper, but some machines also allow microfilm or microfiche. Computer output microform, or COM as it is generally known, is now becoming widely used in the commercial world. COM devices can behave as if they were fast lineprinters and print text on to film using rather ugly lineprinter-type characters at speeds of up to 10,000 lines per minute. 35mm microfilm was the earlier type of microform to be used, but it is not so convenient for the user, as much rewinding is required. Microfiche is now the most frequently used COM output. Normally computer microfiches are 42 or 48 magnification and thus have 270 frames or pages on one fiche. Some also have indexing systems, so that the user can soon identify which frame is required. Microfiche readers can now be purchased quite cheaply. The cost of publishing material by conventional means has risen so sharply that microfiche and microfilm are very real alternatives. Already a number of computer concordances have appeared as microfiche. They may not be as convenient to use as an ordinary book, but they are so much cheaper to produce that the choice is often to publish on microfiche or not at all. Those who are using a computer are at a distinct advantage here because their material can be printed directly from the computer on to microfiche. Microfiche can be produced by many photocomposing machines, and so their text may have many of the qualities of a printed book, with elegant characters, justification and full diacritics.

In this chapter we have seen how textual material can be prepared for the computer and what methods are available for input and output. The best method of input would seem to be a VDU or a teletype with a special purpose keyboard, which can accommodate all the extra characters not

---

Figure 2.8. A page of *A Bibliography of Homeric Scholarship* compiled by David W. Packard and Tania Meyers which was typeset by computer.

614.68.Cheyns A., "La signification religieuse du verbe ἄζομαι dans les poèmes homériques," *RecPhL* 2(1968)109-24.

615.49 Chiliadakis S., Ἡ ὁμηρικὴ φιλοξενία καὶ ὁ τουρισμὸς στὴν ἀρχαία Ἑλλάδα. (Athens 1948).

616.54 Chiodaroli G., "Il Pascoli traduttore." *Acme* 6(1953)207-34.

617.48 Chittenden J., "Diaktoros Argeiphontes," *AJA* 52(1948)24-33.

618.61 Chrestou C. A., "Ὁ Πολύγνωτος καὶ μία ἀγγειογραφία μὲ ἐπεισόδιου ἐκ τῆς Ὁμηρικῆς Νεκυίας," *AE* (1957)168-226.

619.65 Ciani M. G., "La parola omerica τηλύγετος," *AIV* 123(1964-65)157-66.

620.66 Ciani M. G., "Le morti minori nell'Iliade," *AIV* 122(1963-64)403-15.

621.48 Cilento V., "Il dèmone," *PP* 3(1948)213-27.

622.60 Cilento V., "Mito e poesia nelle Enneadi di Plotino," in *Les sources de Plotin*. Entretiens sur l'antiquité classique, 5. (Geneva 1960), 243-323.

623.63 Ciravegna M., "Le traduzioni omeriche di Ugo Foscolo," *NRS* 47(1963)366-74.

624.66 Citti V., "Le edizioni omeriche 'delle città,' " *Vichiana* 3(1966)227-67.

625.67 Citti V., "Eschilo, Supplici 164 s.," *Vichiana* 4(1967)189-91.

626.45 Claes L., *Contribution à l'étude des épithètes d'Apollon dans l'Iliade*. Thèse lic. Louvain (1942-43); cf. *RBPh* 23(1944)582.

627.70 Clark R. J., "Two Virgilian similes and the Ἡρακλέους κατάβασις," *Phoenix* 24(1970)244-55.

628.40 Clark W. P., "Iliad IX, 336 and the meaning of ἄλοχος in Homer," *CPh* 35(1940)188-90.

629.61 Clarke H. W., *The lion and the altar: Myth. rite, and symbol in the Odyssey*. Diss. Harvard (1960); summary in *HSPh* 65(1961)353-55.

630.62 Clarke H. W., "Fire imagery in the Odyssey," *CJ* 57(1961-62)358-60.

631.63 Clarke H. W., "Telemachus and the Telemacheia," *AJPh* 84(1963)129-45.

632.63 Clarke H. W., "Homer and Mickiewicz. Pan Tadeusz and the Odyssean heritage," *Indiana Slavic Stud.* 3(1963)7-25.

633.67 Clarke H. W., *The art of the Odyssey*. (Englewood Cliffs, N.J. 1967).

634.69 Clarke H. W., "The humor of Homer." *CJ* 64(1968-69)246-52.

635.39 Clercx A., *Het noodlot bij Homeros*. Thèse lic. Louvain; cf. *RBPh* 18(1939)285.

636.33 Cluytens F., "Homeros als kunstenaar," *N&V(B)* 14(1932)320-25.

637.55 Cocco V., "D'un' antichissima designazione mediterranea della malva, preell. μῶλυ, pianta magica, malva," *AGI* 40(1955)10-28.

638.61 Cocco V., "Relitti semitici a Creta. Hom. Ἠλύσιον πεδίον," *Biblos*. Revista da Fac. de Letras da Univ. de Coimbra 31(1955)401-22.

639.53 Codino F. (comm.), *Dolonia*. (Bari 1952).

640.59 Codino F., "Sui rapporti fra l'Iliade e la storia," *Belfagor* 14,1(Messina 1959)1-13.

641.60 Codino F., "Presupposti religiosi e tendenza comico-realistica nella mitologia omerica," *Belfagor* 15(Messina 1960)551-66.

normally in the computer's character set that a text may require, although some care may be needed in interpreting results as non-standard characters may appear as different characters when another output device, such as a lineprinter, is used for checking intermediate results. However, the non-standard terminal could be used for proof-reading and correcting the text until it is free of error. If such a terminal is not available, it is always possible to prepare material on punched cards. Many texts now in computer-readable form have been prepared in this medium. Results are best output by a photocomposing machine or computer typesetter. The lineprinter is adequate and necessary for a fast turn-round of intermediate results, but for publication the quality of its printing is not suitable. The photocomposer or COM machine is capable of producing print equal to that achieved by conventional typesetting methods, and it should be used for any final version for publication, whether in book form or on microfiche.

REFERENCES

1. W.P. Cole, Computer Output Microfiche in the Catalogue of American Portraits. *Computers in the Humanities*, 175-83 (ed. J.L. Mitchell). Edinburgh: Edinburgh University Press (1974)

2. Terence D. Crawford and Glyn E. Jones, Automated Concordancing of Welsh Dialects with Output in the IPA. *Bulletin of the Board of Celtic Studies*, 27 (1976) 45-50

3. Lucie Fossier and Gian Piero Zarri, *L'indexation automatique des Sources Documentaires Anciennes*. Paris: Centre National de la Recherche Scientifique (1975)

4. R. Hirschmann, G. Clausing and E. Purcell, Microcomputers and Computer-Assisted Instruction. *Computing in the Humanities*, 175-80 (eds Serge Lusignan and John S. North). Waterloo: University of Waterloo Press (1977)

5. Susan Hockey, Input and Output of Non-Standard Character Sets. *ALLC Bull.* 1 No. 2 (1973) 32-7

6. Susan M. Hockey, A Concordance to the Poems of Hafiz with Output in Persian Characters. *The Computer and Literary Studies*, 291-306 (eds A.J. Aitken, R.W. Bailey and N. Hamilton-Smith). Edinburgh: Edinburgh University Press (1973)

7. R.W. Last, Publishing Computer Output of Processed Natural Language – I. *ALLC Bull.* 1 No. 3 (1973) 5-7

8. R.W. Last, Publishing Computer Output of Processed Natural Language – II. *ALLC Bull.* 2 No. 2 (1974) 38-41

9. K.-F. Lee, Input/Output Problems of Chinese Characters and the Use of COCOA. *ALLC Bull.* 4 (1976) 4-10

10. U. Muller, On Computerising Medieval German Lyric Manuscripts. *ALLC Bull.* 2 No. 2 (1974) 4-12

11. Wilhelm Ott, The Emancipated Input/Output, *The Computer in Literary and Linguistic Studies (Proceedings of the Third International Symposium)*, 27-37 (eds Alan Jones and R.F. Churchhouse) Cardiff: University of Wales Press (1976)

12. D.W. Packard, Can Scholars Publish Their Own Books? *Scholarly Publishing* (October 1973) 65-74

13. David W. Packard and Tania Meyers, *A Bibliography of Homeric Scholarship: Preliminary Edition 1930-1970.* Malibu, California: Undena Publications (1974)

14. D.W. Packard, Teaching Ancient Greek (with the Help of a Computer). *ALLC Bull.* 3 (1975) 45-51

15. B.R. Schneider, Optical Scanning as a Method of Input: the Experience of *The London Stage* Project. *The Computer and Literary Studies*, 283-9 (eds A.J. Aitken, R.W. Bailey and N. Hamilton-Smith). Edinburgh: Edinburgh University Press (1973)

16. J.B. Smith, Encoding Literary Texts: Some Considerations. *ALLC Bull.* 4 (1976) 190-8.

17. Thesaurus Linguae Graecae, *Guide for the Preparation of Text for the Thesaurus Linguae Graecae Project.* Irvine: TLG (1973)

18. F. de Tollenaere, Encoding Techniques in Dutch Historical Lexicography. *Computers and the Humanities* 6 (1972) 147-52

19. G.E. Weil and G. Opsomer, Processus Interactif de Saisie de Visualisation et d'Impression des Données Sémitiques Anciennes et Modernes. *ALLC Bull.* 4 (1976) 223-37

Further Reading

Susie Andres and S. Ramani, Codification of the Devangari Script for Automatic Data-Processing. *Indian Linguistics* 31 (1970) 91-102

R.F. Churchhouse and Susan Hockey, The Use of an SC4020 for Output of a Concordance Program. *The Computer in Literary and Linguistic Research,* 221-31 (ed. R.A. Wisbey). Cambridge: Cambridge University Press (1971)

S. Duncan, T. Mukaii and S. Kuno, A Computer Graphics System for Non-Alphabetic Orthographies. *Computer Studies in the Humanities and Verbal Behavior* 2 (1969) 113-32

H. Hayashi, S. Duncan and S. Kuno, Graphical Input/Output of Non-Standard Characters. *Communications of the ACM* 11 (1968) 613-18

J.G.B. Heal, What to Tell the Programmer. *The Computer in Literary and Linguistic Research,* 201-8 (ed. R.A. Wisbey). Cambridge: Cambridge University Press (1971)

J.A. Moyne, Sasanian Pahlavi Inscriptions: A Concordance. *Computers and the Humanities* 8 (1974) 27-39

David W. Packard, Publishing Scholarly Compilations by Computer. *Computers and the Humanities* 4 (1969) 75-80

William Stallings, The Morphology of Chinese Characters. *Computers and the Humanities* 9 (1975) 13-24

G.P. Zarri, L'Enregistrement Informatique de Documents Non-Littéraires Rédigés dans une Langue Ancienne: Observations et Suggestions. *ALLC Bull.* 4 (1976) 115-24

A bibliography of computer typesetting compiled by W. Ott is in *ALLC Bull.* 2 No. 1 (1974) 79-80

3. Word Indexes, Concordances and Dictionaries

The production of word indexes and concordances is the most obvious application of the computer in literary research. Indeed it was the earliest, beginning with Roberto Busa's work on the *Index Thomisticus*. A word index is simply an alphabetical list of the words in a text usually with the number of times each individual word occurs and some indication of where the word occurs in the text. When each occurrence of each word is presented with the words that surround it, the word index becomes a concordance. The compilation of such word indexes or concordances is a very mechanical process and therefore well suited to the computer. There has indeed been a large number of such concordances in the past fifteen years or so. The computer can count and sort words much faster and more accurately than the human brain. The days when a person devoted his life to the manual preparation of an index of a text are over, but we shall see that using a computer does not remove the need for human thought and judgment.

Some examples of word indexes and concordances made by the COCOA program appear as Figures 3.1, 3.2 and 3.3. The first shows a word count, a list of all the words in the text in alphabetical order, with a count of the number of times each word occurs. References, indicating where each occurrence of each word comes in the text, are added in Figure 3.2. Figure 3.3 shows a concordance. Each word in the text is given in alphabetical order and the number of occurrences or 'frequency count' for each keyword appears at the top of the entries for that word – somewhat unnecessary if the word occurs only once, but very useful in a large text where a word can occur many thousands of times. The text accompanying each occurrence of each keyword is usually referred to as the context, and the indication of where the keyword occurs in the text is known as the reference. In this concordance the keywords are aligned down the middle of the page. This is known as a KWIC or 'keyword in context' index, and is the form adopted by David Packard in his Livy concordance, among others. The lines of context can also be aligned to the left of the page, as in Figure 3.4. The first form is generally considered easier to use, but it does take up considerably more space across the page.

Many reviewers of computer-produced concordances have been critical of them in a number of respects. In particular, they have cited the lack of lemmatisation, the failure to distinguish homographs and the indiscriminate choice of context. I hope now to demonstrate which of these criticisms, if any, are attributable to the computer itself and which can be altered to the choice of the compiler or editor of the concordance.

The examples from verse shown above give just one line of context. This is the most frequently used choice of context. It is eminently suitable for verse where the lines are of a reasonable length, but is not so applicable for verse with short lines or for prose text. It is quite possible to program the computer to supply context of a specific number of words on either side of the keyword or to ask it to extend the context up to a specific character or

2	A	1	AFTERWARDS
1	AM	4	AND
2	AWAY	2	BE
1	BETTER	3	BY
1	CAN	1	CORRUPTION
1	COUNSEL	1	DARKNESS
2	DAY	1	DO
2	FAR	2	FOR
2	FORGET	1	FUTURE
1	GO	2	GONE
1	GRIEVE	1	HAD
1	HALF	1	HAND
1	HOLD	3	I
2	IF	1	INTO
1	IT	1	LAND
1	LATE	1	LEAVE
0	ME	2	MORE
2	NO	1	NOR
1	NOT	2	OF
1	ONCE	1	ONLY
1	OR	1	OUR
1	PLANNED	1	PRAY
5	REMEMBER	1	SAD
3	SHOULD	1	SILENT
1	SMILE	1	STAY
1	TELL	1	THAN
3	THAT	4	THE
1	THEN	1	THOUGHTS
2	TO	1	TURN
1	TURNING	1	UNDERSTAND
1	VESTIGE	3	WHEN
1	WHILE	1	WILL
2	YET	7	YOU

Figure 3.1 A word count in alphabetical order.

```
THE  4
2,3,11,12,

THEN  1
8,

THOUGHTS  1
12,

TO  2
4,8,

TURN  1
4,

TURNING  1
4,

UNDERSTAND  1
7,

VESTIGE  1
12,

WHEN  3
1,3,5,

WHILE  1
9,

WILL  1
8,

YET  2
4,9,

YOU  7
3,6,6,7,9,13,14,
```

Figure 3.2. Part of a word index.

ROS REM 2		GONE FAR AWAY INTO THE SILENT LAND:
ROS REM 3		WHEN YOU CAN NO MORE HOLD ME BY THE HAND,
ROS REM 11		FOR IF THE DARKNESS AND CORRUPTION LEAVE
ROS REM 12		A VESTIGE OF THE THOUGHTS THAT I ONCE HAD,

          1   THEN

ROS REM 8   IT WILL BE LATE TO COUNSEL THEN OR PRAY.

          1   THOUGHTS

ROS REM 12   A VESTIGE OF THE THOUGHTS THAT I ONCE HAD,

          2   TO

ROS REM 4   NOR I HALF TURN TO GO YET TURNING STAY.
ROS REM 8   IT WILL BE LATE TO COUNSEL THEN OR PRAY.

          1   TURN

ROS REM 4   NOR I HALF TURN TO GO YET TURNING STAY.

          1   TURNING

ROS REM 4   NOR I HALF TURN TO GO YET TURNING STAY.

          1   UNDERSTAND

ROS REM 7   ONLY REMEMBER ME; YOU UNDERSTAND

```
                    1   VESTIGE
          A VESTIGE OF THE THOUGHTS THAT I ONCE HAD,
ROS REM 12

                    3   WHEN
         REMEMBER ME WHEN WHEN I AM GONE AWAY,
              WHEN YOU CAN NO MORE HOLD ME BY THE HAND,
         REMEMBER ME WHEN NO MORE DAY BY DAY
ROS REM  1
ROS REM  3
ROS REM  5

                    1   WHILE
YET IF YOU SHOULD FORGET ME FOR A WHILE
ROS REM  9

                    1   WILL
         IT WILL BE LATE TO COUNSEL THEN OR PRAY.
ROS REM  8

                    2   YET
NOR I HALF TURN TO GO YET TURNING STAY.
              YET IF YOU SHOULD FORGET ME FOR A WHILE
ROS REM  4
ROS REM  9

                    7   YOU
              WHEN YOU CAN NO MORE HOLD ME BY THE HAND.
YOU TELL ME OF OUR FUTURE THAT YOU PLANNED:
              YOU TELL ME OF OUR FUTURE THAT YOU PLANNED:
         ONLY REMEMBER ME; YOU UNDERSTAND
              YET IF YOU SHOULD FORGET ME FOR A WHILE
         BETTER BY FAR YOU SHOULD FORGET AND SMILE
              THAN THAT YOU SHOULD REMEMBER AND BE SAD.
ROS REM  3
ROS REM  6
ROS REM  6
ROS REM  7
ROS REM  9
ROS REM 13
ROS REM 14
```

Figure 3.3. Part of a concordance showing keywords centrally aligned.

4   THE

ROS REM 2   GONE FAR AWAY INTO THE SILENT LAND;
ROS REM 3   WHEN YOU CAN NO MORE HOLD ME BY THE HAND,
ROS REM 11 FOR IF THE DARKNESS AND CORRUPTION LEAVE
ROS REM 12 A VESTIGE OF THE THOUGHTS THAT I ONCE HAD,

1   THEN

ROS REM 8   IT WILL BE LATE TO COUNSEL THEN OR PRAY.

1   THOUGHTS

ROS REM 12 A VESTIGE OF THE THOUGHTS THAT I ONCE HAD,

2   TO

ROS REM 4   NOR I HALF TURN TO GO YET TURNING STAY.
ROS REM 8   IT WILL BE LATE TO COUNSEL THEN OR PRAY.

1   TURN

ROS REM 4   NOR I HALF TURN TO GO YET TURNING STAY.

1   TURNING

ROS REM 4   NOR I HALF TURN TO GO YET TURNING STAY.

1   UNDERSTAND

ROS REM 7   ONLY REMEMBER ME; YOU UNDERSTAND

```
                          1  VESTIGE

ROS REM 12    A VESTIGE OF THE THOUGHTS THAT I ONCE HAD,

                          3  WHEN

ROS REM  1    REMEMBER ME WHEN I AM GONE AWAY,
ROS REM  3    WHEN YOU CAN NO MORE HOLD ME BY THE HAND,
ROS REM  5    REMEMBER ME WHEN NO MORE DAY BY DAY

                          1  WHILE

ROS REM  9    YET IF YOU SHOULD FORGET ME FOR A WHILE

                          1  WILL

ROS REM  8    IT WILL BE LATE TO COUNSEL THEN OR PRAY.

                          2  YET

ROS REM  4    NOR I HALF TURN TO GO YET TURNING STAY.
ROS REM  9    YET IF YOU SHOULD FORGET ME FOR A WHILE

                          7  YOU

ROS REM  3    WHEN YOU CAN NO MORE HOLD ME BY THE HAND,
ROS REM  6    YOU TELL ME OF OUR FUTURE THAT YOU PLANNED:
ROS REM  6    YOU TELL ME OF OUR FUTURE THAT YOU PLANNED:
ROS REM  7    ONLY REMEMBER ME; YOU UNDERSTAND
ROS REM  9    YET IF YOU SHOULD FORGET ME FOR A WHILE
ROS REM 13    BETTER BY FAR YOU SHOULD FORGET AND SMILE
ROS REM 14    THAN THAT YOU SHOULD REMEMBER AND BE SAD.
```

Figure 3.4. Part of a concordance showing keywords left aligned.

characters, like full stops, commas, etc. With some programs it is also possible to fill up the width of the lineprinter's line or to a specified number of characters on either side of the keyword. In this case the context may be broken off in the middle of a word, as in Figure 3.5, possibly giving a misleading interpretation of the text. If a KWIC format is chosen and the keyword is at the very beginning or end of the context – that is, it comes just before or after the chosen cut-off character – the computer may be programmed to extend the context into the other half of the line, and make it appear to 'curl round'. An example of this appears in Figure 3.6. This again leads to a slightly unsatisfactory and misleading appearance and the context which has curled round could be omitted, as shown in Figure 3.7. Therefore the choice of context for each keyword can be programmed to suit a variety of criteria although it is not so easy to choose the context for each word individually. The best overall criteria must be chosen, but the selection of criteria is entirely up to the editor of the concordance.

The amount and choice of information to be given as the reference for each citation is another matter for the editor of the concordance to determine. When the text is fed into the computer, it can be given reference markers indicating line number, page number and title of the work, and act, scene or speaker in the case of a play. It is then possible to instruct the machine to accompany each citation with whatever combination of these references the editor thinks appropriate. The important point is that it is much easier for the computer program if all the references in the concordance have the same format. Some form of manual intervention or editing would be required if parts of a concordance were to be referenced in one format and parts in another format. References are an important part of a concordance, for they enable a word to be located in a much wider context by pointing to the actual place in a text where it occurs. They also help to show if a word occurs more frequently in any part of a text or does not occur at all in any particular part. It is usually best to specify as much detail in the references as possible, as long as too much space across the page is not occupied. Referencing the words in a play merely by line numbers does not provide much useful information, but the inclusion of act, scene and speaker for each word could indicate which characters favoured which word forms and whether the language of one particular scene or act deviated from another. Abbreviated forms of references, like the ones shown in our examples, are adequate, provided their meaning is clear.

Those who have prepared manual indexes or concordances to texts have tended to omit or ignore words which occur very frequently, mostly on the grounds that the information to be gained from a list of all these words was not worth the effort involved in indexing them. It is well known that very few different words make up a high proportion of the words used in a particular language or text. The editor of a concordance must decide whether to include these or not. For a computer-produced concordance, the extra effort is on the part of the computer. It may take a little longer for the machine to include every word, but it requires no more effort on the part of the editor. It is usually best to produce a simple word count first on the computer. This enables the editor to decide whether to include high-frequency words, since he can then calculate how many entries or pages of printout would be produced if all the words were to be concorded. In a concordance of the Roman historian Ammianus Marcellinus produced in 1972, there were over 125,000 words, of which the word 'et' occurred 4501 times. That is only one entry in a word count, but at 65 lines per page of printout, it would produce almost 70 pages of concordance.

These high frequency words are often of most interest to those studying linguistic usage. I would suggest that they be produced on microfilm or microfiche if their volume was such that they could not be included in a published concordance. Alternatively they could be kept on magnetic tape, so that the occurrences of selected words could be inspected if required. With most concordance programs it is possible to omit all words which occur above a given frequency, or simply to specify a list of words which are not required as keywords. The latter ensures that words which are required are not omitted simply because they occur frequently. The omitted words would of course still appear in the context of other keywords. Most of the published concordances either omit completely the most frequently occurring words, or they present them in a condensed form, either by giving only the number of times which each occurs, or by giving their references without the context.

Another problem facing the editor of a concordance is the order in which the occurrences of a particular word should be listed. The most usual method is to put them in the order in which they occur in the text as we have seen so far. They can, however, also be listed according to the alphabetical order of what comes to the right of the keyword (Figure 3.8) or to the left of the keyword (Figure 3.9). In this way all the instances of a particular phrase can be grouped together. It is also possible to place the keywords in alphabetical order of their endings. Such a concordance is known as a reverse concordance and is useful in the study of morphology, rhyme schemes and syntax. Figure 3.10 shows an example. Once the text is ready to be processed by the computer, little human effort is required to produce any or all four kinds of concordances which have so far been described.

The editor of a concordance must consider if there are any words which are to be treated separately, for example, quotations from another author. If the text includes a sizeable amount of quoted material, the vocabulary counts will be distorted. There are several ways of dealing with quotations.

```
                                               4    THE

ROS REM  2    WHEN I AM GONE AWAY, GONE FAR AWAY INTO THE SILENT LAND; WHEN YOU CAN NO MORE HO
ROS REM  3    T LAND; WHEN YOU CAN NO MORE HOLD ME BY THE HAND, NOR I HALF TURN TO GO YET TURN
ROS REM 11    ERWARDS REMEMBER, DO NOT GRIEVE: FOR IF THE DARKNESS AND CORRUPTION LEAVE A VEST
ROS REM 12    KNESS AND CORRUPTION LEAVE A VESTIGE OF THE THOUGHTS THAT I ONCE HAD, BETTER BY

                                               1    THEN

ROS REM  8    U UNDERSTAND IT WILL BE LATE TO COUNSEL THEN OR PRAY. YET IF YOU SHOULD FORGET M

                                               1    THOUGHTS

ROS REM 12    S AND CORRUPTION LEAVE A VESTIGE OF THE THOUGHTS THAT I ONCE HAD, BETTER BY FAR

                                               2    TO

ROS REM  4    RE HOLD ME BY THE HAND, NOR I HALF TURN TO GO YET TURNING STAY. REMEMBER ME WHEN
ROS REM  8    MBER ME; YOU UNDERSTAND IT WILL BE LATE TO COUNSEL THEN OR PRAY. YET IF YOU SHOU

                                               1    TURN

ROS REM  4    NO MORE HOLD ME BY THE HAND, NOR I HALF TURN TO GO YET TURNING STAY. REMEMBER ME

                                               1    TURNING

ROS REM  4     BY THE HAND, NOR I HALF TURN TO GO YET TURNING STAY. REMEMBER ME WHEN NO MORE D

                                               1    UNDERSTAND

ROS REM  7    THAT YOU PLANNED: ONLY REMEMBER ME; YOU UNDERSTAND IT WILL BE LATE TO COUNSEL TH
```

```
                          1    VESTIGE

ROS REM 12    IF THE DARKNESS AND CORRUPTION LEAVE A VESTIGE OF THE THOUGHTS THAT I ONCE HAD,

                          3    WHEN

ROS REM  1    THE SILENT LAND;         REMEMBER ME WHEN I AM GONE AWAY, GONE FAR AWAY INTO
ROS REM  3    AY, GONE FAR AWAY INTO THE SILENT LAND; WHEN YOU CAN NO MORE HOLD ME BY THE HAND
ROS REM  5    URN TO GO YET TURNING STAY. REMEMBER ME WHEN NO MORE DAY BY DAY YOU TELL ME OF O

                          1    WHILE

ROS REM  9    PRAY. YET IF YOU SHOULD FORGET ME FOR A WHILE AND AFTERWARDS REMEMBER, DO NOT GR

                          1    WILL

ROS REM  8    ED: ONLY REMEMBER ME: YOU UNDERSTAND IT WILL BE LATE TO COUNSEL THEN OR PRAY. YE

                          2    YET

ROS REM  4    D ME BY THE HAND, NOR I HALF TURN TO GO YET TURNING STAY. REMEMBER ME WHEN NO MO
ROS REM  9    T WILL BE LATE TO COUNSEL THEN OR PRAY. YET IF YOU SHOULD FORGET ME FOR A WHILE

                          7    YOU

ROS REM  3    ONE FAR AWAY INTO THE SILENT LAND: WHEN YOU CAN NO MORE HOLD ME BY THE HAND, NOR
ROS REM  6    AY. REMEMBER ME WHEN NO MORE DAY BY DAY YOU TELL ME OF OUR FUTURE THAT YOU PLANN
ROS REM  6    Y BY DAY YOU TELL ME OF OUR FUTURE THAT YOU PLANNED: ONLY REMEMBER ME: YOU UNDER
ROS REM  7    URE THAT YOU PLANNED: ONLY REMEMBER ME: YOU UNDERSTAND IT WILL BE LATE TO COUNSE
ROS REM  9    BE LATE TO COUNSEL THEN OR PRAY. YET IF YOU SHOULD FORGET ME FOR A WHILE AND AFT
ROS REM 13    THOUGHTS THAT I ONCE HAD, BETTER BY FAR YOU SHOULD FORGET AND SMILE THAN THAT YO
ROS REM 14    R YOU SHOULD FORGET AND SMILE THAN THAT YOU SHOULD REMEMBER AND BE SAD.
```

Figure 3.5. Part of a concordance showing context which fills the page.

```
                              4    THE

ROS REM   2    GONE FAR AWAY INTO THE SILENT LAND:
ROS REM   3    WHEN YOU CAN NO MORE HOLD ME BY THE HAND,
ROS REM  11  E            FOR IF THE DARKNESS AND CORRUPTION LEAV
ROS REM  12               A VESTIGE OF THE THOUGHTS THAT I ONCE HAD.

                              1    THEN

ROS REM   8    IT WILL BE LATE TO COUNSEL THEN OR PRAY.

                              1    THOUGHTS

ROS REM  12       A VESTIGE OF THE THOUGHTS THAT I ONCE HAD,

                              2    TO

ROS REM   4       NOR I HALF TURN TO GO YET TURNING STAY.
ROS REM   8       IT WILL BE LATE TO COUNSEL THEN OR PRAY.

                              1    TURN

ROS REM   4          NOR I HALF TURN TO GO YET TURNING STAY.

                              1    TURNING

ROS REM   4    NOR I HALF TURN TO GO YET TURNING STAY.

                              1    UNDERSTAND

ROS REM   7    ONLY REMEMBER ME; YOU UNDERSTAND
```

```
                           1    VESTIGE

ROS REM 12 NCE HAD,              A VESTIGE OF THE THOUGHTS THAT I 0


                           3    WHEN
ROS REM 1                    REMEMBER ME WHEN I AM GONE AWAY,
ROS REM 3 THE HAND,          REMEMBER ME WHEN YOU CAN NO MORE HOLD ME BY
ROS REM 5                    REMEMBER ME WHEN NO MORE DAY BY DAY


                           1    WHILE                              YE
ROS REM 9 T IF YOU SHOULD FORGET ME FOR A WHILE


                           1    WILL
                                IT WILL BE LATE TO COUNSEL THEN OR
ROS REM 8 PRAY.


                           2    YET
ROS REM 4         NOR I HALF TURN TO GO YET TURNING STAY.
ROS REM 0 A WHILE                YET IF YOU SHOULD FORGET ME FOR


                           7    YOU
ROS REM 3 AND,                WHEN YOU CAN NO MORE HOLD ME BY THE H
ROS REM 6 OU PLANNED:           YOU TELL ME OF OUR FUTURE THAT Y
ROS REM 6 YOU TELL ME OF OUR FUTURE THAT YOU PLANNED:
ROS REM 7              ONLY REMEMBER ME; YOU UNDERSTAND
ROS REM 0                     YET IF YOU SHOULD FORGET ME FOR A WHILE
ROS REM 13            BETTER BY FAR YOU SHOULD FORGET AND SMILE
ROS REM 14            THAN THAT YOU SHOULD REMEMBER AND BE SAD.
```

Figure 3.6. Part of a concordance showing the context curling round into the other half of the line.

ROS REM   2   GONE FAR AWAY INTO THE SILENT LAND;
ROS REM   3   WHEN YOU CAN NO MORE HOLD ME BY THE HAND,
ROS REM 11   FOR IF THE DARKNESS AND CORRUPTION LEAV
ROS REM 12   A VESTIGE OF THE THOUGHTS THAT I ONCE HAD,

        1   THEN

ROS REM   8   IT WILL BE LATE TO COUNSEL THEN OR PRAY.

        1   THOUGHTS

ROS REM 12   A VESTIGE OF THE THOUGHTS THAT I ONCE HAD,

        2   TO

ROS REM   4   NOR I HALF TURN TO GO YET TURNING STAY.
ROS REM   8   IT WILL BE LATE TO COUNSEL THEN OR PRAY.

        1   TURN

ROS REM   4   NOR I HALF TURN TO GO YET TURNING STAY.

        1   TURNING

ROS REM   4   NOR I HALF TURN TO GO YET TURNING STAY.

        1   UNDERSTAND

ROS REM   7   ONLY REMEMBER ME; YOU UNDERSTAND

```
                    1    VESTIGE

                         A VESTIGE OF THE THOUGHTS THAT I O
ROS REM 12

                    3    WHEN

                         REMEMBER ME WHEN I AM GONE AWAY,
ROS REM  1               WHEN YOU CAN NO MORE HOLD ME BY
ROS REM  3               REMEMBER ME WHEN NO MORE DAY BY DAY
ROS REM  5

                    1    WHILE

                    O T IF YOU SHOULD FORGET ME FOR A WHILE
ROS REM  9

                    1    WILL

                         IT WILL BE LATE TO COUNSEL THEN OR
ROS REM  8

                    2    YET

                         NOR I HALF TURN TO GO YET TURNING STAY.
ROS REM  4               YET IF YOU SHOULD FORGET ME FOR
ROS REM  9

                    7    YOU

                         WHEN YOU CAN NO MORE HOLD ME BY THE H
ROS REM  3               YOU TELL ME OF OUR FUTURE THAT Y
ROS REM  6     YOU TELL ME OF OUR FUTURE THAT YOU PLANNED:
ROS REM  6               ONLY REMEMBER ME; YOU UNDERSTAND
ROS REM  7               YET IF YOU SHOULD FORGET ME FOR A WHILE
ROS REM  9               BETTER BY FAR YOU SHOULD FORGET AND SMILE
ROS REM 13               THAN THAT YOU SHOULD REMEMBER AND BE SAD.
ROS REM 14
```

Figure 3.7. Part of a concordance omitting the context which curls round.

```
ROS REM 11                    4        THE
ROS REM 3                          FOR IF THE DARKNESS AND CORRUPTION LEAVE
ROS REM 2            WHEN YOU CAN NO MORE HOLD ME BY THE HAND,
ROS REM 12                 GONE FAR AWAY INTO THE SILENT LAND;
                            A VESTIGE OF THE THOUGHTS THAT I ONCE HAD,

ROS REM 8                          1        THEN
                     IT WILL BE LATE TO COUNSEL THEN OR PRAY.

ROS REM 12                         1        THOUGHTS
                            A VESTIGE OF THE THOUGHTS THAT I ONCE HAD,

ROS REM 8                          2        TO
ROS REM 4                     IT WILL BE LATE TO COUNSEL THEN OR PRAY.
                              NOR I HALF TURN TO GO YET TURNING STAY.

ROS REM 4                          1        TURN
                         NOR I HALF TURN TO GO YET TURNING STAY.

ROS REM 4                          1        TURNING
                     NOR I HALF TURN TO GO YET TURNING STAY.

ROS REM 7                          1        UNDERSTAND
                     ONLY REMEMBER ME; YOU UNDERSTAND
```

```
                                    1   VESTIGE
ROS REM 12         A VESTIGE OF THE THOUGHTS THAT I ONCE HAD,

                                    3   WHEN
ROS REM 1     REMEMBER ME WHEN I AM GONE AWAY,
ROS REM 5     REMEMBER ME WHEN NO MORE DAY BY DAY
ROS REM 3                WHEN YOU CAN NO MORE HOLD ME BY THE HAND,

                                    1   WHILE
ROS REM 9     YET IF YOU SHOULD FORGET ME FOR A WHILE

                                    1   WILL
ROS REM 8            IT WILL BE LATE TO COUNSEL THEN OR PRAY.

                                    2   YET
ROS REM 9            YET IF YOU SHOULD FORGET ME FOR A WHILE
ROS REM 4     NOR I HALF TURN TO GO YET TURNING STAY.

                                    7   YOU
ROS REM 3            WHEN YOU CAN NO MORE HOLD ME BY THE HAND,
ROS REM 6     YOU TELL ME OF OUR FUTURE THAT YOU PLANNED:
ROS REM 13         BETTER BY FAR YOU SHOULD FORGET AND SMILE
ROS REM 9            YET IF YOU SHOULD FORGET ME FOR A WHILE
ROS REM 14         THAN THAT YOU SHOULD REMEMBER AND BE SAD.
ROS REM 6     YOU TELL ME OF OUR FUTURE THAT YOU PLANNED:
ROS REM 7     ONLY REMEMBER ME; YOU UNDERSTAND
```

Figure 3.8. Part of a right-sorted concordance.

```
                          4    THE

                  FOR IF  THE DARKNESS AND CORRUPTION LEAVE
              A VESTIGE OF THE THOUGHTS THAT I ONCE HAD,
              GONE FAR AWAY INTO THE SILENT LAND;
  WHEN YOU CAN NO MORE HOLD ME BY THE HAND,

                          1    THEN

  IT WILL BE LATE TO COUNSEL THEN OR PRAY.

                          1    THOUGHTS

              A VESTIGE OF THE THOUGHTS THAT I ONCE HAD,

                          2    TO

              IT WILL BE LATE TO COUNSEL THEN OR PRAY.
              NOR I HALF TURN TO GO YET TURNING STAY.

                          1    TURN

                  NOR I HALF TURN TO GO YET TURNING STAY.

                          1    TURNING

  NOR I HALF TURN TO GO YET TURNING STAY.

                          1    UNDERSTAND

              ONLY REMEMBER ME; YOU UNDERSTAND
```

ROS REM 11
ROS REM 12
ROS REM 2
ROS REM 3

ROS REM 8

ROS REM 12

ROS REM 8
ROS REM 4

ROS REM 4

ROS REM 4

ROS REM 7

```
                        1   VESTIGE

ROS REM 12                  A VESTIGE OF THE THOUGHTS THAT I ONCE HAD,

                        3   WHEN
ROS REM  3                  REMEMBER ME WHEN I AM GONE AWAY,
ROS REM  1                  REMEMBER ME WHEN NO MORE DAY BY DAY
ROS REM  5      WHEN YOU CAN NO MORE HOLD ME BY THE HAND,

                        1   WHILE
ROS REM  9   YET IF YOU SHOULD FORGET ME FOR A WHILE

                        1   WILL
ROS REM  8                  IT WILL BE LATE TO COUNSEL THEN OR PRAY.

                        2   YET
ROS REM  4      NOR I HALF TURN TO GO YET TURNING STAY.
ROS REM  9                  YET IF YOU SHOULD FORGET ME FOR A WHILE

                        7   YOU
ROS REM  7              ONLY REMEMBER ME; YOU UNDERSTAND
ROS REM  9                  YET IF YOU SHOULD FORGET ME FOR A WHILE
ROS REM  3                  WHEN YOU CAN NO MORE HOLD ME BY THE HAND,
ROS REM 13          BETTER BY FAR YOU SHOULD FORGET AND SMILE
ROS REM  6   YOU TELL ME OF OUR FUTURE THAT YOU PLANNED:
ROS REM 14          THAN THAT YOU SHOULD REMEMBER AND BE SAD.
ROS REM  6                  YOU TELL ME OF OUR FUTURE THAT YOU PLANNED:
```

Figure 3.9. Part of a left-sorted concordance.

Reference		Context	Count	Keyword
ROS REM 10		AND AFTERWARDS REMEMBER, DO NOT GRIEVE:	1	DO
ROS REM 4		NOR I HALF TURN TO GO YET TURNING STAY.	1	GO
ROS REM 3		WHEN YOU CAN NO MORE HOLD ME BY THE HAND,	2	NO
ROS REM 5		REMEMBER ME WHEN NO MORE DAY BY DAY		
ROS REM 4		NOR I HALF TURN TO GO YET TURNING STAY.	2	TO
ROS REM 8		IT WILL BE LATE TO COUNSEL THEN OR PRAY.		
ROS REM 2		GONE FAR AWAY INTO THE SILENT LAND;	1	INTO
ROS REM 2		GONE FAR AWAY INTO THE SILENT LAND;	2	FAR
ROS REM 13		BETTER BY FAR YOU SHOULD FORGET AND SMILE		
ROS REM 1		REMEMBER ME WHEN I AM GONE AWAY,	5	REMEMBER
ROS REM 5		REMEMBER ME WHEN NO MORE DAY BY DAY		
ROS REM 7		ONLY REMEMBER ME; YOU UNDERSTAND		
ROS REM 10		AND AFTERWARDS REMEMBER, DO NOT GRIEVE:		
ROS REM 14		THAN THAT YOU SHOULD REMEMBER AND BE SAD.		
ROS REM 13		BETTER BY FAR YOU SHOULD FORGET AND SMILE	1	BETTER

ROS REM 8   IT WILL BE LATE TO COUNSEL THEN OR PRAY.   1   OR

ROS REM 9   YET IF YOU SHOULD FORGET ME FOR A WHILE   2   FOR
ROS REM 11   FOR IF THE DARKNESS AND CORRUPTION LEAVE

ROS REM 4   NOR I HALF TURN TO GO YET TURNING STAY.   1   NOR

ROS REM 6   YOU TELL ME OF OUR FUTURE THAT YOU PLANNED: 1   OUR

ROS REM 10   AND AFTERWARDS REMEMBER, DO NOT GRIEVE: 1   AFTERWARDS

ROS REM 11   FOR IF THE DARKNESS AND CORRUPTION LEAVE   1   DARKNESS

ROS REM 12   A VESTIGE OF THE THOUGHTS THAT I ONCE HAD,   1   THOUGHTS

ROS REM 6   YOU TELL ME OF OUR FUTURE THAT YOU PLANNED: 3   THAT
ROS REM 12   A VESTIGE OF THE THOUGHTS THAT I ONCE HAD,
ROS REM 14   THAN THAT YOU SHOULD REMEMBER AND BE SAD.

ROS REM 9   YET IF YOU SHOULD FORGET ME FOR A WHILE   2   FORGET
ROS REM 13   BETTER BY FAR YOU SHOULD FORGET AND SMILE

Figure 3.10. Part of a reverse concordance.

They could be marked by special characters in the text, such as square brackets, and the computer would then be instructed to omit all words with square brackets from the main concordance. Another method is to mark quotations by a special reference character and then compile additional concordances of all the quoted material, maybe even one for each author from whom the quotations are made. If necessary, the quotations could be included in the context of words which are required as keywords. A better solution still might be to retain the quoted words in the main concordance and include them in a separate appendix as well.

Stage directions in a play are another example of words which require special treatment. It has been known for them to be included as ordinary words, which leads to high count of occurrences for words like 'enter' and 'exit'. It seems most sensible to omit them from the concordance by enclosing them in special characters or by not putting them into the text when it is typed into the computer. Foreign words could also be treated in a special way. For example, the Italian word 'come' should not be included in the occurrences of the English word 'come'. The most obvious way to deal with foreign words is to mark them by some special character at the beginning of the word, such as an asterisk. The computer could then be instructed to list all the words beginning with that symbol as a separate concordance, which would produce an appendix of foreign words separate from the main concordance. Proper names could also be listed separately. In some concordances of classical texts made in Oxford, all proper names are input preceded by a dollar sign, e.g. $CLAUDIUS. The editor of the concordance can then choose whether to instruct the machine to treat the dollar as a letter of the alphabet for sorting, and thus list all the proper names together, or whether to ignore the dollar completely and thus put CLAUDIUS in its true alphabetical position under the letter C. Using such marker symbols when the text is prepared for the computer does not necessarily mean that they are printed in the concordance. It is easy enough to omit them from the printout if desired.

A difficulty of much larger dimension is that of homographs – words which are spelled the same but have a different meaning. A particular example in English is 'lead', which is both a verb and a noun, with a different pronunciation and meaning for each one. The treatment of homographs is an area where reviews of computer-produced concordances have been most critical, and it is a problem which does not have any clear solution except extensive human intervention based on careful appraisal of the circumstances. When preparing a text for the computer, proper names are easily apparent and can be marked almost automatically. The same is true of stage directions and foreign words and to a lesser extent quoted material. But, until a complete concordance of a work has been inspected carefully, the editor may not realise that some homographs exist. To the computer 'lead' the verb and 'lead' the noun appear to be instances of the same word, as they are both spelled the same. Some computer concordances group the occurrences of homographs together indiscriminately, so that, for example, Latin *canes*, meaning 'dogs' and *canes*, meaning 'you will sing', are listed as two occurrences of the same word. It is then left to the user of the concordance to separate them and to take appropriate action when comparing word counts. Another means of dealing with homographs is to pre-edit the text in such a way that the words are listed separately or correctly. This involves considerable work and is unlikely to be error-free. It is probably only possible to discover all the homographs in a text by making a complete concordance without separating them and then looking through it carefully. Some marker symbol can then be inserted in the text before those words which need to be distinguished from their homographs, and then the complete concordance can be re-run. Homographs are recognised to be a difficulty. It is for the editor to select the method of dealing with them that is most appropriate to his needs or the needs of the scholars he serves. Three points should be borne in mind. One is that homographs can easily be deduced from the context but can cause erroneous results when only word counts are used. Secondly, in some texts, particularly poetry, words are deliberately ambiguous, and it may even be possible to have a separate entry for these. A third difficulty arises if the editor has chosen to omit some frequent words and these words are homographs of other words which are to be included. Such may be the case with the English words 'will' and 'might', which are both auxiliary verbs and nouns. Pre-editing seems to be the only solution here.

The discussion of homographs leads to the difficult question of lemmatisation – that is, the classification of words under their dictionary heading. Many computer-produced concordances have been criticised for their failure to do this. One dictionary defines a concordance as 'an alphabetical arrangement of the chief words or subjects in a book or author, with citations of the passages concerned'. This does not necessarily imply that words are to be placed under their dictionary heading.

Wisbey, like most other concordance makers, does not lemmatise, but he provides a useful look-up table of infinitives of verbs, although nouns should perhaps also be included. Father Busa decided to pre-edit his text for the *Index Thomisticus*, a mammoth task which has produced what is perhaps a more useful concordance. I would say that for most concordances lemmatisation is not worth the effort involved. In most cases, words from the same lemma are grouped fairly closely together. It is only in languages where there are prefixes and infixes that real difficulties arise.

Hyphenated words and words containing apostrophes or diacritics need careful consideration. Most concordance programs offer some flexibility in the treatment of hyphens. They can either be ignored, as far as the ordering of words is concerned, or partially ignored, or treated as word separators. Treating the hyphen as a character which affects the sorting of words seems to be the best approach, so that for example all the occurrences of LADY-LIKE would appear as a separate entry in the concordance immediately after all those of LADYLIKE. If the hyphen was ignored completely, the occurrences of both forms would be listed as one entry. If the hyphen was treated as a word separator, the two halves would be considered as separate words thus distorting the vocabulary counts for LADY and LIKE. Some editors have chosen to make a separate word-index of all hyphenated forms, as well as listing them in the main concordance. This would be important if the printing of the text was being studied. Whichever method is chosen, the point to remember is that the computer cannot treat one hyphenated word differently from another. Hyphens must never be inserted into the text as continuation characters at the ends of lines as they are in normal typescript. These would be treated in the same way as genuine hyphens and give rise to some curious words appearing in the concordance.

Words containing apostrophes are a similar case. Obvious examples are I'LL and ILL or CAN'T and CANT. Ideally all the instances of I'LL should come immediately after all the instances of ILL but under a separate keyword heading. If the computer was told to treat all the apostrophes as word separators, the concordance would then no doubt include a large number of words which consisted solely of the letter S. Inclusion of I'LL under ILL would distort the word counts of two words that are under no circumstances the same. A similar treatment could be given to characters which have been used to mark accents in French. *A*, part of *avoir*, should not be confused with *à*, the preposition. If *à* was coded for the computer as A#, the # indicating a grave accent, the computer could be instructed to list all the occurrences of *à* immediately after but under a separate heading from all those of *a*.

Diacritical marks in Greek can also be dealt with in the same manner. Suppose that the letter H is used to represent the Greek *η* in the computer coding. An *η* can occur with a variety of diacritics in several combinations such as ἥ ἤ ἥ ἥ ἤ ἥ ἥ etc. These diacritics can be coded for the computer using different marker symbols preceding or following the H, and the various forms with different diacritics would then appear as separate entries in the concordance.

It is not true that a computer sorts words only according to the English alphabet order. It can be programmed to sort according to any alphabet order and include in its alphabet symbols, such as asterisks, which are not alphabetic. Concordances of Greek or Russian or Semitic languages which appear in the English alphabet order are the result of lazy use of programs which assume the normal sequence of characters. The computer manufacturers' own sorting programs usually only allow the English alphabet order and have a rigid sequence of non-alphabetic characters. Most program packages which have been written for analysing literary text allow the user to specify which computer symbols constitute the alphabet to be used for sorting and also to specify which symbols are word separators, which are to have no effect on the sorting of words, and which are to function as diacritics. The manufacturers' sorting programs are unsuitable for text, as their specifications are too inflexible. Careful programming allows a bilingual text to be sorted according to two alphabet orders, e.g. Greek and English or Russian and English. Provided that the machine was given instructions as to which language it was sorting at any one time, this would be feasible.

Concordances of bilingual texts have been made and can be useful in language teaching or studying bilingual texts where one language is undeciphered or not well understood. If a text exists in two languages and is prepared for the computer in such a way that a line from one text is followed immediately by the corresponding line from the other text, and those two lines are specified as the context of any word appearing in them, a bilingual concordance can be produced. This can be used to find which occurrences of a word are translated by one form and which by others.

Some computer-produced concordances have been criticised heavily for the choice of a particular edition of a text. Some reviewers have even gone so far as to blame the computer for the use of a particular edition. It is, of course, entirely up to the editor to decide which version of the text to use. There are several points which he could consider in choosing his text. If a concordance is to be published and made generally available, it becomes a tool for other people to use. It is essential for them to be aware of which text has been used. It would seem sensible not to make any alteration or emendation to a text to be concorded, and to choose an edition which is well known and generally available, such as the Oxford Classical Texts for Greek and Latin. Even typographical errors should also be left as they are. Corrections to them can be inserted in brackets in the text, but the original should not be deleted. If the editor of a concordance does make his own emendations, his concordance is less useful, as it is based on a text which is not published and which therefore cannot be consulted by other scholars. The choice of a controversial text should always be justified and adequate information should be included about the basis of the text if it has not been previously published.

We have now seen that there are a number of decisions to be made by anyone proposing to produce a concordance by computer. If a concordance is only for the benefit of an individual research project and not for publication, the editor will obviously be aware of its shortcomings and be able to make allowances for them. He may for example be able to compile a list of all the words which he would like to see under one particular lemma without setting out the list in a form suitable for publication. He will also be able to mark those homographs which are important for his research, while ignoring the others. A concordance which is to form the basis of further research for one or two individuals only can therefore be produced with fewer clerical alterations to the computer output.

It must be emphasised that for publication the editor must take considerably more care. A published concordance should have a good introduction explaining in clear terms exactly how the concordance should be used and setting out any defects which may be attributed to the computer. If no attempt has been made to separate homographs or lemmatise words, it must explain that this is the case. The introduction should describe the chosen method of referencing and relate it to the particular edition of the text with an indication of what, if any, emendations have been made. The methods of dealing with hyphenated words, apostrophes, proper names and quoted matter should all be set out clearly, so that the user of the concordance knows exactly where and how to locate entries. A simple word count of forms is useful as an appendix.

It is perhaps appropriate now to consider how some published concordances have dealt with these problems.

The Oxford Shakespeare Concordances, one volume per play, were published from 1969 to 1972. Professor T.H. Howard-Hill began work on them in 1965. He chose to use as his text the old-spelling edition of the plays. His concordances have been criticised on this count, a criticism which is not at all related to the use of a computer. About the same time work on another series of Shakespeare concordances was begun by Marvin Spevack, an American now working in Germany. Spevack chose to use a new text, the Riverside edition. Inevitably the two have been compared in reviews, though Howard-Hill was aiming to make concordances of individual plays in the old-spelling edition, whereas Spevack used a new edition for a complete concordance to Shakespeare.

Howard-Hill puts the keyword to the left of the page (see Figure 3.11), followed by the number of times which the word occurs. In some cases, the number of occurrences of the keyword is given as two distinct figures separated by an asterisk. The introduction explains that the figure after the asterisk is the number of times the word occurs in so-called 'justified' lines, where the spellings may have been affected by the compositor's need to fit the text to his measure. It would perhaps be more meaningful to add the two together and indicate the number of justified lines within this total. The justified lines themselves are marked by an asterisk. His context is aligned to the left, and in almost all cases one line is given, a sensible choice

BURIED = *1
*of many a tall ship lie buried, as they say, if my gossip report   1224
BURNING = 1
  Por. That light we see is burning in my hall: 2503
BURNISHT = 1
  The shadowed liuerie of the burnisht sunne,   519
BURTHENS = 1
why sweat they vnder burthens, let their beds   2001
BUSHELS = *1
*two bushels of chaffe: you shall seeke all day ere you finde them,   125
BUSINES = 4
  I take it your owne busines calls on you,   70
  That purpose merriment: but far you well, | I haue some busines.   767
  slumber not busines for my sake *Bassanio*,   1095
  Por. O loue! dispatch all busines and be gone.   1679
BUT *l*.6 30 36 39 43 78 85 110 117 136 156 162 167 182 *203 *213
  *215 *226 *233 *239 *249 *263 *300 *345 *347 *361 367 383 394
  420 424 462 534 549 *591 *605 *606 *614 *620 *633 *641 *645
  *650 *664 *675 *684 742 746 754 762 767 770 775 *783 789 800
  849 851 *860 870 874 883 921 931 937 947 953 1003 1007 1008
  1019 1030 1031 1042 1062 1096 1120 1140 1161 1180 1189 *1228
  *1254 1283 1294 *1306 *1307 1308 1325 1334 1345 1348 1349
  1352 1354 1358 1363 1370 1374 1382 1397 1422 1424 1427 1433
  1443 1450 1470 1504 1508 1509 1514 1516 1530 1567 1578 1622
  1639 1672 *1677 1681 1693 1731 1781 1787 1809 *1819 1820
  *1852 *1856 1894 1912 1923 1930 1948 1961 1988 2032 2033 2049
  *2061 2104 2175 2179 2193 2195 2199 2224 2239 2243 2244 2248
  2260 2317 2353 2399 2434 2445 2448 2473 2476 2484 2488 2495
  2535 2544 2551 2554 2606 2610 2621 2632 2634 2669 2673 2677
  2699 2710 2734 = 144*37
BUY = 2*1
  They loose it that doe buy it with much care,   83
  *Prophet the Nazarit coniured the deuill into: I wil buy with you,   358
  To buy his fauour, I extend this friendship,   497
BUZZING = 1
  among the buzzing pleased multitude.   1527
BY *see also* be = 88*16
CACKLING = 1
  when euery Goose is cackling, would be thought   2519
CALL = 9*2
  which hearing them would call their brothers fooles,   108
  You call me misbeleeuer, cut-throate dog,   439
  Ant. I am as like to call thee so againe,   457
  Shy. Who bids thee call? I doe not bid thee call.   843
  Iessica. Call you? what is your will?   847
  *they call the place, a very dangerous flat, and fatall, where the
  car-|casses   1222
  *he was wont to call me vsurer, let him looke to his bond, hee
  was   1260
  First goe with me to Church, and call me wife,   1661
  Duke. Goe one and call the Iew into the Court.   1918
  Duke. Bring vs the letters? call the Messenger?   2017
CALLD = 2
  Portia. Yes, yes, it was *Bassanio*, as I thinke so was he calld.   306
  You calld me dogge: and for these curtesies   455
CALLDST = 1
  thou call'dst me dogge before thou hadst a cause,   1692

for lines the length of Shakespeare's; but a few entries have more than one line, and a vertical stroke is then used to indicate the end of the first line in them. The criterion for listing more than one line of context is not apparent, and those entries must have been selected manually. He includes the speakers' names as part of the context on those lines which begin a speech. They are included as keywords in the concordance but are indexed separately in all but the first few volumes.

No attempt is made at lemmatisation; but for English text the various forms of one lemma are usually close to each other in alphabetical order. The introduction also explains the arrangement of the entries, indicating that the old spelling may occasionally lead the reader astray in the search for a word. In some cases cross-references have been inserted in the concordances to direct the reader to the appropriate place.

High-frequency words are treated in one of two different ways. Only frequency counts are given for some very common words, including pronouns, parts of the verb 'to be' and some prepositions. A larger number of words, mostly variant spellings, have been given a fuller treatment in that the line number references of where they occur in the text are also provided.

One further point can be made about Howard-Hill's choice of layout. When a word occurs more than once in a line, that line occurs only once in the contexts given for that word. Thus it is not so easy for the reader to see that a word occurs more than once in the same line. A better alternative is to list a line once for each time a word occurs in it. This may be monotonous for a line in which the same word is repeated several times, but at least all the information is there. If a KWIC-type concordance was used, each occurrence of the word would in turn be aligned in the centre of the page so that its position in a line would be easier to see. Another possibility is to underline the keywords in the context lines or to print them in italics.

Howard-Hill used computer typesetting for his concordances, and the results are pleasing to the eye. The keywords stand out well and it is very easy for the reader to find the entries for a particular word, but perhaps not so easy once the individual contexts need to be inspected. Spevack's first publication of his concordances consisted of a reproduction of computer-printout upper case only and looked very ugly. Since then a complete concordance of all Shakespeare's plays has been published by him and is much more pleasing in appearance.

In his *Index Thomisticus*, Busa provides a different layout. His entries are given in columns down the page with about two and a half lines of context for each word. The forms of each lemma all appear as sub-entries under the dictionary heading. For this purpose the text was pre-edited as it was input. Following the lemma, each of its forms appears in alphabetical order. The keyword and succeeding word are printed in bold type in the contexts, and the keyword is also printed some distance above the contexts. The layout of keywords and contexts is clear, but the references are not easy to follow. They appear at the end of the context for each entry and consist of very short abbreviations and numbers. Their format is described in the introduction, which is itself a separate volume, written in six languages. The completed index will comprise over 60 volumes, but unfortunately its price puts it out of the reach of all but the most affluent libraries. Publishing on microfiche would have reduced the cost considerably and might now be a more suitable medium for such a large work.

Concordances need not necessarily be made from texts made up of alphabetic words. In his decipherment of Linear B, Ventris compiled grids of the frequencies of all the Linear B symbols by hand. The computer can perform the same task on symbols of undeciphered scripts. A coding system has to be devised to represent each symbol, and then the computer can be programmed to compile a concordance of each symbol. When the symbols are sorted by right or left context, the frequency of groups of consecutive symbols is apparent. The symbols can be drawn on a computer graphics device and the concordance output in the original script. One such concordance was that produced by Koskenniemi, Parpola and Parpola on the Indus Valley inscriptions (see Figure 3.12). A similar method of investigating sign frequencies has also been applied to Linear A and Minoan hieroglyphs.

The making of concordances and word indexes is thus a largely automatic task well suited to the computer. We have seen that some manual intervention is normally required to deal with the problems posed by automation, but this is slight compared with the amount of work which the computer itself performs as it counts and sorts words. Lexicography, on the other hand, demands human effort on a much larger scale. There are three basic stages in compiling a dictionary. The first stage consists of assembling the material, usages of words which are potentially interesting, the traditional method being to record each usage of each word on a slip. The second stage is to sort the slips into alphabetical order and file them under the appropriate lemma. The third stage is to edit the examples for each lemma so as to produce the article for each word.

A number of successful attempts have been made to use the computer for stage one, the collection of material. This means that all the material to be scanned must be in computer-readable form, which entails a mammoth task if the dictionary is to cover a complete language. This is the procedure adopted by the *Trésor de la Langue Française*. In order to collect their 'slips', the editors have made concordances to texts from over 1000 different authors from the nineteenth and twentieth centuries. The examples have

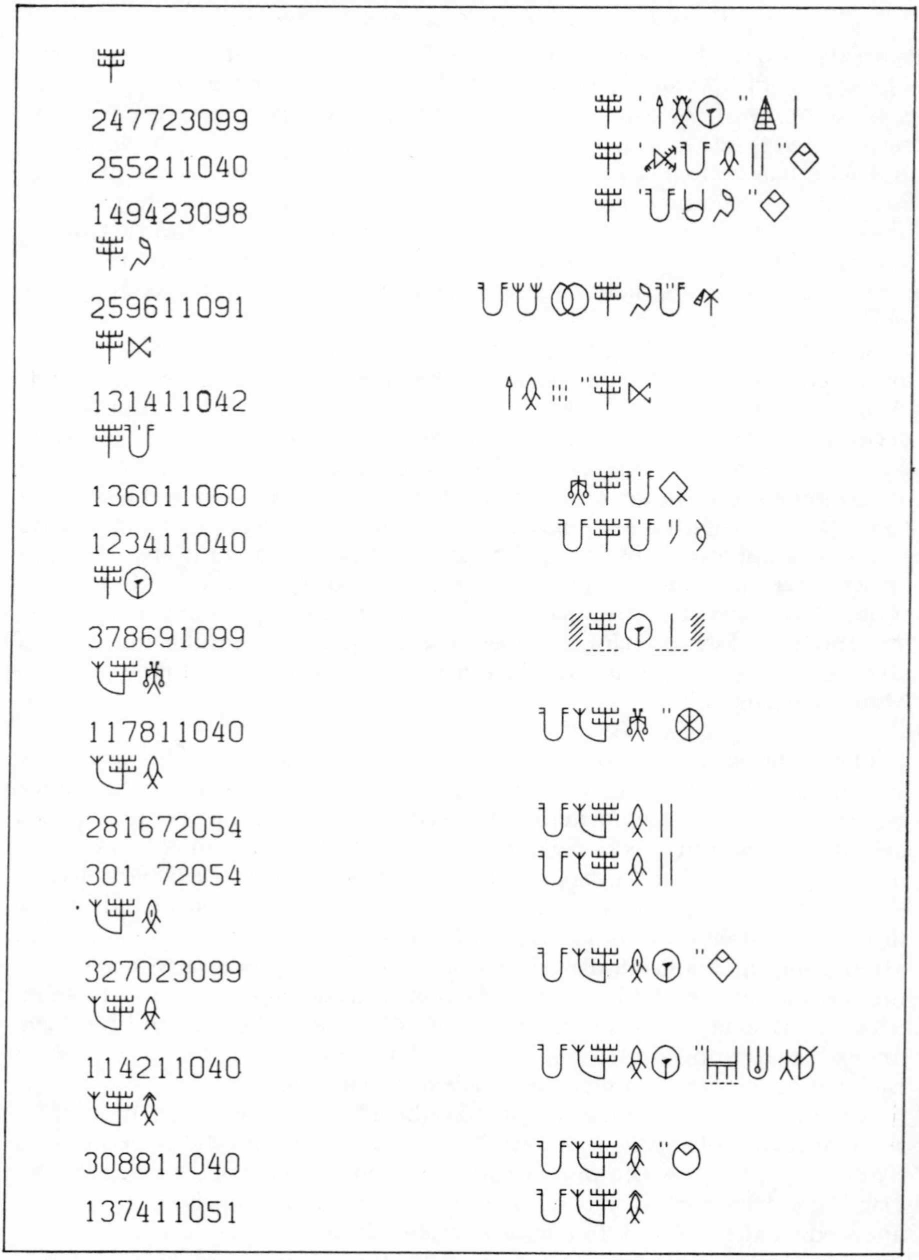

247723099

255211040

149423098

259611091

131411042

136011060

123411040

378691099

117811040

281672054

301 72054

327023099

114211040

308811040

137411051

Figure 3.12. A page from the concordance of Indus Valley inscriptions *Materials for the Study of the Indus Script* edited by Koskenniemi, Parpola and Parpola.

then been collected from these concordances. The *Dictionary of Old English* based in Toronto and the *Dictionary of the Older Scottish Tongue* based in Edinburgh have adopted the same method, though on much smaller corpora of material. A by-product of this method is, of course, a comprehensive archive of texts in computer-readable form, which may be used for other purposes and possibly become more important than the original work. Using such a comprehensive archive is the only way of ensuring that all possible material has been scanned and that no significant usages have been omitted. It does, however, require large resources for preparing material for the computer, processing the concordances and then scanning the concordances for interesting usages. This method is practical only if there are large resources available or the volume of material is not too large – for example, a dictionary of a specific author, or authors, or a short period of a language, or a language for which there are few known texts.

The problem of the context in computer-aided lexicography has been discussed at some length, particularly by de Tollenaere. The dictionary-maker does not wish to refer back to the original text in order to determine the meaning of a word. He must therefore have at his disposal sufficient context for this purpose, which may be up to seven or eight lines. The keyword would most probably appear somewhere in the middle of this context, which would consist of one or more complete sentences. The lineprinter could be loaded with special stationery and the machine programmed to print slips on that stationery, which could then be filed in the traditional manner. Figure 3.13 shows an example of computer-generated dictionary slips. In this case the keyword is offset to the left at the top and surrounded by asterisks for clarity in the context.

The computer is most useful at stage two of the dictionary-making process, the filing and sorting of slips. It is no longer necessary for the dictionary-maker to have a large number of shoe-boxes containing slips filed in alphabetical order. The computer can be used to hold the information contained on the slips, and when new slips are made the machine will insert them into the correct alphabetical position. If the slips are themselves generated by computer as described above, they can be printed if necessary; but it is more likely that they will be stored on magnetic tape or disc.

Accuracy and speed are the main advantages of using the computer here. In a manual system, a slip misfiled is almost always a slip lost for ever. The computer should never lose material once it is stored correctly, and the slips should always be in the correct alphabetical order. If the slips have been created manually, an indication can be given if the word is a homograph so that it will be filed with the appropriate lemma.

If the computer has been used for excerption, some method of

think

They point out that by the excision of the epilogue and all the references to
such undramatic and tedious matters as the Church, the feudal system, the
Inquisition, the theory of heresy and so forth, all of which, they point out,
would be ruthlessly blue pencilled by any experienced manager, the play could be
considerably shortened. I **think** they are mistaken. The experienced knights
of the blue pencil, having saved an hour and a half by disembowelling the play,
would at once proceed to waste two hours in building elaborate scenery,
B. SHAW, *Saint Joan* 83 [1924]

audience

The intervals between the acts whilst these splendors were being built up and
then demolished by the stage carpenters would seem eternal, to the great profit
of the refreshment bars. And the weary and demoralized **audience** would lose
their last trains and curse me for writing such inordinately long and
intolerably dreary and meaningless plays.
B. SHAW, *Saint Joan* 83 [1924]

public

Nobody who knows the stage history of Shakespear will doubt that this is what
would happen if I knew my business so little as to listen to these well
intentioned but disastrous counsellors: indeed it probably will happen when I am
no longer in control of the performing rights. So perhaps it will be as well for
the **public** to see the play while I am still alive.
B. SHAW, *Saint Joan* 84 [1924]

Figure 3.13. Computer generated dictionary slips. (de Tollenaere)

lemmatisation must be adopted. There are three ways in which the computer can be instructed to lemmatise forms. First, it may be given rules by means of a program so that it can assign the correct lemma to each word. Such a computer program is very complicated and must allow for many exceptions and is never very satisfactory. Secondly the text can be pre-edited as it is input, so that each word is accompanied by its lemma; but this entails much extra labour at the input stage. The third method is to use a kind of 'dictionary' which is already in computer-readable form.

The word 'dictionary' is here used in its computing sense. It does not imply a complete listing of all words in the language – a kind of computerised Webster or *Oxford English Dictionary*. Rather it is applied to a computer file which contains definitions of, or further information on, terms or words which a program may encounter. Such a dictionary is likely to be consulted or 'searched' by a number of different programs, and may be built up over a long period, with new forms added to it when required. In the context of lemmatisation a dictionary would contain the lemma of each word likely to be encountered.

It would be useful at this point to explain the functions involved in a search of a computer dictionary. The human mind learns: it looks a word up two or three times and then memorises it; no more searches are required. The computer cannot do this. Every word must be looked up every time that it is encountered. Therefore an efficient use of searching methods can make all the difference to whether a program runs well or not.

Let us suppose that we have a computer dictionary of 1000 words. This dictionary would be stored in alphabetical order on magnetic tape or disc. If the computer were large enough, it could all be held in the machine's main memory throughout the duration of the program. Let us suppose that we are searching in the dictionary for the word 'cat'. If our dictionary was in alphabetical order we might have to start at the beginning and ask if each word in turn was 'cat'. As the letter 'c' is near the beginning of the alphabet, 'cat' would be found fairly soon, probably around the seventieth attempt. If 'cat' was not in the dictionary, we could determine that by recognising when we had come to a word later in the alphabet. But consider what would happen if the word was 'zebra'. If we started at the beginning and compared every word with 'zebra' we would have made almost 1000 comparisons, which is very wasteful of machine time.

Another method is to construct a small table, which is stored with the dictionary. This table would contain information indicating where each letter of the alphabet starts in the dictionary. We would then establish that our word begins with a c, look up c in our table and find which position in our dictionary the cs start and also how many there are. We could then make a straightforward search through the cs to find our word. This method would reduce the number of comparisons to be made for a word at the end of the alphabet to the same number as for any letter. When new words are added to the dictionary they will be inserted in the correct alphabetical position, usually by sorting them into alphabetical order and then merging them with the words already there. A special program would also update the table indicating where each letter begins and ends.

Another more commonly used method of computer searching approximates to the way in which a reader would look up a word in an ordinary dictionary. He opens it at one page and then flips backwards and forwards from there until he isolates the page which contains the word. The computer opens its dictionary in the middle and looks to see whether the word comes before or after that point. If it finds that it comes before, it takes the middle again of this first section and asks the same question. It goes on taking the middle of each section found until it has arrived almost at the correct place. It can then do a straightforward sequential search through the last five or so items to find the exact one. This method is known as a *binary search* because each section that is found is split into two before being searched again. If our 'cat' was at position 70 out of 1000, it would be found in only ten comparisons. A binary search such as this combined with the table look-up one described above would provide an even more efficient search technique. The computer would use the table to find the beginning and end of the 'c's and then do a binary search on the 'c's.

Yet another method of dictionary look-up is called hashing. This requires some fairly complex programming, but in essence the method consists of converting each word to a number which indicates its position in the dictionary. The SNOBOL programming language includes a feature for table look-up using a hashing procedure which relieves the programmer from having to write all the program for dictionary searches.

This process of collecting lexicographic material and filing it inside the computer may take several years of work. With such a lapse of time, one disadvantage of using a computer must be recognised. The life of a computer is only about eight or ten years. The time taken to collect material for a dictionary may be much longer than this and so the editor must ensure that the files he is creating can easily be transferred from one machine to another. It is all too easy to exploit the idiosyncrasies of one machine and then discover that programs have to be completely rewritten for another machine. Those who are fortunate enough to have their own computer for a dictionary project may avoid this problem completely if they can use one machine from start to finish.

The third stage of lexicography, that of editing the quotations for each word to form a dictionary article, is basically a task for the human mind. The computer cannot decide whether to include specific quotations, as it has no sense of meaning. However it can be instructed to print out all the slips it has assembled for a particular lemma. The editor can then select the quotations he requires from the printout and organise them into specific categories of meaning.

By using a computer to edit the material for each word in the computer files he can create the final article for his dictionary inside the computer. This may involve some reordering of the entries, but the bulk of the work will consist of deleting superfluous quotations and reducing the length of those required, both of which are simple tasks to perform at a computer terminal. The advantage of this method of editing is that the material remains in computer-readable form and can be typeset directly thus eliminating any further need for extensive proofreading.

The computer can therefore only completely replace the mechanical process of filing, sorting and organising the slips. This can itself make a significant contribution to the speed and accuracy with which a dictionary is compiled. The machine cannot make any kind of judgment on what to include or select in each article. That is and always will be the work of the lexicographer.

REFERENCES

1. A.J. Aitken, Historical Dictionaries and the Computer. *The Computer in Literary and Linguistic Research*, 3-17 (ed. R.A. Wisbey). Cambridge: Cambridge University Press (1971)

2. A.J. Aitken and P. Bratley, An Archive of Older Scottish Texts for Scanning by Computer. *English Studies* 48 (1967) 60-1

3. M.H.T. Alford, The Computer and Lexicography. *ALLC Bull.* 1 No. 3 (1973) 8-9

4. G.L.M. Berry-Rogghe, COCOA: A Word Count and Concordance Generator. *ALLC Bull.* 1 No. 2 (1973) 29-31

5. Godelieve L.M. Berry-Rogghe and T.D. Crawford, Developing a Machine Independent Concordance Program for a Variety of Languages. *The Computer and Literary Studies*, 309-15 (eds A.J. Aitken, R.W. Bailey and N. Hamilton-Smith). Edinburgh: Edinburgh University Press (1973)

6. Godelieve L.M. Berry-Rogghe and T.D. Crawford, *COCOA Manual*. Atlas Computer Laboratory (1973)

7. Paul Bratley and Serge Lusignan, Information Processing in Dictionary Making: Some Technical Guidelines. *Computers and the Humanities* 10 (1976) 133-43

8. Roberto Busa S.J. (ed.), *Index Thomisticus*. Stuttgart: Fromann-Holzboog (1973-)

9. A. Cameron, The Dictionary of Old English and the Computer. *Computing in the Humanities*, 101-6 (eds Serge Lusignan and John S. North). Waterloo: University of Waterloo Press (1977)

10. John Chadwick, *The Decipherment of Linear B*. Cambridge: Cambridge University Press (1958)

11. Roberta Frank and Angus Cameron (eds), *A Plan for the Dictionary of Old English*. Toronto: University of Toronto Press (1973)

12. N. Hamilton-Smith, A Versatile Concordance Program for a Textual Archive. *The Computer in Literary and Linguistic Research*, 235-44 (ed. R.A. Wisbey). Cambridge: Cambridge University Press (1971)

13. Susan M. Hockey and V. Shibayev, The Bilingual Analytical Literary and Linguistic Concordance (BALCON). *ALLC Bull.* 3 (1975) 133-9

14. T.H. Howard-Hill, The Oxford Old Spelling Concordances. *Studies in Bibliography* 22 (1969) 143-64

15. T.H. Howard-Hill (ed.) *Oxford Shakespeare Concordances*. Oxford: Oxford University Press (1969-72)

16. T.H. Howard-Hill, *Literary Concordances*. New York: Pergamon Press (1979)

17. Paul Imbs (ed.), *Trésor de la Langue Française: Dictionnaire de la Langue du XIX et du XX Siècle* (1789-1960). Paris: Editions du Centre National de la Recherche Scientifique (1971-)

18. William Ingram, Concordances in the Seventies. *Computers and the Humanities* 8 (1974) 273-7

19. R.I. Ireland, (ed.), *Concordance to Ammianus Marcellinus*. (unpublished)

20. Seppo Koskenniemi, Asko Parpola and Simo Parpola (eds), *Materials for the Study of the Indus Script*. Helsinki: Suomalainen Tiedeakatenia (1973)

21. D.W. Packard (ed.), *A Concordance to Livy*. Harvard: Harvard University Press (1968)

22. D.W. Packard, *Minoan Linear A*. Berkeley and Los Angeles: University of California Press (1974)

23. Stephen M. Parrish, Problems in the Making of Computer Concordances. *Studies in Bibliography* 15 (1962) 1-14

24. Joseph Raben, The Death of the Handmade Concordance. *Scholarly Publishing* 1 (1969) 61-9

25. J.L. Robinson and R.W. Bailey, Computer-produced Microfilm in Lexicography: Toward a Dictionary of Early Modern English. *The Computer and Literary Studies*, 3-14 (eds A.J. Aitken, R.W. Bailey and N. Hamilton-Smith). Edinburgh: Edinburgh University Press (1973)

26. M. Spevack (ed.) *The Harvard Concordance to Shakespeare*. Cambridge, Mass.: Belknap Press of Harvard University Press (1974)

27. Marvin Spevack and H. Joachim Neuhaus, SHAD (A Shakespeare Dictionary): Toward Volume One. *ALLC Bull.* 5 (1977) 15-22

28. M. Spevack, H.J. Neuhaus and T. Finkenstaedt, SHAD: a Shakespeare Dictionary. *Computers in the Humanities*, 111-23 (ed. J.L. Mitchell). Edinburgh: Edinburgh University Press (1974)

29. F. de Tollenaere, The Problem of the Context in Computer-aided Lexicography. *The Computer and Literary Studies*, 25-35 (eds A.J. Aitken, R.W. Bailey and N. Hamilton-Smith). Edinburgh: Edinburgh University Press (1973)

30. R.A. Wisbey, Publications from an Archive of Computer-Readable Literary Texts. *The Computer in Literary and Linguistic Research*, 19-34 (ed. R.A. Wisbey). Cambridge: Cambridge University Press (1971)

Further Reading

R.W. Bailey and J.L. Robinson, The University of Michigan Early Modern English Dictionary Project. *Shakespeare Research and Opportunities* 4 (1968) 120-1

Leonard Brandwood (ed.), *A Word Index to Plato*. Leeds: W.S. Maney (1976) (Vol. 8 in COMPENDIA series)

Angus Cameron, Roberta Frank and John Leyerle (eds), *Computers and Old English Concordances*. Toronto: University of Toronto Press (1969)

A.T. Crosland, The Concordance and the Study of the Novel. *ALLC Bull.* 3 (1975) 190-6

L.A. Cummings, A Homily on Wulfstan's Homilies: Concordance Making and Publishing. *ALLC Bull.* 5 (1977) 113-8

J.E.G. Dixon, A Prose Concordance: Rabelais. *ALLC Bull.* 2 No. 3 (1974) 47-54

N. Hamilton-Smith, *CONCORD: User's Specification*. Edinburgh Regional Computer Centre (1970)

T.H. Howard-Hill, On Literary Concordances: An Early View. *ALLC Bull.* 4 (1976) 215-20

D.J. Koubourlis, On Concordances and their Uses. *Slavic and East European Journal* 19 (1975) 246-53

L.F. Lara, On Lexicographical Computing: Some Aspects of the Work for a Mexican Spanish Dictionary. *ALLC Bull.* 4 (1976) 97-104

H. Joachim Neuhaus and Marvin Spevack, A Shakespeare Dictionary (SHAD): Some Preliminaries for a Semantic Description. *Computers and the Humanities* 9 (1975) 263-70

Robert L. Oakman, Concordances from Computers: a Review Article. *Proof* 3 (1973) 411-25

M. Spevack, Concordances: Old and New. *Computer Studies in the Humanities and Verbal Behavior* 4 (1973) 17-19

M. Spevack, SHAD (A Shakespeare Dictionary): Toward a Taxonomic Classification of the Shakespeare Corpus. *Computing in the Humanities*, 107-14 (eds Serge Lusignan and John S. North). Waterloo: University of Waterloo Press (1977)

F. de Tollenaere, The Leiden Thesaurus. *Computer Studies in the Humanities and Verbal Behavior*, 3 (1972) 169-72

Felicien de Tollenaere and Randall L. Jones (eds), *Word Indices and Word-Lists to the Gothic Bible and Minor Fragments*. Leiden: E.J. Brill (1976)

F. de Tollenaere, Word Indexes and Word-Lists to the Gothic Bible: Experiences and Problems. *The Computer in Literary and Linguistic Studies (Proceedings of the Third International Symposium)*, 118-32 (eds Alan Jones and R.F. Churchhouse). Cardiff: University of Wales Press (1976)

David Wells, Roy Wisbey and Brian Murdoch (eds), *Concordances to the Early Middle High*

German Biblical Epic the 'Vorauer Bücher Moses' the 'Altdeutsche Exodus' and the 'Anegenge', 8 microfiches. Cambridge: Cambridge University Press (1976)

R.A. Wisbey, Concordance Making by Electronic Computer: Some Experiences with the Wiener Genesis. *Modern Language Review* 57 (1962) 161-72

R.A. Wisbey, The Analysis of Middle High German Texts by Computer – Some Lexicographical Aspects. *Transactions of the Philological Society* (1963) 28-48

G.P. Zarri, A Project of a New and Updated edition of the Fifth Volume of the Corpus Inscriptionum Latinarum with Automatic Preparation of Indexes. *ALLC Bull.* 2 No. 3 (1974) 7-15

4. Vocabulary Studies, Collocations and Dialectology

In this chapter we shall explore some of the ways in which the computer can be used in the study of vocabulary, and in particular words in relation to other words, or co-occurrences or collocations as they are sometimes called. Counting occurrences of words is, of course, nothing new. T.C. Mendenhall at the end of the last century was one of the earliest workers in this field and in 1944 George Udny Yule published *The Statistical Study of Literary Vocabulary*. Yule's *K* characteristic has been widely used as a measure of diversity or richness of vocabulary. It is of course now much easier and more accurate to make the word counts by computer and also to use the machine to make statistical calculations on the numbers collected.

A simple word frequency count produced by the COCOA program is shown in Figure 4.1. All words occurring once are listed in alphabetical order, followed by all those occurring twice and so on up to the most frequent. The COCOA program can also provide what is called a frequency profile, telling us how many words occur once, how many twice, etc., and giving cumulative totals of the number of different words, or *types* and the usages of those words, sometimes called *tokens*. An example of such a word frequency profile appears in Figure 4.2 showing that in this text, 42 words occur once, 14 occur twice, 5 occur 3 times and so on up to the most frequent word occurring 7 times.

Vocabulary counts like these are used increasingly in the design of language courses. Teaching can then concentrate on those words and grammatical forms which occur most frequently in the language. This was the approach of the University of Nottingham when they undertook to design a German course for chemists. The aim was to teach chemists sufficient German to enable them to read technical articles. Word counts were made on a number of German chemical journals and a course was designed which concentrated on the most frequent forms. For example it was found that the first and second persons of the verb occurred so infrequently in the technical literature that it was decided not to include them in the course.

The Nottingham German course is just one example of the many computer projects which are used in the specification of language courses.

The fact that the computer does not lemmatise forms or classify them under their dictionary heading is of some advantage here as those grammatical forms which occur most frequently can be determined. A frequency count of words sorted in alphabetical order of their endings can also be made. This would be of particular use in inflected languages to

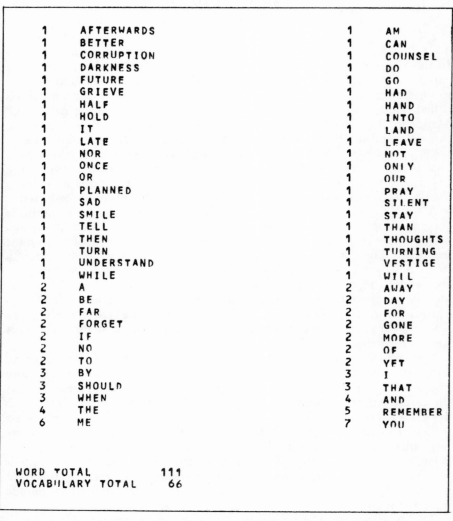

1	AFTERWARDS		1	AM
1	BETTER		1	CAN
1	CORRUPTION		1	COUNSEL
1	DARKNESS		1	DO
1	FUTURE		1	GO
1	GRIEVE		1	HAD
1	HALF		1	HAND
1	HOLD		1	INTO
1	IT		1	LAND
1	LATE		1	LEAVE
1	NOR		1	NOT
1	ONCE		1	ONLY
1	OR		1	OUR
1	PLANNED		1	PRAY
1	SAD		1	SILENT
1	SMILE		1	STAY
1	TELL		1	THAN
1	THEN		1	THOUGHTS
1	TURN		1	TURNING
1	UNDERSTAND		1	VESTIGE
1	WHILE		1	WILL
2	A		2	AWAY
2	BE		2	DAY
2	FAR		2	FOR
2	FORGET		2	GONE
2	IF		2	MORE
2	NO		2	OF
2	TO		2	YET
3	BY		3	I
3	SHOULD		3	THAT
3	WHEN		4	AND
4	THE		5	REMEMBER
6	ME		7	YOU

```
WORD TOTAL          111
VOCABULARY TOTAL     66
```

Figure 4.1. A word count in frequency order.

WORD COUNT	NUMBER SUCH	VOCAB TOTAL	WORD TOTAL	PERC. OF VOCABULARY	PERC. OF WORDS
1	42	42	42	63.64	37.84
2	14	56	70	84.85	63.06
3	5	61	85	92.42	76.58
4	2	63	93	95.45	83.78
5	1	64	98	96.97	88.29
6	1	65	104	98.48	93.69
7	1	66	111	100.00	100.00

Figure 4.2. A word frequency profile.

determine which morphological features should be taught first. In one project reported by Dudrap and Emery, a study of French nominal genders was undertaken. All nouns from the *Nouveau Petit Larousse* were prepared for the computer, each noun being terminated by a numerical code indicating its gender. The words were then sorted by their endings and the distribution of nouns according to their endings noted.

Another use of vocabulary counts in language teaching is to control the introduction of new vocabulary into courses. Kanocz and Wolff describe the preparation of a German language course for the British Broadcasting Corporation. The computer was used to provide frequency counts of a number of German texts from which words to be included in the course were chosen. As each course unit was prepared, its vocabulary was input to the computer and checked against the vocabulary of the previous units to ensure that new words were being introduced at a reasonable rate and that there was some repetition of words already introduced. A similar method was employed by Burnett-Hall and Stupples in their preparation of a Russian course.

Large frequency counts have been made of a number of texts or languages. One of the earliest was Sture Allén's frequency count of present-day Swedish. This was taken from some one million words of newspaper material. In all 1387 signed articles by 569 different writers in five Swedish morning newspapers published in 1965 were selected. The articles were chosen so as to be representative of the modern language and thus excluded material written by foreigners, letters to the editor and articles which contained long quoted passages. Unsigned articles were also excluded on the grounds that they might have been written by someone whose native language was not Swedish. Allén has produced three volumes of frequency counts so far and more are planned.

Newspapers are a good choice of material for an examination of the current use of language. They were also the choice of Alan Jones in Oxford who has been studying modern Turkish. There have been enormous changes in the Turkish language since the alphabet was romanised in 1928. Many Arabic and Persian loan words have been replaced by newly coined words formed from old Turkish roots or by loan words from European languages, principally French. Seven newspapers and one magazine were chosen as representatives of the language, and a computer program which generates random numbers was used to select samples totalling 40,000 words from each of the eight journals, all from 1968-9. Word frequency counts were made on all of these samples and thus the proportion of Arabic, Persian and English or French loan words was noted. The process is being repeated on samples taken from the same newspapers five years later, and the changes which have taken place in the language over that period are being noted.

The use of frequency counts to study loan words in a language entails a considerable amount of manual work to read through the word lists marking all the loan words. A number of attempts have therefore been made to program the computer to select loan words. The approach has been to compile a set of letter combinations which could appear in loan words but not in the native language. One such study of English loan-words in modern French is described in an article by Suzanne Hanon. Letter combinations which would designate an English loan word include the use of rare letters like *w* and *k* and English suffixes such as *-ing* and *-man*. At total of about 100 graphical entities found was reduced to about 70 because some were redundant (such as -g/-ing) and some were represented in different positions in a word. The next stage was to write a program to recognise these character strings in the relevant positions in the word. If it found them, the program would indicate that the word was English. The program was first tested on a number of known loan-words, which were themselves chosen manually from newspapers. The test program found about 80% of the test data supplied to it. More criteria were devised from the words which it failed to find, but there were still 31 words out of a total of 881 which it was impossible to deal with automatically. They were mostly forms like 'bluffeur' which consists of a French ending on an English word. The experiment concluded by trying the program on some genuine French text, about thirty pages of a novel. Again the results had to be checked manually. Out of 8952 words, 75 were identified as loan-words. Of these, only 10 were found to be genuine English loans. It was established manually that the program had not missed any genuine loans, but the high number of erroneous finds indicates that this method of selecting loan words by computer is not very satisfactory. It would of course require a different program for each borrowing language and each lending language. As in the case of the Turkish newspaper project, there could be loan words from a number of languages in any one language. It would appear to be more sensible to approach the study of loan-words by using a word frequency count and select the words manually, although more work is involved.

The study of the vocabulary of a specific author or authors can be assisted considerably by the use of a computer. More of this will be found in Chapter Six, but here we can describe some simple applications. Martin, a Belgian who has been studying Dutch vocabulary with the aid of a computer, indicates the sort of methods which may be successful. He describes his work on a poem of 32,235 words, a lyrical epic called *May* which is rich in vocabulary and was thought to contain a number of 'new words'. Martin was able to compare his text with a computer-readable version of a thesaurus of Dutch and could thus ascertain that 460 words which occurred in the poem were not in the dictionary. Of these only 16 had a frequency of more than one and only two occurred more than twice. He then went on to investigate the distribution of these words in the poem. This was done by dividing the poem into eleven roughly equal sections. He was then able to calculate the number of new words in each section which would be expected on the assumption that they were evenly distributed. By comparing the actual values with the expected values it was found that a significantly high proportion of the new words came in one section of the poem, that of the song of the god Balder, thus confirming the special character of this part of the work.

Martin also investigated the richness of the vocabulary measured by the type/token ratio. This was found to be 5.69, compared with a value of just over 8 for two other Dutch texts of the same length, which confirmed that there was a relatively extensive vocabulary. A further study showed that at least half the surplus of types were concentrated on words which occurred at the ends of lines – that is, words which were chosen to satisfy the rhyme requirements. Martin's study shows the kind of vocabulary investigation which can be made very easily using a computer, but would not really be feasible without.

One very early computer-aided vocabulary study was that by Joseph Raben on the influence of Milton on Shelley. Raben's method could well be applied to study the influence of any one author on another. He attempted to find those lines in one work which consciously or unconsciously echo lines in another work. This does not necessarily mean that the lines are identical, but that a similarity may be recognised such as

> Whence and what art thou, execrable shape,
> That dars't, though grim and terrible, advance
> Thy miscreated Front athwart my way
> To yonder gates? through them I mean to pass,

and

> Horrible forms,
> What and who are ye? Never yet there came
> Phantasms so foul through monster-teeming Hell
> From the all-miscreative brain of Jove;
> Whilst I behold such execrable shapes,

Raben could have adopted several methods of dealing with this problem, such as coding his material in a phonemic transcription or attempting to put words in their semantic categories. The method he chose was quite successful. Complete word lists of the texts of both Milton and Shelley were made – these lists were then modified so that some words, such as prepositions, were omitted. Proper names were retained. Most of the words were converted to what he calls their canonised form, a sort of lemmatisation. Suffixes and prefixes were also stripped off for this purpose, so that for example 'miscreated' would be reclassified as 'create', and 'disobeyed', 'obedience', 'obedient' would all become 'obey'. The texts were then recoded automatically in this canonised form and a simple concordance made. It was then very easy to see which patterns of words were echoed by Shelley from Milton. This kind of vocabulary study can provide concrete evidence to support a subjective impression that one author consciously, or unconsciously, echoes another. A straightforward concordance of one author can provide some material. By looking up words from the second author, similarities of phrases or whole lines can be found. A concordance of two texts combined can provide yet more evidence of these similarities, but would not find combinations such as 'disobeyed' and 'obeyed' unless prefixes were separated from the root forms. Raben's method ensures that all combinations can be found at the cost of a little extra computing.

Thematic analysis can also be attempted by computer, but the machine must be told which words (and grammatical forms of words) denote a particular theme or themes. This kind of study can be based on a concordance, but a program devised by Fortier and McConnell at Manitoba has attempted to reduce the human work. A list of synonyms is supplied to the program, which will then produce frequency and distribution tables for certain sections of the text. The program also draws a histogram on the computer's lineprinter indicating which sections of the work have a high density of a particular theme. Fortier and McConnell's system contains ten synonym dictionaries of French words, and is therefore specific to French, but it could easily be adapted for use with other languages. It is possible to separate words denoting primary or strong evocation of a theme from those denoting secondary or weaker evocation.

Figure 4.3 shows a histogram drawn by a section of the program called GRAPH. It uses colons for showing primary evocation, in this case of words denoting jealousy in Céline's *Voyage au Bout de la Nuit*. The numbers indicate the number of times which the theme occurs in each chapter. The histograms can also be used to denote secondary evocations, in which case full stops are used instead of colons. These programs are called THEME and represent an extension of the concordance. Results have also been published on the analysis of words evoking doubt in Beckett's *En Attendant Godot*.

```
CHAPTER=1        29:::::::::::::::::::::::::::

CHAPTER=2        39:::::::::::::::::::::::::::::::::::::

CHAPTER=3        16::::::::::::::::

CHAPTER=4        61:::::::::::::::::::::::::::::::::::::::::::::::::::::::::::::

CHAPTER=5        38:::::::::::::::::::::::::::::::::::::

CHAPTER=6        38:::::::::::::::::::::::::::::::::::::

CHAPTER=7        81::::::::::::::::::::::::::::::::::::::::::::::::::::::::::::::::::::::::::::::::

CHAPTER=8        67:::::::::::::::::::::::::::::::::::::::::::::::::::::::::::::::::::::

CHAPTER=9        16::::::::::::::::
```

Figure 4.3. GRAPH output from the THEME system showing the distribution of words denoting jealousy in Celine's *Voyage au Bout de la Nuit*. (Fortier and McConnell)

We can now move on to look at the study of collocations, a term first introduced by J.R. Firth in 1951. Firth does not give an exact definition of collocation but rather illustrates the notion by way of examples, e.g. one of the meanings of 'ass' is its habitual collocation with an immediately preceding 'you silly …' In other words we are looking at lexical items which frequently associate with other lexical items. It is only recently that the notion of collocations has been seriously studied, largely because of the practical restrictions imposed on any large scale investigation of collocating words. The advent of computers has remedied this drawback and led to several linguistic collocational studies.

Dr Lieve Berry-Rogghe has been one of the leaders in the field of computer-aided collocation studies. She aims to compile a list of those lexical items 'collocates' which co-occur significantly with a given lexical item called the *node* within a specified distance called the *span* which is measured as a number of words. In order to obtain a comprehensive

Span = 3				Span = 4			
Collocate	K	Fc	*z-score*	*Collocate*	K	Fc	*z-score*
sold	6	7	24·0500	sold	6	7	20·7566
commons	4	4	21·2416	commons	4	4	18·3415
decorate	2	3	19·9000	decorate	3	3	15·8837
this	22	252	13·3937	this	22	252	10·7863
empty	3	7	11·9090	empty	3	7	10·2360
buying	2	4	10·5970	buying	2	4	9·0697
painting	2	4	10·5970	painting	2	4	9·0697
opposite	2	6	8·5192	opposite	2	6	7·5951
loves	2	10	6·4811	loves	2	10	5·5975
outside	2	12	5·8626	*entered*	2	10	5·5975
lived	2	13	5·6067	*near*	2	11	5·2373
family	2	20	4·3744	outside	2	12	4·9038
remember	2	26	3·9425	lived	2	13	4·7583
full	2	25	3·8209	remember	3	26	4·9102
my	8	271	3·6780	*rooms*	2	15	4·3255
into	3	92	3·5792	*flat*	2	18	3·8170
the	35	2368	3·2978	*big*	2	19	3·7878
has	2	50	2·9359	*Bernard*	2	20	3·6876
				family	2	20	3·6676
				my	9	271	3·3055
				full	2	23	3·2845
				into	3	92	2·8326
				the	42	2368	2·3182
				every	3	59	2·7971
				Mrs	2	29	2·6713

Figure 4.4. The significant collocates of '*house*' for span size three, four, five and six. (Berry-Rogghe)

picture of collocation relations, it would be necessary to process a very large volume of text. Berry-Rogghe's initial experiment was conducted on some 71,000 words, which she herself admits is not sufficient. A concordance-type program was written which limits the context for each keyword to the specified span. All items occurring within the span are then conflated into an alphabetical list and their number of co-occurrences with the node is counted. This list is compared to a previously compiled dictionary consisting of an alphabetical frequency list for the whole text. She then computes what she calls the *z-score* for each collocate. The z-score measures the frequency of the item occurring as a collocate as against its overall frequency in the text. For example, if the word 'table' was selected as the node, the word 'the' would appear frequently as it is collocated within a

Span=5				Span=6			
Collocate	K	Fc	z-score	Collocate	K	Fc	z-score
sold	7	7	21·6383	sold	8	7	22·5581
commons	4	4	16·3571	commons	4	4	14·8871
decorate	3	3	14·1356	decorate	3	3	13·8456
fronts	2	2	11·5635	fronts	2	2	10·5971
this	22	252	9·6080	*cracks*	2	2	10·5971
empty	3	7	9·0914	this	22	252	8·4908
buying	2	4	8·0577	empty	3	7	8·2410
painting	2	4	8·0577	buying	2	4	7·3117
opposite	2	6	6·1350	painting	2	4	7·3117
loves	2	10	4·8677	opposite	2	6	5·8695
entered	2	10	4·8677	loves	2	10	4·3741
near	2	11	4·6050	entered	2	10	4·3741
outside	2	12	4·6050	black	2	12	3·9168
black	2	12	4·3742	near	2	11	4·1308
remember	3	26	4·2689	outside	2	12	4·1308
lived	2	13	4·1691	remember	2	26	3·7847
rooms	2	15	3·9122	lived	2	13	3·7118
garden	2	17	3·5230	rooms	2	15	3·6698
flat	2	18	3·4019	God	5	64	3·6806
big	2	19	3·2829	*stop*	3	27	3·2550
into	5	92	3·2795	garden	2	17	3·1308
God	4	64	3·1869	flat	2	18	3·0115
family	2	20	3·1728	every	4	59	2·9325
Bernard	2	20	3·1728	big	2	19	2·9009
my	9	271	2·8011	my	11	271	2·8854
full	2	25	2·7980	into	5	92	2·8849
				family	2	20	2·7310
				Bernard	2	20	2·7310
				whole	2	23	2·6771

small span. 'The' would also appear frequently in many other places in the text and would therefore give a small z-score. However, a word which appears only within the span for 'table' would give a very high z-score.

The first keyword chosen was 'house' with a span of three and as expected those items which co-occur most frequently with 'house' are function words, being 'the', 'this', 'a', 'of', 'in', 'I'. Of these words only 'this' gives a high 'z' score and it is indeed fourth in the list when the collocates are listed by z score, coming after 'sold', 'commons' and 'decorate'. The incidence of 'commons' of course occurs through the phrase 'House of Commons'. Figure 4.4 shows the significant collocates of 'house' for span size three, four, five and six. Increasing the span size to four introduced the new words 'entered' and 'near' at positions nine and ten in the z-score ordered list. More words come into the list as the span size increases but it can be seen that the words which enter high up the list like 'fronts' for span size five and 'cracks' for span size six occur only twice in the text and both times in collocation with 'house'.

In another experiment Berry-Rogghe used a total of 200,000 words to study what she calls 'phrasal verbs' – that is, those occurrences of a verb followed by a particle which are idiomatic, e.g. 'look after', 'give in'. Phrasal verbs can then be identified by examining the second part of the phrase, that is the particle, and applying to it similar methods of calculation as in the example 'house' in the earlier study, but this time with a span of zero. 'In' was chosen as the first particle to be studied and a left-sorted concordance used to find all the words which occur to the left of 'in'. This would include incidences of 'in' used in a phrasal verb as well as its normal use as a preposition. The computation of z-scores as shown in Figure 4.5 indicates that words like 'interested', 'versed', 'believe' are more closely associated with 'in' than with items such as 'walk' and 'sit'. By contrast the words to the right of 'in' are completely different and can broadly be broken into three categories:

1. Nouns denoting time, e.g. summer
2. Idiomatic phrases such as 'in spite', 'in short'
3. Nouns denoting places, e.g. 'town'.

Dr Berry-Rogghe's papers are both based on what she admits is a very small amount of text for collocational studies, and the distribution of the vocabulary in them is governed to some extent by the subject matter. Her first study was compiled from *A Christmas Carol* by Charles Dickens, *Each his own Wilderness* by Doris Lessing and *Everything in the Garden* by Giles Cooper. For the study of phrasal words the Lessing text was used again, together with *St Mawr* by D.H. Lawrence and *Joseph Andrews* by Henry Fielding. A corpus of text which is representative of the language as a whole would have been more suitable for this kind of linguistic study. Such a collection of text has been compiled at Brown University and is known as the Brown University Corpus of Present Day American English, or more simply the Brown Corpus. It consists of a million words of American English, divided into 500 different prose sections each of approximately 2000 words long. The samples were chosen randomly from fifteen different categories of prose including newspapers, religious material, books on skills and hobbies, popular lore, government reports, learned journals and various kinds of fiction. All the material in the Corpus was first published in 1961.

The different categories of prose are well-marked, so that it is possible to determine whether one feature occurs significantly higher in one section than another. This corpus therefore provides a representative sample of the

collocate	z-score	K	Fc	collocate	z-score	K .	Fc
interested	19·5417	10	15	sat	6·0168	7	60
versed	15·6253	4	4	died	5·5652	4	25
lived	10·8156	12	62	interest	5·5016	5	38
believe	10·4247	21	180	life	5·4178	14	220
found	9·7332	15	107	rode	4·7597	4	32
live	9·6771	9	44	stood	4·3505	6	73
ride	8·6582	9	53	walk	4·3205	4	37
living	7·9694	8	49	find	4·3059	6	74
dropped	7·3877	4	12	house	3·9535	11	213
appeared	7·2358	6	34	arrived	3·8899	4	43
travelled	6·9987	4	17	came	3·4035	9	184
die	6·3513	6	42				

collocate	z-score	K	Fc	collocate	z-score	K	Fc
spring	28·1354	3	4	world	9·8196	8	203
spite	26·9920	5	12	London	7·3727	3	53
short	25·4783	10	53	country	7·2987	4	93
reality	24·1014	5	15	voice	7·0130	3	58
afternoon	23·3767	7	31	opinion	6·8814	3	60
fact	21·6487	7	36	pocket	6·8355	2	28
daytime	21·6483	2	3	way	6·7730	5	160
vain	20·3351	6	30	garden	6·3556	2	23
Russia	18·7215	2	4	town	6·3556	2	23
summer	17·5262	4	18	minutes	6·2503	2	33
manner	16·4620	7	61	road	5·6985	2	39
case	14·4996	4	26	night	5·5240	3	88
order	13·5211	5	46	book	5·4666	2	42
morning	13·0070	7	95	America	5·3249	2	44
sense	11·7287	4	39	days	5·3249	2	44

Figure 4.5. Significant left-hand (above) and right-hand (below) collocates of *in* for span size zero (Berry-Rogghe)

language of the time and was designed specifically for computer analysis of vocabulary and other features. The University of Lancaster has been attempting to compile a similar corpus of British English. This has now been taken over by the International Computer Archive of Modern English in Oslo and when it is complete it should also provide a valuable source of linguistic material for computer analysis.

Complete word counts of the Brown Corpus have in fact been published, but the texts have been used in many other studies. In one particular collocational study carried out by Peggy Haskel, the keywords were carefully selected. The 28 words finally chosen came initially from the published word counts of the Brown Corpus and included only words which occurred more than 200 times. Words which had several meanings were excluded. The final choice of keywords was made using Buck's *Dictionary of Selected Synonyms in Principal Indo-European Languages* to ensure that there was at least one word from each of his 22 groups. A computer program then scanned the text for the keywords and extracted all collocating words for a span of up to four words on either side of the keyword. In this case function words were ignored in finding the span. Their occurrence could make a difference in the final results of such a study, and it would seem advantageous to perform another computer run including function words to see whether there is any significant difference in the results. It would require only a small change to a computer program to do this. The collocating words are conflated into an alphabetical dictionary in a similar manner to Berry-Rogghe's. The third stage of the program calculates the percentage of cases in which the word appears with each of the several keywords that it may on occasion accompany. This is another way of denoting the significance of the collocation, which Berry-Rogghe does by z-scores.

A few preliminary results are reported in the article and it is interesting to compare the different categories of prose in the Corpus. In fiction the word 'cut' is normally used literally and it associates with 'open', 'belly', 'concussion', 'boy'. In newspapers its figurative meaning is more common and it co-occurs more frequently with 'inflate', 'modest', 'expenses' and 'estimates'. Similar tendencies were found for the word 'dead', where 'issues' are dead in the press, but in fiction 'dead' co-occurs with 'fight', 'mourned', 'wounded'. 'Top' gives 'steeple', 'head', 'stairs', and 'wall' in fiction, and 'officials', 'personnel' and 'executive' in the press.

Berry-Rogghe and Haskel's work are only two examples of an increasingly wide variety of collocational studies using a computer. The Centre de Recherche de Lexicologie Politique at St Cloud have been making a comprehensive study of the political documents circulated in Paris in May 1968. They have approached the question of collocations by making a chain from which they can construct what they call a multistorey lexicograph, where the relationships and distances between words are shown in a network-like diagram. Similar work is reported on by Pêcheux and Wesselius who have made a particular study of the word 'lutte'.

Experimental psychologists have adopted similar methods in dealing with word associations. A number of people are asked to give their response to a particular word and these words again used as further 'stimulant'. Gradually a thesaurus of associative terms can be built up and a network diagram constructed showing the word relationships. Figure 4.6 shows the network surrounding the initial word 'butterfly' taken from an article by

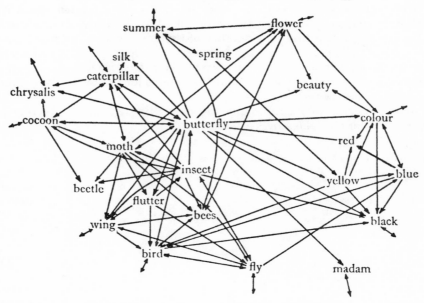

Figure 4.6. Part of the association network around *butterfly*. (Kiss, Armstrong, Milroy and Piper)

Kiss, Armstrong, Milroy and Piper on an associative thesaurus of English. Such a thesaurus of terms can then be stored in the computer in dictionary form. A program could be instructed to start at a particular keyword, or node, and find all the words up to a certain span from the node. The dictionary can be searched interactively by sitting at a video screen. One word would then be typed in and the computer would respond by displaying a list of associated words.

The vocabulary of dialects has also been studied with the computer. The dialectologist typically goes out and collects large quantities of linguistic data and then needs to classify and organise the material collected, usually by sorting and comparing items on many bases. Either the choice of vocabulary or the pronunciation, or both, may be investigated, and the results may be presented in tabular format or as isoglosses drawn on a map.

One vocabulary study in dialectology, described by Shaw, adopts a technique new to language studies known as cluster analysis. It originated in the biological sciences where there are problems of grouping species into genera and genera into families. In recent years this technique has been used much more widely in the humanities, for example, in archaeology and textual criticism as well as in the study of vocabulary. In order to group a number of items together we need to measure the similarity or dissimilarity between them according to a number of different criteria or variables. In the case of dialects, we are attempting to group together or cluster a number of villages according to the vocabulary they use for specific terms. Most computer centres have standard programs for cluster analysis which are not difficult to use.

Shaw gives a useful example showing six fictitious villages and ten sets of alternatives for lexical features as follows:

Alternate lexical features			Villages					
1	2	3	A	B	C	D	E	F
field	close		1	1	1	2	2	1
manger	crib	trough	1	1	1	2	2	3
ladder	stee		1	1	1	2	2	1
rung	stave	step	1	1	1	2	2	3
cowhouse	byre	shippon	1	1	2	2	2	3
scarecrow	mawkin		1	1	2	1	1	1
boar	brawn	hog	1	1	2	1	1	3
tire	rim	hoop	1	2	1	2	2	3
handle	shaft	stale	1	2	1	1	2	1
lamb	heeder		1	2	2	2	1	2

It can be seen that Village A has reading one in every case, Village B has reading one in the first seven cases and reading two in the last three and so on. The figures are converted to percentages and similarity matrix formed showing the relationship of each village with all the others.

	A	B	C	D	E
B	70				
C	60	50			
D	30	40	30		
E	30	40	10	80	
F	40	40	40	30	10

The villages are then clustered according to their similarity as follows. Villages D and E use the same term eight out of ten times and therefore form the nucleus of the first cluster. A and B agree with each other in seven out of ten times, and so they too form another cluster. C agrees with A six times, and so it then joins the A and B cluster. Gradually all the villages join one of the two clusters, which will eventually join together into one large group. The clusters can either be represented graphically on a map using a computer graphics device, or they can be shown in the form of a dendrogram which illustrates the levels of similarity at which they are linked. Shaw gives an example of fourteen East Midlands villages showing the levels of similarity as a percentage (see Figure 4.7).

There are several different mathematical ways of performing cluster analysis. One large computer program called CLUSTAN is able to use many of them. It is advisable to try several methods on the same set of data to see whether similar results are produced. Shaw's initial experiment used only 60 features for 14 localities in three independent sets of data. It would still take some considerable time to perform all the calculations by hand for these numbers, but the advantage of using a computer can clearly be seen when much larger sets of data require to be analysed. It would be then impossible to perform all the calculations by hand.

The study of dialects often requires the representation of particular dialect items on maps. Lance and Slemons describe a project where the data was taken from the *Dictionary of American Regional English* and consisted of vocabulary items recorded in response to questions asking the names of things. Such a question might be 'What do you call a stream of water not big enough to be a river?'. Each different response (they have sixteen in all for this item) is allocated a letter as an identifier and only the letters are marked on the map. Figure 4.8 shows one of their maps, drawn on a lineprinter. This map would look much better if it was done on a graph plotter. No attempt has been made to draw isoglosses separating those places with different responses. If it were done on an ordinary pen plotter which uses several different colours of ink, a different colour could be used for each isogloss, thus making them much easier to see. Not all computer centres have graph plotters and in some cases the lineprinter must be used for drawing.

Dialect maps were also drawn by Rubin who used the *Survey of English Dialects* to study pronunciation, in particular the voicing of initial fricative sounds in the south west of England. The survey had reported on 75 locations in ten counties in England. Each location was identified for the computer by a four-digit number, with two digits indicating the county and two the locality, so that for example 3906 was Burley, the sixth (06) locality in county number 39 (Hampshire). Sixty-eight words were listed for each of the 75 localities, giving a total of 5100 items. A coding system was devised for the words which preserved all significant features of the phonetic transcription. An example here

3101   FINGER   F19G)R   677

shows that the word 'finger' (item VI.7.7. of the SED) is pronounced

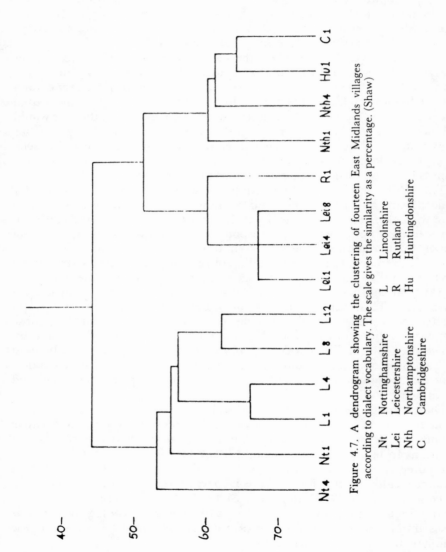

Figure 4.7. A dendrogram showing the clustering of fourteen East Midlands villages according to dialect vocabulary. The scale gives the similarity as a percentage. (Shaw)

Nt   Nottinghamshire   L   Lincolnshire
Lei Leicestershire   R   Rutland
Nth Northamptonshire   Hu   Huntingdonshire
C   Cambridgeshire

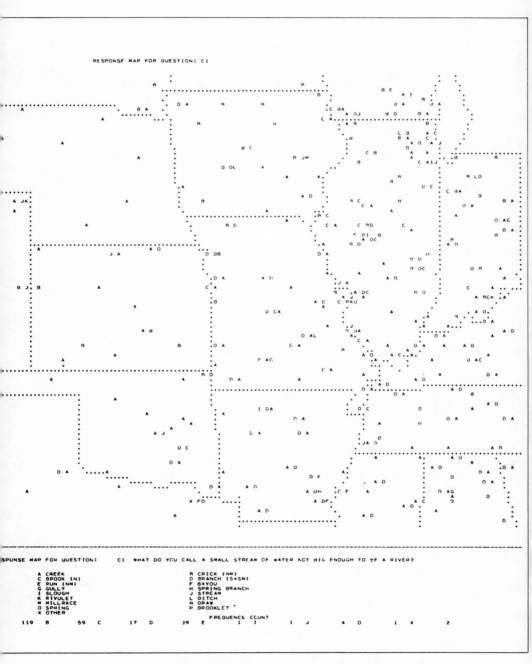

Figure 4.8. A dialect response map drawn on a lineprinter. (Lance and Slemons)

[fingər] at location 01 of county 31 Weston in Somerset). Rubin was then able to sort his data by keyword, citation and location. Inspection of his lists showed that there was wide variation within the area from word to word and from locality to locality. It was then decided to produce dialect maps by computer. An offline plotter was used to draw first an outline map of southern England. The positions of each locality relative to the map were stored inside the computer. A map could then be drawn for each of the 68 words, indicating whether they started with a voiced or unvoiced fricative. Figure 4.9 shows the map drawn for the word 'furrow' showing the initial consonant used in each of the 75 localities. Other maps were drawn showing the proportion of voiced to unvoiced words for each place.

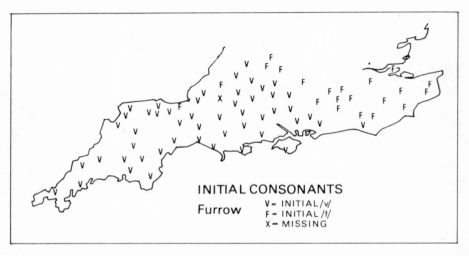

Figure 4.9. A dialect map drawn on a graph plotter showing the initial consonant for the word *furrow* in seventy-five localities. (Rubin)

A simpler method was adopted by the Welsh Language Research Unit at University College, Cardiff, who use concordances to investigate the phonetics of Welsh dialects. Extensive tape recordings are first taken in the selected dialect area. These recordings are then subjected to a detailed phonetic analysis and transcribed into symbols of the International Phonetic Alphabet. These transcriptions are processed by a straightforward concordance program which sorts the words on both the beginnings and endings of words using the phonetic alphabet as a key. The researchers have then been able to print their output in the phonetic alphabet using a computer microfilm recorder (Figure 4.10).

II a

1   ꭏ par o gɛfɔlɛ gʋaiθ da ni, a ꭏ tʃain vaχ i·Kadu nʋ vθ i qilið, ne vɔsɛn nʋ

2 ð, ne vɔsɛn nʋ n tani mas bɔbman, χi n gʋeld. a ʋedin ꭏ lɔin bɔb oχor. na bɛθ ɔin i nɔid gɔnt

4 pan dɔsɛn i i r Kɑ, pɛgo peder ꝉɑθ rɑʋnd i r Kɑ a Kal marK baχ i ðodi mɛʋn, a tɔni r arad mɑs sɛ

5 ɛr ꝉɑθ rɑʋnd i r Kɑ a Kal marK baχ i ðodi mɛʋn, a tɔni r arad mɑs sɛχ χi n dod i bɛn tir χi n gʋ

5 ni r arad mɑs sɛχ χi n dod i bɛn tir χi n gʋel. a ꭏ gɔment rʋidaχ troir talarɛ ar dueð ɔs bɔsɛχ

7 ɔs bɔsɛχ χi ʋedi nɔid dʒobin tɔidi vθ vind mɛʋn a mɔs, ꭏ raid Kal ꝉe i droi nol χi n gʋel, ag o

10 ʋg gɛnol ɔ Kɑ nɑʋr. ɔiχ χi nɔid marK baχ, pɛgo, a mɪnd lan dors ɔ Kɑ mor gʋmus a alsɛχ χi a dod

10 pɛgo, a mɪnd lan dors ɔ Kɑ mor gʋmus a alsɛχ χi a dod nol oχor arɑꝉ ʋedin. a na le oχ χi n mɪn r

10 marK baχ, pɛgo, a mɪnd lan dors ɔ Kɑ mor gʋmus a alsɛχ χi a dod nol oχor arɑꝉ ʋedin. a na le oχ

11 mor gʋmus a alsɛχ χi a dod nol oχor arɑꝉ ʋedin. a na le oχ χi n mɪn rɑʋn abɔʋt i hʋn nɑʋr o id o

12 e oχ χi n mɪn rɑʋn abɔʋt i hʋn nɑʋr o id o hɪd. a oχ χi n nɔid r in peθ nɛs bɔti pɔmθeg ꝉɑθ nɛs

I abɔʋt

11 d nol oχor arɑꝉ ʋedin. a na le oχ χi n mɪn rɑʋn abɔʋt i hʋn nɑʋr o id o hɪd. a oχ χi n nɔid r in

I ag

8 ɛʋn a mɔs, ꭏ raid Kal ꝉe i droi nol χi n gʋel, ag ꭏ din gaꝉi nɔid e beder ꝉɑθ. ʋel, na beθ ꭏ

I alsɛχ

10 arK baχ, pɛgo, a mɪnd lan dors ɔ Kɑ mor gʋmus a alsɛχ χi a dod nol oχor arɑꝉ ʋedin. a na le oχ χ

I ar

6 tir χi n gʋel. a ꭏ gɔment rʋidaχ troir talarɛ ar dueð ɔs bɔsɛχ χi ʋedi nɔid dʒobin tɔidi vθ vin

I arad

5 ʋnd i r Kɑ a Kal marK baχ i ðodi mɛʋn, a tɔni r arad mɑs sɛχ χi n dod i bɛn tir χi n gʋel. a ꭏ

Figure 4.10. Part of a concordance of a phonetic transcription of a North Breconshire Dialect of Welsh printed in the International Phonetic Alphabet using a computer microfilm recorder. (Crawford and Jones)

It is clear then that the computer has considerable possibilities in the study of vocabulary, whether it be individual words or relationships of words with other words. From the design of language courses to the study of word relationships in political documents, a whole range of uses is apparent. Though simple vocabulary studies have been carried out long before the use of computers, the machine can clearly make much faster and more accurate counts than the human brain. Cluster analysis techniques in the study of dialects or other vocabulary would be almost impossible without the computer. The machine has also made feasible the study of collocations which was previously impossible even on a small scale. The advent of larger storage devices could lead to much more work being done in the field of collocations and allow much larger networks of associative words.

REFERENCES

1. Sture Allén (ed), *A Frequency Dictionary of Present-Day Swedish Based on Newspaper Material.* 3 vols, Stockholm: Almqvist and Wiksell (1970, 1971 and 1975)

2. Godelieve L.M. Berry-Rogghe, The Computation of Collocations and their Relevance in Lexical Studies. *The Computer and Literary Studies*, 103-12 (eds A.J. Aitken, R.W. Bailey and N. Hamilton-Smith). Edinburgh: Edinburgh University Press (1973)

3. Godelieve L.M. Berry-Rogghe, Automatic Identification of Phrasal Verbs. *Computers in the Humanities*, 16-26 (ed. J.L. Mitchell). Edinburgh: Edinburgh University Press (1974)

4. D.G. Burnett-Hall and P. Stupples, The Use of Word Frequency in Language Course Writing. *The Computer in Literary and Linguistic Research*, 103-14 (ed. R.A. Wisbey). Cambridge: Cambridge University Press (1971)

5. Christopher S. Butler, Syntactic Analysis of German Chemical Texts: On Constructing a Short Course in German for Chemists. *International Review of Applied Linguistics in Language Teaching* 8 (1975) 320-6

6. Terence D. Crawford and Glyn E. Jones, Automated Concordancing of Welsh Dialects with Output in the IPA. *Bull. of the Board of Celtic Studies* 27 (1976) 45-50

7. C. Dudrap and G. Emery, Sorting the French Vocabulary According to Word Endings. *The Computer in Literary and Linguistic Research,* 87-92 (ed. R.A. Wisbey). Cambridge: Cambridge University Press (1971)

8. P.A. Fortier and J.C. McConnell, Computer-Aided Thematic Analysis of French Prose Fiction. *The Computer and Literary Studies*, 167-81 (eds A.J. Aitken, R.W. Bailey and N. Hamilton-Smith). Edinburgh: Edinburgh University Press (1973)

9. Paul Fortier and J. Colin McConnell, Computer-Aided Thematic Analysis of French Prose Fiction: II. Analysis of Texts and Preparation Costs. *The Computer in Literary and Linguistic Studies (Proceedings of the Third International Symposium),* 215-22 (eds Alan Jones and R.F. Churchhouse). Cardiff: University of Wales Press (1976)

10. W.N. Francis, *Manual of Information to Accompany a Standard Sample of Present-Day Edited American English for Use with Digital Computers.* Providence, Rhode Island: Department of Linguistics, Brown University (1964, revised 1971)

11. Annie Geffroy, P. Lafon, Gill Seidel and M. Tournier, Lexicometric Analysis of Co-occurrences. *The Computer and Literary Studies,* 113-33 (eds A.J. Aitken, R.W. Bailey and N. Hamilton-Smith). Edinburgh: Edinburgh University Press (1973)

12. Suzanne Hanon, The Study of English Loan Words in Modern French. *Computers and the Humanities* 7 (1973) 389-98

13. Peggy I. Haskel, Collocations as a Measure of Stylistic Variety. *The Computer in Literary and Linguistic Research*, 159-68 (ed. R.A. Wisbey). Cambridge: Cambridge University Press (1971)

14. Alan Jones, Some Oxford Projects in Oriental Languages. *The Computer in Literary and Linguistic Research*, 191-7 (ed. R.A. Wisbey). Cambridge: Cambridge University Press (1971)

15. Stephen Kanocz and Al Wolff, The Role of the Computer in Selecting Contemporary German Prose for a Beginners' (Second Stage) Course. *The Computer in Literary and Linguistic Research*, 93-102 (ed. R.A. Wisbey). Cambridge: Cambridge University Press (1971)

16. G. Kiss, Chrisine Armstrong, R. Milroy and J. Piper, An Associative Thesaurus of English and its Computer Analysis. *The Computer and Literary Studies*, 153-65 (eds A.J. Aitken, R.W. Bailey and N. Hamilton-Smith). Edinburgh: Edinburgh University Press (1973)

17. Henry Kučera and W. Nelson Francis, *Computational Analysis of Present-Day English*. Providence, Rhode Island: Brown University Press (1967)

18. Donald M. Lance and Stephen V. Slemons, The Use of the Computer in Plotting the Geographical Distribution of Dialect Items. *Computers and the Humanities* 10 (1976) 221-9

19. Rosemary Leonard, Some Possible Uses of the Computer Archive of Modern English Texts, *ALLC Bull.* 2 No. 2 (1974) 13-18

20. W. Martin, Some Quantitative Vocabulary Aspects of a Dutch Poem. *The Computer and Literary Studies*, 61-8 (eds A.J. Aitken, R.W. Bailey and N. Hamilton-Smith). Edinburgh: Edinburgh University Press (1973)

21. J. Colin McConnell and Paul A. Fortier, *THEME: A System for Computer-Aided Theme Searches of French Texts*. University of Manitoba, Department of French and Spanish Research Reports 1 (1975)

22. M. Pêcheux and Jacqueline Wesselius, Students and Workers in May 68 Student Tracts. *The Computer and Literary Studies*, 135-51 (eds A.J. Aitken, R.W. Bailey and N. Hamilton-Smith) Edinburgh: Edinburgh University Press (1973)

23. Joseph Raben and David V. Lieberman, Text Comparison: Principles and a Program. *The Computer in Literary and Linguistic Studies (Proceedings of the Third International Symposium)*. 297-308 (eds Alan Jones and R.F. Churchhouse). Cardiff: University of Wales Press (1976)

24. Gerald M. Rubin, Computer-Produced Mapping of Dialectal Variation. *Computers and the Humanities* 4 (1970) 241-46

25. David Shaw, Statistical Analysis of Dialectal Boundaries. *Computers and the Humanities* 8 (1974) 173-7

26. David Wishart, *CLUSTAN 1C User Manual*. London: University College Computer Centre (1975)

27. G. Udny Yule, *The Statistical Study of Literary Vocabulary*. Cambridge: Cambridge University Press (1944)

Further Reading

S. Jones and J. McH. Sinclair, English Lexical Collocations: a Study in Computational Linguistics. *Cahiers de Lexicologie* 24 (1974) 15-61

J.A. Leavitt and J.L. Mitchell, SPAN: A Lexicostatistical Measure and Some Applications. *Computing in the Humanities*, 59-71 (eds Serge Lusignan and John S. North). Waterloo: University of Waterloo Press (1977)

J. McH. Sinclair, S. Jones and R. Daley, *English Lexical Studies*. OSTI Report. University of Birmingham Department of English (1970)

5. Morphological and Syntactic Analysis, Machine Translation

We have seen in the discussion on concordances in Chapter Three that the computer cannot classify a word under its dictionary heading without prior instructions. This could only be done if the machine is presented with a series of rules from which it can uniquely categorise a word into its correct form, or if a computer dictionary is available which holds the lemma, or dictionary heading, for every word. Usually these two methods are combined so that a series of rules is applied to remove a possible flectional ending and the resulting 'stem' is looked up in a dictionary to ensure that it exists. It follows that a separate program and dictionary must be used for each natural language. In general highly inflected and agglutinative languages are easier to analyse than languages like English in which words are sometimes inflected and sometimes not.

A case study from Swedish lexicology described by Hellberg demonstrates the procedures required for lemmatisation. This study was made in connection with the word-frequency counts of modern Swedish mentioned in Chapter Four, which were taken from newspaper material. A dictionary of all possible endings was first stored. An alphabetical word list could then be lemmatised simply by grouping in each lemma words with the same stem but different inflectional endings. The 'stem' of the lemma was defined as that part of the word that was identical in all its inflectional forms. The endings therefore did not correspond exactly with the usual linguistic ones. For example, the word 'titel', whose plural is 'titlar', was assigned the stem 'tit-' and endings '-el', '-lar' etc., though the linguistic stem is 'titl-'. Irregular or strong nouns which occurred frequently in compounds were treated as extra paradigms. The word 'man,' plural 'män' appeared in so many compounds that it was established as a separate paradigm. The list of possible endings was shortened in one way. The ending '-s' always occupies the last position and can be added to almost every form of noun and adjective having a genitive function or to verbs having a passive function. This would have meant nearly doubling the ending list. Therefore the 's' was removed first and then the ending treated as if it was not there. Homographs in the alphabetical list were always treated on the assumption that a verb preceded a noun. In all, some

112,000 words were lemmatised in this way, and a manual test check revealed an error rate of 3.5%. These errors included fictitious lemmas which the program had derived from foreign words, such as one consisting of the English word 'fair' and the French word 'faire'.

Meunier's system for lemmatising contemporary French follows the Swedish method closely. His text is first converted into an alphabetical list. Words are then looked up in a function-word dictionary, which includes the more common words in all parts of speech. The remaining forms are then treated in the same way as the Swedish words – that is, each word is compared with the next to see if they could be variants of the same lemma. One of the features of this system is the automatic construction of the dictionary of possible endings from which the computer can determine whether two endings are compatible.

A similar method was adopted by David Packard for use with Greek, another highly inflected language. This program was written originally to assist the preparation of a textbook to teach elementary Greek, by finding the most frequently occurring forms, but it has more general applications in the study of Greek text. Words are analysed in the order in which they come in the text, not from an alphabetical list. Each word is first looked up in a dictionary of what he calls 'indeclinables', which consists of prepositions, adverbs and particles as well as highly irregular forms. About half the words are found in this list. Greek morphological rules are then applied and the program attempts to remove endings from the stem, starting with the final letter only. If the single final letter is not found in the list of possible endings, the length of the ending is increased by one letter and the search made again. If an ending is found, the remainder of the word is looked up in a dictionary of stems. If it is found and is consistent with the ending, the program identifies this as a possible analysis. However, it does not then move on to the next word, but continues to search for other longer endings in case the form is ambiguous.

Contracted forms are treated as separate paradigms, though this procedure produces false stems. Nouns of the third declension are also given special treatment. The nominative νύξ and dative plural νυξί are placed in the list of indeclinables as they cannot be reconstructed from the stem νυκτ-. Augmented forms which prefix an initial ε are found by program, but verbs with irregular augments are included in the stem dictionary, as are reduplicated perfect stems. Many Greek words are also formed by prefixing a preposition to a stem, and in some cases the final consonant of the preposition is assimilated to the following letter. The prefix συν- may appear as συν-, συλ-, συγ-, συμ- or συ-. The verbal augments come between the prefix and the stem. Packard's program attempts to remove prepositional prefixes from the beginning of a word if the word is not found in the stem dictionary. It can also reconstruct elided forms, but crasis (the merging of two words into one) is more difficult to recognise automatically. The more common forms of it are therefore included in the dictionary of indeclinables. In many cases the program generates more than one analysis for a form. Instead of printing them all it is allowed to opt for the most likely version. In almost every case of ambiguity between a verbal and a nominal analysis, the nominal form is correct in Greek and so the program always prefers the latter.

The program can accommodate 4000 stems, 2000 endings and 1000 indeclinables. It uses a binary search for the dictionary look-up and so the dictionaries are re-sorted into alphabetical order whenever a new entry is added. For those words which are not found in the indeclinables, several searches would be required for all possible analyses. The dictionary of endings is generated by program. From a nucleus of words, the other dictionaries are added to as required, an approach which is considered quite satisfactory. Packard's program is designed for a large computer and it can hold all the dictionaries in core. He claims that it can analyse 2000 words per second, although he does not give the error rate.

Bathurst's account of a system to alphabetise Arabic words does not give sufficient indication of the success level. Arabic has an abundance of prefixed and infixed letters. Each word is built up of a root, which is normally three consonants, together with a combination of infixes, prefixes and suffixes. An added difficulty is that one or more of the radical letters may be one of three weak consonants, such as 'w', which are liable to mutation or elision. Bathurst comments that there can be up to 2300 different combinations of prefixes preceding the first letter of a verb stem and more than 1600 for nouns. Infixes within the stems add more than 500 additional patterns. No examples are given, but there is an indication that there was some success in selecting the radicals from a number of words which were then used to sort the words into alphabetical order. It seems that quadriliterals and words with weak radicals were dealt with separately by a dictionary look-up.

A suffix removal program for English is described by John Dawson of the Literary and Linguistic Computing Centre, Cambridge. Like most lemmatisation programs the Cambridge system starts by compiling a list of possible suffixes. Following a paper by Julie Beth Lovins, a list of about 250 English suffixes was constructed. This list lacked plurals and combinations of simple suffixes, and when these were added the total came to some 1200 entries. With each suffix was stored a condition code, a numeric marker indicating in which circumstances a suffix could be removed from a word. To cope with a dictionary of some 1200 items, the suffixes were stored by length, and then in reverse alphabetical order (i.e. in alphabetical order of their final letters). The condition codes consisted of:

1. A number which represented the minimum stem length which may be left after the suffix is removed.
2. An inclusion list, indicating that the suffix may only be removed after these strings of characters.
3. An exclusion list, which gives those character strings after which the suffix may not be removed.

Several of these conditions may be combined for each suffix.

Following the conditions, we can perhaps look at the suffix -ITE in the words ERUDITE, DOLOMITE and SPRITE. The program will find the suffix -ITE in ERUDITE, but it has been instructed not to remove it in DOLOMITE because it comes after the letter M, or in SPRITE because there are only three letters left then and they begin with an S.

The text is dealt with one word at a time so that the order of words is immaterial. The program attempts to remove the longest suffix first, always allowing for a minimum stem length of two characters. All but the first two characters of the word are removed and looked up in the suffix dictionary. If this does not make a known suffix, the first letter of this hypothetical suffix is ignored and the remainder looked up again.

Allied to the suffix removal process is a procedure for what is described as word conflation – that is, grouping together all forms of the same stem. This procedure has been developed empirically and allows for the matching of such forms as

ABSORB   ABSORB/- and ABSORPT/-

This is done by keeping sets of standard stem endings which can be considered equivalent. The conflation process is applied to blocks of words which are already in alphabetical order. The procedure for matching the groups is described by Dawson in some detail. Fifty-five stem ending sets are used and these do not include many irregular verb inflections. A considerable degree of success was reported as the following examples show:

ending set	*example*
B/BB+	ROB ROBBING
D/DD+	PAD PADDING
G/GG+	TAG TAGGING

But following the same principle, HIS was grouped together with HISSED. It is always important to note the percentage of errors in such a lemmatisation system. Dawson does not give this, but he does make the point that the scholar should be provided with a list of all the forms which have been classified with each stem so that errors can be determined easily.

A number of other lemmatisation systems have been reported much more recently than those already discussed. It appears that after a lull of several years the possibilities of automatic lemmatisation are once again being explored. Maegaard's procedure to recognise finite verbs in Frencl texts reports 100% success in recognising all the words that could possibly be finite verbs, although the number of erroneous forms is not given. Success with homographs was about 90%. This system again uses a dictionary of stems and a dictionary of endings. The roots were taken from a standard dictionary of French verbs and each root is accompanied by a numerical code indicating what paradigms can be applied to it. The program tests each word for endings by the same method as Packard – that is, by removing the shortest possible ending first. When a legitimate ending and stem are found, the numerical codes are checked to see whether they are compatible. In French about 25% of the forms which are recognised as possible finite verbs are homographs, in the sense that they can be either a finite verb or something else. These are marked in the stem dictionary which also gives an indication of which homography tests can be applied. For example, the participles ending in '-s' like *mis* and *pris* can only be finite verbs if preceded by a subject pronoun *je* or *tu*. These programs operate on basic text and appear to be quite successful in searching for this one type of verb feature.

There have also been attempts at automatic lemmatisation on a number of other languages including Latin, Spanish, German and Russian. It seems clear that a success rate of about 95% can be attained for highly inflected languages. Packard's Greek system seems to be the most comprehensive and his method of looking for a word first in a list of function words and irregular forms immediately takes care of about half the words in a text. One can either begin as Maegaard did on the French finite verbs by constructing a word list of stems from a standard dictionary, or the stems can be compiled from a word list of a text or texts. Whichever way the dictionaries are compiled, once production begins it seems preferable to operate on the basic text if possible rather than on an alphabetical word list.

Both Packard and Meunier generate their ending dictionaries automatically merely to facilitate their compilation. Automatic generation of word endings or prefixes can also be applied to the compilation of language dictionaries or in language teaching.

Shibayev's CARLEX project was designed specifically for the teaching of Russian but it was planned to extend it to other inflected languages. A basic Russian dictionary was compiled of the 4000 most frequent stems. Each stem was punched on a computer card with a code giving information about its possible parts of speech and the type of inflexion for each part of speech, together with a tentative English translation. A second set of input cards consisted of a complete set of flectional endings given separately for nouns and pronouns, adjectives, verbs and all invariables with the cases they govern. The number of possible forms of these endings combined with all 4000 stems was therefore very large indeed.

The computer was then programmed to generate the required inflexion in accordance with the code numbers of the stem data and to print out the entire grammatical structure of any one or more stems. The aim was to generate small amounts of output in response to specific requests rather than create a voluminous quantity of results from large runs. The ideal would be to operate such a program interactively from a terminal, and this was planned by Shibayev before his death. The student could type in either the stem or the English word and the terminal would then display the required inflection. CARLEX operated in transliterated form, but given a video terminal with Russian characters it could be operated successfully as a language teaching system for students of Russian. Further developments to the program could allow the user to request a specific form of a word and display just that form rather than the entire paradigm. Figure 5.1 shows part of an example giving all possible forms for the adjective transliterated PREKRASNY1.

An algorithm for generating Hebrew or Arabic word forms is much more complicated, because both languages allow infixes and prefixes as well as suffixes to indicate various flectional forms. In a project described by Price each stem was stored in a dictionary together with numerical codes indicating which infixes, suffixes or prefixes can be added to the stem. Each word was then transcribed into a series of input descriptors from which the Hebrew word could be generated. This algorithm is part of a research project in machine translation from Hebrew to English, for generating Hebrew words was considered a useful way of examining the procedures required to parse them.

Assigning the correct grammatical form or part of speech to a word in order to determine syntax can be a much more complicated process than the removal of flectional endings, but syntax can be studied with the aid of a computer in more simple ways. It may of course require no more than a straightforward search for word forms. Such an investigation is described by Dowsing where some aspects of Old English syntax were studied with the aid of a computer. Her main interest was in the use of 'have' and 'be' with the past participle and in the development of compound tenses. The use of inflexional endings in Old English meant that the past participle might have several forms. A very simple method was adopted for finding all examples of the past participle. The built-in editor on the computer's terminal system was used to find all the lines which contained any of some

```
21142542AM    PREKRASN-Y123 1BEAUTIFUL, FINE, EXCELLENT              31832469

NOMINATIVE SINGULAR MASCULINE                      PREKRASNY1
GENITIVE SINGULAR MASCULINE                        PREKRASNOGO
DATIVE SINGULAR MASCULINE                          PREKRASNOMU
ACCUSATIVE SINGULAR MASCULINE INANIMATE            PREKRASNY1
ACCUSATIVE SINGULAR MASCULINE ANIMATE              PREKRASNOGO      PREKRASNE1WEGO
INSTRUMENTAL SINGULAR MASCULINE                    PREKRASNYM       PREKRASNE1WIM
LOCATIVE SINGULAR MASCULINE                        PREKRASNOM       PREKRASNE1WEM

NOMINATIVE SINGYLAR FEMININE                       PREKRASNAÅ       PREKRASNE1WAÅ
GENITIVE SINGULAR FEMININE                         PREKRASNO1       PREKRASNE1WE1
DATIVE SINGULAR FEMININE                           PREKRASNO1       PREKRASNE1WE1
ACCUSATIVE SINGULAR FEMININE                       PREKRASNUÅ       PREKRASNE1WUÅ
INSTRUMENTAL SINGULAR FEMININE                     PREKRASNO1       PREKRASNE1WEÅ
LOCATIVE SINGULAR FEMININE                         PREKRASNO1       PREKRASNE1WE1

NOMINATIVE SINGULAR NEUTER                         PREKRASNOE       PREKRASNE1WEE
GENITIVE SINGULAR NEUTER                           PREKRASNOGO      PREKRASNE1WEGO
DATIVE SINGULAR NEUTER                             PREKRASNOMU      PREKRASNE1WEMU
ACCUSATIVE SINGULAR NEUTER                         PREKRASNOE       PREKRASNE1WEE
INSTRUMENTAL SINGULAR NEUTER                       PREKRASNYM       PREKRASNE1WIM
LOCATIVE SINGULAR NEUTER                           PREKRASNOM       PREKRASNE1WEM

NOMINATIVE PLURAL (ALL GENDERS)                    PREKRASNYE       PREKRASNE1WIE
GENITIVE PLURAL (ALL GENDERS)                      PREKRASNYX       PREKRASNE1WIX
DATIVE PLURAL (ALL GENDERS)                        PREKRASNYM       PREKRASNE1WIM
ACCUSATIVE PLURAL (ALL GENDERS) INANIMATE          PREKRASNYE       PREKRASNE1WIE
ACCUSATIVE PLURAL (ALL GENDERS) ANIMATE            PREKRASNYX       PREKRASNE1WIX
INSTRUMENTAL PLURAL (ALL GENDERS)                  PREKRASNYMI      PREKRASNE1WIMI
LOCATIVE PLURAL (ALL GENDERS)                      PREKRASNYX       PREKRASNE1WIX

COMPARATIVE                                        PREKRASNEE

SUPERLATIVE:
NOMINATIVE SINGULAR MASCULINE                      PREKRASNE1WI1
GENITIVE SINGULAR MASCULINE                        PREKRASNE1WEGO
DATIVE SINGULAR MASCULINE                          PREKRASNE1WEMU
ACCUSATIVE SINGULAR MASCULINE INANIMATE            PREKRASNE1WI1
```

Figure 5.1. Printout from CARLEX showing all possible forms of the adjective transliterated PREKRASNY1. (Shibayev)

60 different finite forms of 'have' and 'be'. Those lines containing any of them were edited into a second computer file, which was then searched for all occurrences of participial endings. This search inevitably picked up some spurious material which was later removed manually, leaving the participles in a file, which could then be interrogated to find the distribution of specific verbal forms.

A concordance would also have provided her with the material she wanted to find. Using the editor on the terminals is easier, but it requires more computer resources. A special purpose program to identify all the past participles would have taken much longer to write but is another way of approaching the problem. Green's study of formulas and syntax in Old English poetry depends much more on manual specification of the syntax.

Each line of his input text is accompanied by a code indicating the syntactic features in that line and the machine is only used to sort the lines by syntactic feature.

If therefore only one or two syntactic features are being investigated which can be identified by specific forms, it is much easier to use a concordance-type program to locate occurrences of those forms and then identify the required words manually after that. However, most syntactic studies require a fuller analysis of a text, both to classify words into their grammatical form and to determine their function in a sentence. As the rules for sentence structure and word usage vary from language to language, there can be no general purpose program to perform syntactic analysis. A special program is required for each natural language.

One well-known syntactic analysis program which has been used for literary text in English is EYEBALL, developed at the University of Minnesota by Donald Ross and Robert Rasche. The original EYEBALL was written in FORTRAN. Three other versions of the program exist, one from Ohio written in SNOBOL, which is also called EYEBALL, one from the University of Southern California called HAWKEYE, which is written in FORTRAN, and one at the University of Oxford called OXEYE, which was developed from the Ohio EYEBALL and therefore written in SNOBOL. EYEBALL, HAWKEYE and OXEYE all attempt to parse English text, albeit in a limited fashion, and to produce frequency distributions of each part of speech. The parsing rules for the Minnesota EYEBALL are described in some detail in an article by Ross and the other programs are similar.

All set out to parse a basic text, to which no additional symbols have been added to facilitate the parsing. OXEYE accepts text in a format identical to that required by COCOA, and the two packages can therefore easily be used on the same text. All but the Ohio program work in several stages. At each stage the user may intervene and correct any mistakes in the parsing before going on to attempt the next stage.

Ross's EYEBALL has a built-in dictionary of about 200 function words. The program looks up each word in the dictionary. If the word is in the dictionary, some additional information about the word will be found there. For 'and' the dictionary indicates that it is always a conjunction. 'The' is always an article, but some function words like 'for' can fulfil more than one syntactic category, e.g. conjunction or preposition. EYEBALL has a hierarchy for dealing with situations like this. It looks for phrases before it looks for clauses, since prepositional phrases are usually short and are therefore easier to identify than clauses. It tries to find the end of a phrase and then works backwards from that. The end of a phrase could be punctuation, a preposition or an interjection, or possibly the word 'not', or a word which introduces a clause, or another preposition, or an interjection. All words which can begin clauses and all prepositions or interjections would be found in the dictionary. Clauses are more difficult to analyse, especially if they are long, since it is very difficult to identify the end of a clause if it is not signalled by punctuation. Ross and Rasche attempted to include one or two other automatic features in their program. One was to mark all words ending in '-ly' as adverbs, but a number of exceptions were found by the program like 'family', 'ally' and 'belly'. OXEYE does mark '-ly' words as adverbs, but it includes the main exceptions to the '-ly' rule in its dictionary.

Ross's EYEBALL, HAWKEYE and OXEYE both work in several stages. A computer file of words is first produced from the text and each word is given a tentative grammatical category. Figure 5.2 shows such a word file created by OXEYE before any human intervention. The file can be corrected manually before any statistics are printed. Each part of speech is identified by a letter category as shown here.

Adjective	J	Noun	N
Adverb 'ly'	A	Participle	L
Adverb function	B	Particle prep	R
Auxiliary	X	Preposition	P
Coordinator	C	Pronoun	U
Determiner	D	Subordinator	S
'To' infinitive	T	'There' signal	H
Infinitive verb	F	Verb	V
Intensifier Adverb	I	Miscellaneous	M
'Not'	O	Unknown	?

Syntactic functions can be resolved further in a second stage of the program. They are indicated by the following symbols:

Subject	S
Predicate	V
Predicate adjunct	A
Prepositional adjunct	P
Complement	C
Unknown	?

When the parts of speech have been modified, the parsing can be attempted and the results of that are shown in Figure 5.3. Figure 5.4 shows the text printed with the corrected grammatical categories and parsing underneath each word. The Ohio EYEBALL does not allow manual intervention and one result is seen in Figure 5.5, where 'Hammersmith' is parsed as an infinitive verb showing one major problem in the automatic parsing of

```
----1:6-------------------------------------------------------------
  10000 ▲   MARLEY        0NJV45
  10000     WAS           1XV65
  10000     DEAD          0NJV45  ,
  10000     TO            1PTR
  10000     BEGIN         0NJV45
  10000     WITH          1P      .
----2:7-------------------------------------------------------------
  10000     THERE         1HN6
  10000     IS            1XV65
  10000     NO            1J
  10000     DOUBT         0NJV45
  20001     WHATEVER      0NJV45
  20001     ABOUT         2P
  20001     THAT          1SDU45  .
----3:18------------------------------------------------------------
  20001     THE           1D
  20001     REGISTER      0NJV45
  20001     OF            1P
  20001     HIS           1DU45
  20001     BURIAL        0J
  20001     WAS           1XV65
  20001     SIGNED        0VJ55
  30002     BY            1PR
  30002     THE           1D
  30002     CLERGYMAN     0NJV45  ,
  30002     THE           1D
  30002     CLERK         0NJV45  ,
  30002     THE           1D
  30002     UNDERTAKER    0NJV45  ,
  30002     AND           1C
  30002     THE           1D
  30002     CHIEF         0NJV45
  40003     MOURNER       0NJV45  .
----4:3-------------------------------------------------------------
  40003     SCROOGE       0NJV45
  40003     SIGNED        0VJ55
  40003     IT            1U45    .
----5:16------------------------------------------------------------
  40003     AND           1C
  40003     SCROOGE'S     0NJV65
  40003     NAME          0NJV45
  40003     WAS           1XV65
  50004     GOOD          1JB5
  50004     UPON          2P
  50004     CHANGE        0NJV45  ,
  50004     FOR           1PS
  50004     ANYTHING      3N4
  50004     HE            1U44
  50004     CHOSE         0NJV45
  50004     TO            1PTR
  50004     PUT           0NJV45
  50004     HIS           1DU45
  60005     HAND          0NJV45
  60005     TO            1PTR    .
----6:8-------------------------------------------------------------
 '70006     OLD           0NJV45
  70006     MARLEY        0NJV45
  70006     WAS           1XV65
  70006     AS            1S
  70006     DEAD          0NJV45
  70006     AS            1S
  70006     A             1D
  70006     DOOR-NAIL     0NJV45  .
```

Figure 5.2. Part of a word file created by OXEYE before any human intervention.

```
----1:6----------------------------------------------------
 10000     MARLEY           0N  S
 10000     WAS              1V  V
 10000     DEAD             0J  C    ,
 10000     TO               1T  ?
 10000     BEGIN            0F  ?
 10000     WITH             1P  ?    .
----2:7----------------------------------------------------
 10000     THERE            1H  A
 10000     IS               1X  V
 10000     NO               1J  C
 10000     DOUBT            0J  C
 20001     WHATEVER         0N  C
 20001     ABOUT            2P  P
 20001     THAT             1U  P    .
----3:18---------------------------------------------------
 20001     THE              1D  ?
 20001     REGISTER         0N  ?
 20001     OF               1P  P
 20001     HIS              1U  P
 20001     BURIAL           0J  ?
 20001     WAS              1X  V
 20001     SIGNED           0V  V
 30002     BY               1R  A
 30002     THE              1D  ?
 30002     CLERGYMAN        0N  ?    ,
 30002     THE              1D  ?
 30002     CLERK            0J  ?    ,
 30002     THE              1D  ?
 30002     UNDERTAKER       0NJV?    ,
 30002     AND              1C  ?
 30002     THE              1D  ?
 30002     CHIEF            0J  C
 40003     MOURNER          0N  C    .
----4:3----------------------------------------------------
 40003     SCROOGE          0NJV?
 40003     SIGNED           0VJ ?
 40003     IT               1U  ?    .
----5:16---------------------------------------------------
 40003     AND              1C  ?
 40003     SCROUGE'S        0J  S
 40003     NAME             0N  S
 40003     WAS              1V  V
 50004     GOOD             1J  C
 50004     UPON             2P  P
 50004     CHANGE           0N  P
 50004     FOR              1S  A
 50004     ANYTHING         3N  ?
 50004     HE               1U  S
 50004     CHOSE            0V  V
 50004     TO               1T  V
 50004     PUT              0F  V
 50004     HIS              1D  C
 60005     HAND             0N  C
 60005     TO               1R  A    .
----6:8----------------------------------------------------
 70006     OLD              0J  S
 70006     MARLEY           0N  S
 70006     WAS              1V  V
 70006     AS               1S  A
 70006     DEAD             0NJV?
 70006     AS               1S  A
 70006     A                1D  ?
 70006     DOOR-NAIL        0N  ?    .
```

Figure 5.3. The word file shown in figure 5.2. after being parsed and before being corrected.

```
 1      2    3     4   5      6
MARLEY WAS DEAD, TO BEGIN WITH.
 N      V    J     T   F      R
 S      V    C     ?   ?      ?

 1     2  3  4     5        6     7
THERE IS NO DOUBT WHATEVER ABOUT THAT.
 H     V  J  N     I        P     U
 A     V  C  C     ?        P     P

 1   2        3  4   5      6   7      8  9   10        11  12     13  14         15  16
THE REGISTER OF HIS BURIAL WAS SIGNED BY THE CLERGYMAN, THE CLERK, THE UNDERTAKER, AND THE
 D   N        P  D   N      X   Y      P  D   N          D   N      D   N           C   D
 ?   ?        P  P   ?      V   V      ?  ?   A ?         ?   ?      ?   ?           ?   ?

 17    18
CHIEF MOURNER.
 J     N
 C     ?

 1       2      3
SCROOGE SIGNED IT.
 N       V      U
 ?       ?      ?

 1   2         3    4   5    6    7       8   9        10 11    12 13  14  15   16
AND SCROOGE'S NAME WAS GOOD UPON CHANGE, FOR ANYTHING HE CHOSE TO PUT HIS HAND TO.
 C   D         N    V   J    P    N       P   N         U  V     T  F   D   N    R
 ?   S         S    V   C    P    P       A   ?         S  V     V  V   C   C    A

 1   2      3   4  5    6  7 8
OLD MARLEY WAS AS DEAD AS A DOOR-NAIL.
 J   N      V   J  J    S  D N
 S   S      V   A  ?    ?  A ? ?
```

Figure 5.4. OXEYE printout showing the text with the corrected grammatical categories and parsing underneath.

```
1    2    3    4     5      6    7     8       9    10     11    12    13    14     15     16    17  18
THEY TELL ME, MISS, THAT YOU ARE DISPOSED TO TRAVEL, AND THAT YOUR FIRST AIRING WILL BE TO
U    V    U   ?      S   U   X   V        T    F      C     S     D     B     J      N     X   T
S    V         ?     A   S   V   V        V    V      ?     A     ?     ?     S      S     V   V

19
HAMMERSMITH.
F
V


1          2    3     4   5   6    7    8     9   1011  12        13  14   15
WHEREFORE I THINK IT MY DUTY TO WISH YOU A GOOD JOURNEY AND FINE WEATHER.
?          U  V     U   D   N   T    F   U     D   R          J   C    J   N
?          S  V     C   S   S   V    V   C     ??  ??         ?   C    ?   C
```

Figure 5.5. Printout of uncorrected parsing showing Hammersmith as an infinitive verb.

English, the word 'to', which can be either a preposition or part of an infinitive.

Some of the statistics produced by OXEYE using the corrected information are shown in Figure 5.6. It is then possible to ask the computer such questions as how many sentences begin with a noun, or how many sentences have consecutive sequences of two or more adjectives. These questions are formulated as SNOBOL patterns, a feature peculiar to SNOBOL but very easy for the non-programmer to understand. Figure 5.7 shows the printout from such specific questions.

EYEBALL and its derivatives are the only programs which have been used to any extent to parse literary English. Ross himself has worked on Blake's *Songs of Innocence and of Experience* using the program and has been able to calculate the percentage distribution of each category of speech in each poem and overall. EYEBALL and HAWKEYE have been used to study Tennyson, Keats, Coleridge, Blake and Wordsworth, as well as Joyce's *Ulysses*. OXEYE has been used on Mrs Gaskell, as well as on Henry Fielding and Marlowe.

The procedures which have so far been described in this chapter are required for any kind of machine translation system. A sentence in the source language must be analysed grammatically – that is, the function of every word must be determined either by a dictionary search or by suffix removal or by a combination of both, and then the clause structure must be ascertained. The translation of each word must then be determined from a dictionary and a sentence constructed in the target language which is both grammatical and meaningful. It may well be that the word order is quite different in the two languages, or that one displays much more inflection than the other.

In the early days of computing it was thought that machine translation might be the answer to many problems of communication, but the first work in the field soon discovered the difficulties and it was found to be uneconomic. There has been a recent revival of interest in the subject, notably in Hong Kong for translating Chinese, but most effort in the western world is concentrating on the first stage of the procedure, the analysis of the syntax of natural language.

One machine translation system, called BABEL, developed by T.D. Crawford at University College Cardiff, well illustrates the procedures involved. The input text, in this case Russian in transliterated form, is processed sentence by sentence. Each sentence is broken down into words and each word looked up in a dictionary. For each Russian word, the dictionary contains information about its grammatical category and subcategories, an indication as to whether it is a homograph and a provisional English translation. In this case the dictionary includes every form of every word, though it would be equally possible for the program to

```
---------
ADJECTIVE
---------

FREQUENCY PER SENTENCE :        0        1        2        3        7
             NUMBER SUCH :        5        9        2        1        1
             % PROBABILITY :  100.00    72.22    22.22    11.11     5.55


----
NOUN
----

FREQUENCY PER SENTENCE :        0        1        2        3        4        6        7
             NUMBER SUCH :        1        6        4        2        2        1        2
             % PROBABILITY :  100.00    94.44    61.11    38.88    27.77    16.66    11.11


-----------
PREPOSITION
-----------

FREQUENCY PER SENTENCE :        0        1        2        5
             NUMBER SUCH :        9        3        5        1
             % PROBABILITY :  100.00    50.00    33.33     5.55


-------
PRONOUN
-------

FREQUENCY PER SENTENCE :        0        1        2
             NUMBER SUCH :        6        7        5
             % PROBABILITY :  100.00    66.66    27.77


----
VERB
----

FREQUENCY PER SENTENCE :        0        1        2        3
             NUMBER SUCH :        1       10        5        2
             % PROBABILITY :  100.00    94.44    38.88    11.11


---------------
AUXILIARY VERB
---------------

FREQUENCY PER SENTENCE :        0        1        3
             NUMBER SUCH :       10        7        1
             % PROBABILITY :  100.00    44.44     5.55
```

Figure 5.6. Some statistics produced by OXEYE for parts of speech.

```
-----
'DJN'
-----

FREQUENCY PER SENTENCE :          0        1        3        4
            NUMBER SUCH :         12        4        1        1
            % PROBABILITY :   100.00    33.33    11.11     5.55


TOTAL OCCURRENCES : 11



----------------------------
POS(0) 'N' ('V' | 'X')
----------------------------

FREQUENCY PER SENTENCE :          0        1
            NUMBER SUCH :         14        4
            % PROBABILITY :   100.00    22.22


TOTAL OCCURRENCES : 4



--------------------------------------
('DJ' | 'D') 'N' ('DJ' | 'D') 'N'
--------------------------------------

FREQUENCY PER SENTENCE :          0        1
            NUMBER SUCH :         16        2
            % PROBABILITY :   100.00    11.11


TOTAL OCCURRENCES : 2
```

Figure 5.7. Statistics produced by OXEYE for the specific requests:
(1) 'DJN' Determiner noun adjective
(2) POS (0) 'N' ('V' ! 'X') A noun followed by a verb or auxiliary at the beginning of a sentence.
(3) ('DJ' ! 'D') 'N' ('DJ' ! 'D') 'N' The sequence determiner adjective noun, or determiner noun repeated more than once in succession.

strip the morphological ending from the words and then search only for the root. Crawford's view is that the increased space of storage devices on modern computers makes it more economical to retain every form in the dictionary. As in all systems, the amount of storage required is to be balanced against the amount of extra program needed to perform the morphological analysis correctly.

Once all the grammatical categories for a sentence have been found, the machine operates a phrase-structure-type grammar until the sentence has been resolved. If the sentence contains a homograph the grammar is rerun. It may need to be run several times if there are several homographs. When the analysis is complete, even if it has been found impossible, another set of rules operate which attempt to construct a sentence in the target language, in this case English. If the previous grammatical analysis is unsuccessful the resulting English will be ungrammatical.

The chief inadequacy of this system, like many others, is the inability to match meaning to context. It will construct sentences which are grammatically correct but have no sense. Many homographs and other ambiguities cannot be satisfactorily dealt with by machine translation, particularly if they have the same grammatical category. The same Russian word is translated as 'about' and 'in' in English. Crawford's program always prints it as *ABOUT/IN*, as shown in Figure 5.8. Homographs are not found so frequently in technical text and it is on this area that most machine translation systems have concentrated. The somewhat staccato English produced by a program such as BABEL would be acceptable to a scientist if the alternative was not to be able to read the article at all.

The problem of semantics in machine translation has not yet been satisfactorily resolved, and a solution seems unlikely until very large dictionaries of collocations are available. In the future it may be possible to store information with each word which would indicate which words can or cannot be juxtaposed with it. This would result in a much larger dictionary and is beyond the capacity of current computer hardware. Crawford's dictionary consists of some 20,000 items, but each new text to be translated could include words which are not already in the dictionary. Therefore new texts must first be scanned for these words and the dictionary updated before any translation is attempted. More acceptable English is produced by the Chinese University of Hong Kong project, but in that system the source text is pre-edited to alter syntactic irregularities to a form that the machine can recognise, for example, by inserting a subject in sentences which do not already have one, by inserting a copula to link subject and predicate, or by breaking up a complex sentence into simpler ones. The English produced (Figure 5.9) flows much more easily than that of BABEL, but it is doubtful whether the results justify the pre-editing necessary.

```
            ACADEMY OF SCIENCES OF U.S.S.R. .
            INSTITUTE OF RUSSIAN TONGUE .
            * SURVEY OF WORKS ABOUT/IN CONTEMPORARY RUSSIAN
  LITERARY TONGUE OVER 1966 - 1969 (YEARS) .
            RUSSIAN TONGUE IN INVESTIGATIONS ABOUT/IN AUTOMATIC
  TRANSLATION .
            * UNDER EDITORSHIP OF CORRESPONDING MEMBER OF
  ACADEMY OF SCIENCES OF U.S.S.R. F.P. FILIN .
            * ( MATERIALS FOR DISCUSSION ) .
            MOSCOW 1973 .
            EDITOR OF ISSUE IS S.K. SHAUMYAN .
              AUTHORS ARE  : YU.D. APRYESHAN ( PART II. )
     I.A. MYEL'CHUK ( PART I. ) .
            CONTENTS .
            FOREWORD 5 .
            LIST OF LITERATURE 8 .
            PART I. 15 .
            I. MORPHOLOGY 21 .
            II. SYNTAX 23 .
            1. (RE)PRESENTATION/IDEA OF SYNTACTIC STRUCTURE
  24 .
            2. REVELATION OF SYNTACTIC STRUCTURE 27 .
            III. SEMANTICS 39 .
            IV. RUSSIAN TONGUE IN WORKING SYSTEMS OF MT 50 .
            PART II. 56 .
            1. RIGHT SYNTACTIC STRUCTURE 56 .
            2. SYNTACTIC HOMONYMY 64 .
            3. CONCLUSION/IMPRISONMENT 69 .
            FOREWORD /
            FOREWORD .
            *    IN LAST YEARS ALWAYS INCREASES STREAM OF WORKS
  , DEVOTED TO CONTEMPORARY RUSSIAN LITERARY TONGUE . SPECIALIST IN RUSSIAN
  ALREADY CANNOT ATTENTIVELY WATCH OVER ALL THIS LITERATURE . * PHONETICIAN
  OFTEN DOES NOT KNOW OF NEW ACHIEVEMENTS OF WORD-BUILDING
  THEORY . SPECIALIST ABOUT/IN WORD-BUILDING OFTEN DOES
  NO OWNS NEW IDEAS IN PROVINCE OF SYNTAX AND SO ON .
```

Figure 5.8. A translation into English from Russian by the machine translation program BABEL. (Crawford)

Machine translation is regarded by many as merely an academic exercise. It is uneconomic, not only because of the complexity of the computer programs required, but also because of the time taken to keypunch the material initially. But machine translation of technical material, especially if it is available in machine readable form as a by-product of computer typesetting methods, can be of use to scholars who would otherwise be unable to read the material at all. The language of technical texts is usually of a much simpler and more straightforward structure than that of literary material. The same is also true of business correspondence where there is also a need for translation from one language to another. It is in these areas that machine translation has been found to be least unsuccessful, where the translation does not have to be elegant, but does have to give the meaning adequately.

There is a lot of work still to be done on syntax analysers. The best

THE NEED FOR MACHINE TRANSLATION

THE RATE AT WHICH MAN HAS CONTINUOUSLY BEEN ACCUMULATING USEFUL KNOWLEDGE
ABOUT HIMSELF AND THE ENVIRONMENT HAS ACCELERATED GREATLY, PARTICULARLY DURING
THE LAST 100 YEARS. THERE ARE MANY REASONS FOR THIS INCREASE : THERE ARE MORE
SCIENTISTS TO-DAY THAN EVER BEFORE, SCIENTIFIC RESEARCH IS RECEIVING
SUBSTANTIAL GRANTS AND FINANCIAL SUPPORT FROM GOVERNMENT AND INDUSTRY, THE COLD
WAR HAS RESULTED IN A COMPETITIVE ATMOSPHERE IN WHICH NATIONS ARE ENDEAVOURING
FOR MILITARY AND TECHNOLOGICAL SUPREMACY, ETC.

BY THE MOST CONSERVATIVE ESTIMATES, EUROPE WAS PUBLISHING 1000 NEW BOOKS
PER YEAR BEFORE 1500. BY 1950, FOUR AND A HALF CENTURIES LATER, THE RATE
HAS ACCELERATED SO SHARPLY THAT EUROPE WAS PUBLISHING 120,000 NEW BOOKS
PER YEAR. BY THE MID-SEVENTIES, THE PUBLICATION OF BOOKS ON A WORLD SCALE,
EUROPE INCLUDED, REACHED THE FIGURE OF APPROXIMATELY 1,500 NEW BOOKS PER DAY.

THERE ARE MORE SCIENTIFIC SOCIETIES IN EXISTENCE TODAY THAN EVER BEFORE,
AND THESE SOCIETIES ARE HOLDING MORE MEETINGS, CONVENTIONS AND SEMINARS,
AND PUBLISH MORE JOURNALS AND PROCEEDINGS THAN EVER BEFORE. THE FIRST TWO
SCIENTIFIC JOURNALS APPEARED 300 YEARS AGO. IN 1958, THE NUMBER OF RESPONSIBLE
TECHNICAL JOURNALS APPROACHED 100,000; THERE ARE NOW FOUR MILLION JOURNAL
ARTICLES, 120,000 TECHNICAL BOOKS AND 100,000 TECHNICAL REPORTS BEING PUBLISHED
ANNUALLY (ON A WORLDWIDE BASIS APPROXIMATELY 60,000,000 PAGES EVERY YEAR).
AND THIS RATE OF PUBLICATION IS INCREASING EVERY YEAR. . TO-DAY, FOR EXAMPLE,
THE NUMBER OF SCIENTIFIC AND TECHNOLOGICAL JOURNALS AND ARTICLES IS DOUBLING,
LIKE INDUSTRIAL PRODUCTION IN THE INDUSTRIALISED COUNTRIES, ABOUT EVERY FIFTEEN
YEARS.

HOWEVER, WE CAN ARGUE THAT EVERY BOOK IS A GAIN FOR THE ADVANCEMENT OF
KNOWLEDGE. NEVERTHELESS, IT IS TRUE THAT THE ACCELERATION RATE OF BOOK
PUBLICATION IS, IN FACT, PARALLEL TO THE RATE AT WHICH MAN DISCOVERS NEW
KNOWLEDGE.

THE RESULT OF ALL THESE PUBLICATION ACTIVITIES IS THAT THE INDIVIDUAL
SCIENTIST IS STRUGGLING IN AN OCEAN OF INFORMATION AND IS ENDEAVOURING TO SEEK
THE INFORMATION HE NEEDS. FURTHERMORE, ALL JOURNALS AND BOOKS ARE PUBLISHED IN
DIFFERENT NATIONAL LANGUAGES, BECAUSE NO ONE COUNTRY CAN MONOPOLIZE THE
DEVELOPMENT OF SCIENCE AND TECHNOLOGY.

Figure 5.9. A translation into English from Chinese by the Chinese University of Hong
Kong machine translation project. (Loh)

method of dealing with such programs is by no means apparent, but they
are now being increasingly designed for analysing search requests in
information retrieval systems. This would allow a user to submit a request
in natural language, and the computer would then analyse the request
before performing the search. It is arguable whether this is economic.
Training a user to specify a search request in a particular form does not
take long, and it reduces the amount of computing to be done for each
request, freeing more time for the searches themselves.

The recent revival of interest in syntax analysis and machine translation
results from the development of computer hardware to the speed and size

where it might be more feasible and where it might have a useful application. At the present time its practical uses are limited and it is not within the scope of this book to expand further on a subject which is itself the subject of many books. Some references are given which may be a useful introduction to the world of computational semantics and artificial intelligence, but readers of them will note that the success level of those systems applied to literary text is not very high.

REFERENCES

1. R.D. Bathurst, Automatic Alphabetisation of Arabic words. *The Computer in Literary and Linguistic Research*, 185-90 (ed. R.A. Wisbey). Cambridge: Cambridge University Press (1971)

2. Louis Burnard, *OXEYE: A Text Processing Package for the 1906A*. Oxford University Computing Laboratory (1976)

3. T.D. Crawford, Project BABEL: Machine Translation with English as the Target Language. *The Computer in Literary and Linguistic Studies (Proceedings of the Third International Symposium)*, 223-9 (eds Alan Jones and R.F. Churchhouse). Cardiff: University of Wales Press (1976)

4. J.L. Dawson, Suffix Removal and Word Conflation. *ALLC Bull.* 2 No. 3 (1974) 33-46

5. Anita Dowsing, Some Aspects of Old English Syntax. *The Computer in Literary and Linguistic Studies (Proceedings of the Third International Symposium)*, 285-92 (eds Alan Jones and R.F. Churchhouse). Cardiff: University of Wales Press (1976)

6. Donald C. Green, Formulas and Syntax in Old English Poetry: A Computer Study. *Computers and the Humanities* 6 (1971) 85-93

7. Staffan Hellberg, Computerised Lemmatisation without the Use of a Dictionary: A Case Study from Swedish Lexicology. *Computers and the Humanities* 6 (1972) 209-12

8. S.-C. Loh, Machine Translation: Past, Present and Future. *ALLC Bull.* 4 (1976) 105-114

9. Bente Maegaard, The Recognition of Finite Verbs in French Texts. *ALLC Bull.* 4 (1976) 49-52

10. Jean G. Meunier, Serge Boisvert, Francois M. Denis, The Lemmatisation of Contemporary French. *The Computer in Literary and Linguistic Studies (Proceedings of the Third International Symposium)*, 208-14 (eds Alan Jones and R.F. Churchhouse). Cardiff: University of Wales Press (1976)

11. David W. Packard, Computer-Assisted Morphological Analysis of Ancient Greek. Forthcoming in the *Proceedings of the 1973 International Conference on Computational Linguistics*, Pisa 1973

12. James D. Price, An Algorithm for Generating Hebrew Words. *Computer Studies in the Humanities and Verbal Behavior* 1 (1968) 84-102

13. M.B. Pringle and D. Ross, Dialogue and Narration in Joyce's *Ulysses*. *Computing in the Humanities*, 73-84 (eds Serge Lusignan and John S. North). Waterloo: University of Waterloo Press (1977)

14. D. Ross, Beyond the Concordance: Algorithms for Description of English Clauses and Phrases. *The Computer and Literary Studies*, 85-99 (eds A.J. Aitken, R.W. Bailey and N. Hamilton-Smith). Edinburgh: Edinburgh University Press (1973)

15. D. Ross, An EYEBALL view of Blake's *Songs of Innocence and of Experience*. *Computers in the Humanities*, 94-108 (ed. J.L. Mitchell). Edinburgh: Edinburgh University Press (1974)

16. D. Ross and R. Rasche, *Description and Users' Manual for EYEBALL*. University of Minnesota Department of English (1972)

17. D. Ross and R. Rasche, EYEBALL: A Computer Program for Description of Style. *Computers and the Humanities* 6 (1972) 213-21

18. V. Shibayev, The CARLEX Computerised Analytical Russian Dictionary. *The Computer in Literary and Linguistic Studies (Proceedings of the Third International Symposium)*, 240-5 (eds Alan Jones and R.F. Churchhouse). Cardiff: University of Wales Press (1976)

Further Reading

Eugene Charniak and Yorick Wilks (eds), *Computational Semantics: An Introduction to Artificial Intelligence and Natural Language Comprehension*. (Fundamental Studies in Computer Sciences 4) New York: North Holland (1976)

Joseph Denooz, Recherches sur le Traitement Automatique de la Langue Latine. *Revue* No. 3 (1967) 1-89

M.L. Hann, Towards an Algorithmic Methodology of Lemmatisation. *ALLC Bull.* 3 (1975) 140-50

L.F. Lara, On Lexicographical Computing: Some Aspects of the Work for a Mexican Spanish Dictionary. *ALLC Bull.* 4 (1976) 97-104

James D. Price, An Algorithm for Analyzing Hebrew Words. *Computer Studies in the Humanities and Verbal Behavior* 2 (1969) 137-65

Anna-Lena Sågvall, *A System for Automatic Inflectional Analysis (Implemented for Russian)*. Stockholm: Almqvist and Wiksell (1973)

Y. Wilks, *Seven Theses on Artificial Intelligence and Natural Language*. Geneva: Fondazione della Molle (1975)

Terry Winograd, *Understanding Natural Language*. Edinburgh: Edinburgh University Press (1972)

6. Stylistic Analysis and Authorship Studies

Except for the production of concordances, the computer has been used and abused more frequently in the analysis of literary style than for any other form of literary text analysis. In particular, it has been used to 'solve' problems of disputed authorship. In this chapter we shall point out those areas where the misuse of the computer has been common and attempt to demonstrate how it might be used to real advantage in the analysis of style.

Can style be defined? and if so, what definitions of the style lend themselves to computational analysis? Style manifests itself for example in an author's choice of vocabulary, in his use of long or short sentences or in the syntactic constructions he prefers. Traditionally opinions about style have been largely intuitive, but the computer now can provide additional data to make an objective study. However, in order to make any kind of stylistic analysis by computer, specific features must be defined in terms which the machine can understand. Most computer-aided analyses of style have therefore restricted themselves to those features which are easily quantifiable and easily identified by machine. These features fall broadly into two groups: on the one hand, word and sentence length, together with the positions of words within sentences; on the other hand, the study of vocabulary, that is the choice and frequency of words. A third possible category is syntactic analysis once the syntactic features have been adequately defined and classified.

There is of course nothing new in the study of these features. It is merely that their study is facilitated by using a machine. Some of the earliest stylistic analyses were made by T.C. Mendenhall and published at the turn of the century. Among other things, Mendenhall applied himself to the question of the authorship of the Shakespearean plays, studying only word length – that is, the number of letters per word. He employed two ladies to count words, recording the number of words with one letter, with two letters, with three letters and so on. This they did for all the Shakespearean plays as well as for extensive material from Bacon, Jonson, Marlowe and others. In all some two million words were counted. It was shown that Shakespeare and Marlowe were alone in their high usage of four-letter words. All the others peaked at three letters, except for the two-letter peak of John Stuart Mill.

Mendenhall's account of the counting process is of some interest:

... excellent and entirely satisfactory manner in which the heavy task of counting was performed by the (two) ladies who undertook it ... The operation of counting was greatly facilitated by the construction of a simple counting machine by which a registration of a word of any given number of letters was made by touching a button marked with that number.

It is a pity that Mendenhall did not live seventy years later. His results would have been obtained very much faster, although he might not have dispensed completely with his two ladies.

Mendenhall presented his results as a series of graphs showing how many words of each length were found for each author. For comparative purposes the counts for two authors on one graph were placed as shown in Figure 6.1. Mendenhall illustrated his points well by presenting his results visually. Most modern analysts of style have preferred to present tables of numbers and then to manipulate these numbers further.

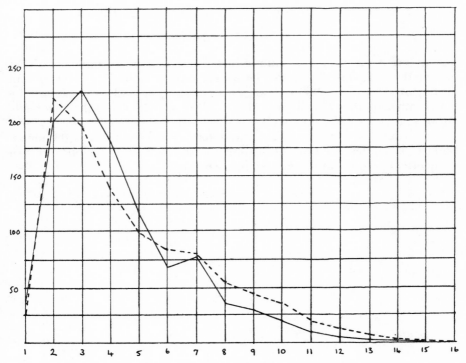

Figure 6.1. A graph showing wordlength distribution of Atkinson (solid line) and Mill (broken line) redrawn from Mendenhall 1887.

This manipulation of numbers inevitably requires statistical methods, and it is in this area where computer-aided stylistic analyses have been heavily criticised. Once numbers have been collected, we need to know how to interpret them and to determine whether they are of any significance or not. The basic mathematics of this are simple and can be understood by the non-scientist. The bibliography to this chapter gives several references for elementary statistics. Muller is good for statistics applied to linguistic analysis. Here we will limit ourselves to a few simple examples.

One of the simplest and most obvious statistics is what is known as the arithmetic *mean*, the commonest of the three 'averages' used in statistics. If we take ten words by author A and see that their lengths in letters are

$$2\ 4\ 2\ 6\ 1\ 7\ 1\ 4\ 2\ 1$$

The average or mean word length is the total of these divided by the number of words, that is

$$30 \div 10 = 3$$

Another ten words by author B might yield the following counts

$$2\ 4\ 3\ 3\ 1\ 3\ 5\ 2\ 4\ 3$$

also giving a mean of 3. A simple inspection of these counts shows that author B's word lengths are grouped more closely around their mean than author A's. Statistically we can measure this spread or variation by performing another calculation, the result of which is called the *standard deviation*. It is derived as follows.

Take each value in turn. Find the difference between it and the mean. Square this difference and add up all the squared values. If the value of each letter count is x and the mean is $\bar{x}$, we have

Author A	x	$x - \bar{x}$	$(x - \bar{x})^2$
	2	−1	1
	4	+1	1
	2	−1	1
	6	+3	9
	1	−2	4
	7	+4	16
	1	−2	4
	4	+1	1
	2	−1	1
	1	−2	4
			——
			42
			——

The total 42 is called the *sum of squares* about the mean. Divided by the number of items, in this case 10, it gives the *variance* 4.2. The standard deviation is the square root of the variance, and this may be obtained from square root tables which yield 2.049.

For author B, we can also calculate the standard deviation this time abbreviating the table to show how many words there are for each count. x is the count, n is the number of times that count occurs and $\bar{x}$ is the mean count.

Author B	x	n	$\bar{x} - x$	$(\bar{x} - x)^2$	$n(\bar{x} - x)^2$
	1	1	2	4	4
	2	2	1	1	2
	3	4	0	0	0
	4	2	−1	1	2
	5	1	−2	4	4
					12

Here we have a sum of squares of 12, a variance of 1.2 and a standard deviation of 1.095. The two sets of words are thus shown to differ in their spread.

These groups of ten words are obviously insufficient to make any representative comments about an author. They merely serve to illustrate the calculation of the simplest of statistics. But how much text should be used? If the whole text is available in machine readable form, it is obviously preferable to work on the entire text, but in many cases it will be impossible to calculate statistics from the entire text or texts under study (the *population*).

However in literary studies as in other disciplines valid statistical conclusions can be drawn from *samples* of text. From the statistics of a sample, such as the mean and standard deviation, it is possible to estimate values for the entire population. How and where to choose samples has been the subject of much discussion particularly in the case of text, since words do not appear in random order in a text but are related to each other in sequence. Traditionally there are two accepted ways of taking samples. One method is to categorise the text in some way (e.g. by genres of literature) and then sample from each category. This ensures that the samples are representative. The other method is to be entirely random. That is not to say that sampling should be haphazard. If you drop your text and just let it fall open, it is far more likely that it will open somewhere near the middle rather than at the first or last page. Similarly if you close your eyes and stick a pin in a page, the pin is far more likely to fall in the middle. True random samples are chosen by inspecting tables of random numbers. The best method of sampling text falls half way between these two methods. Inevitably much is already known about a text which is to be sampled and it can be divided into sections on the basis of this knowledge. Within these sections samples can be chosen using random number tables to indicate the starting page, line or word, and continuous lines of text can be taken from there.

The size of textual samples varies considerably, but for a prose text at least 100 and preferably many more sentences should be taken consecutively. Ellegard reckoned that a sample must contain at least ten occurrences of the feature being tested, and so if the feature is particularly rare a lot of text may be required. If several texts are being used for comparative purposes, two or more samples from the same text can be tested against each other to see whether a particular feature occurs with regularity in that text before it is used in an attempt to discriminate between authors.

A simple statistical test called the χ^2 (chi-square) is frequently used to indicate whether there is any significant difference between two groups of data. This test is much favoured by literary scholars because it is easy to calculate and does not involve any mathematics more complicated than squares and square roots. It should always be based on absolute counts, never on percentages or proportions, and it should not be used where the value in any category is less than five. If this is the case in the 'tail' of a distribution of numbers, those at the end should be added together and treated as a single value.

A χ^2 test would be appropriate for examining the distribution of sentence length within a text. Suppose that the text is divided into four sections A, B, C and D, each of 300 sentences, and we wish to discover whether section A is typical of the text as a whole. The example shows how this could be tested using χ^2. Sentence lengths are first tabulated:

	No. of sentences				
No. of words per sentence	A	B	C	D	Total
1–5	24	12	10	17	63
6–10	36	33	28	29	126
11–15	53	37	39	41	170
16–20	47	58	60	55	220
21–25	52	64	69	66	251
26–30	34	55	48	49	186
31–35	32	24	26	24	106
36–40	15	10	11	13	49
41–45	4	6	5	2	17
46–50	2	1	1	3	7
51–55	0	0	2	1	3
56–60	1	0	1	0	2
	300	300	300	300	1200

Note the way in which the information is grouped into sections of five words. Above the level of forty words per sentence the values are small, in most cases less than five, and so they should be grouped together into a single section for 41+ giving

	A	B	C	D	Total
41+	7	7	9	6	29

From these totals we can calculate what the expected number of words in each section would be if the number of words per sentence was distributed evenly throughout the text i.e. the total for each section divided by four giving

Expected values

No. of words per sentence	No. of sentences
1 – 5	15.75
5 – 10	31.5
11 – 15	42.5
16 – 20	55
21 – 25	62.75
26 – 30	46.5
31 – 35	26.5
36 – 40	12.25
41 +	7.25

The next stage is to subtract the expected values from the observed ones and square the result. This will yield a positive number whatever the result of the subtraction. This figure is then divided by the expected value. For section A this can be tabulated as follows

Observed (o)	Expected (e)	$o-e$	$(o-e)^2$	$(o-e)^2/e$
24	15.75	8.25	68.063	4.321
36	31.5	4.5	20.25	0.643
53	42.5	10.5	110.25	2.594
47	55	−8	64	1.164
52	62.75	−10.75	115.56	1.842
34	46.5	−12.5	156.25	3.360
32	26.5	5.5	30.25	1.142
15	12.25	2.75	7.562	0.617
7	7.25	−0.25	0.0625	0.009

|||||15.692|

The figures in the final column are added up to give a value for χ^2. We then need to know what this value means. We want to know if the counts for section A differ significantly from those for the rest of the text. Therefore we look up our figure for χ^2 in χ^2 tables found in statistics text books, for which we also need to know the number of *degrees of freedom*. This is always one less than the number of values in each column, in other words one less than the number of items measured separately. In our case the values were finally divided into nine groups which gives eight degrees of freedom. In the tables for eight degrees of freedom a *probability* of 0.05 is given for a value of 15.5, which is the nearest value given to our 15.69. Probabilities are always given between 0 and 1. A value of 1 indicates that an event is bound to happen, 0 that it will never happen. A probability of less than 0.05 indicates that the event has less than a 5% chance of occurring – that is, a one in twenty chance of happening thus by chance alone. Likewise a probability of less than 0.01 indicates less than a 1% chance, or one in a hundred chance, of occurring thus by chance alone. A result which has less than a 5% chance of happening is generally considered to be significant, while one which has less than a 1% chance is generally considered highly significant. In our case the probability of obtaining a χ^2 value as high as 15.69 if section A is indeed typical of the text as a whole is less than 0.05, and so we would conclude that the difference between section A and the text as a whole is significant at the 5% level or in other words, there is only a 5% probability that the difference occurred by chance alone.

Examining section B of the text gives the following table.

Observed	Expected	$o - e$	$(o - e)^2$	$(o - e)^2 / e$
12	15.75	−3.75	14.0625	0.893
33	31.5	1.5	2.25	0.071
37	42.5	−5.5	30.25	0.712
58	55	3	9	0.164
64	62.75	1.25	1.5625	0.025
55	46.5	8.5	72.25	1.554
24	26.5	−2.5	6.25	0.236
10	12.25	−2.25	5.0625	0.413
7	7.25	−0.25	0.0625	0.009
				4.077

In the χ^2 tables this gives a probability of about 0.85 indicating that that distribution of values may well have occurred by chance and that the results are not significant. In the two examples given, each section is tested against the entire body of the text including itself. It is also possible to use a χ^2 test to compare one section of the text against all the others excluding itself or against each individual section. These latter tests are more likely to produce significant differences but can be used with discretion.

Means, standard deviation and χ^2 are simple statistics, which in many cases can be computed by a standard computer program, but it is important to understand what these numbers mean. It is useful to perform some of these simple calculations by hand on a small quantity of text to ensure that the principles behind them are thoroughly understood, before allowing the machine to take over. One other point can be noted. Some computer programs when calculating the variance divide not by n, the number of items, but by $n-1$. This may also be true of those pocket calculators which can work out standard deviations. If the number of items is very large, this is not going to make much difference to the results, but it is as well to be aware of the possibility.

As many literary scholars have begun to use statistics, so many statisticians have begun to take an interest in text, as a new and interesting source of data. A number of articles have been published by professional statisticians and mathematicians attempting to find new mathematical ways of describing text. Of particular interest is the distribution of items of vocabulary in a text. This does not conform to any known distribution and has therefore attracted many attempts to find a new one. No one has yet succeeded in finding a measure which describes all vocabulary. Non-mathematicians should be warned that these articles require a fair knowledge of mathematics.

We have now established some of the ground work for the statistical analysis of literary style and for authorship studies. Whether using a computer or not, it is necessary to understand some simple statistics in order to quantify the results. With a χ^2 test the 1% and 5% probability levels can be used to indicate whether an event is likely to have happened by chance or not. If at all possible, it is advisable to operate on the whole text, not on samples. If samples have to be taken, they must be chosen with care applying random number principles. It is useful to test individual samples from a known work against each other for homogeneity before attempting to make comparisons with disputed texts. A feature of style which is not consistent in known works cannot serve as a discriminant. As many features as possible should be investigated in authorship studies, and external evidence must not be forgotten. Good historical evidence may carry more weight than stylistic analysis. In the simplest case of a disputed work known by external evidence to be by one of two or more candidates, the work can be compared with text by all the possible candidates. If the test is merely to question the authorship of a work and not an attempt to assign it to another author, it must be compared with a representative set of material by the author, and it must not be forgotten that an author's style may change throughout his life or may depend on the subject matter. These tests are very rarely conclusive. Frequently they may only provide negative evidence. In only a very few cases have problems of disputed authorship been solved totally and these have been ideally suited to computer analysis. Using such quantitative methods will however accumulate as much evidence as possible and will allow many different tests to be applied systematically.

One feature of style which has attracted some interest recently is syntax. We have seen in Chapter Five how the computer may (or may not) be used to parse a text. Here we shall investigate those syntactic analyses which have been performed primarily for stylistic purposes. In many cases this has entailed manual parsing of the material rather than computer parsing. In other cases using computer programs like EYEBALL and OXEYE, the computer coding can be modified to correct any errors. Statistics from OXEYE have already been illustrated in Chapter Five. Another example in Figure 6.2 also shows means and standard deviations

Milic in his work on Swift adopted a different method of coding which used a series of numbers rather than letter codes. Though written as long ago as 1967, his book gives some useful information for the quantitative analysis of prose style, but the method does have some drawbacks. A two-digit code is assigned to each word indicating its part of speech, and a separate code is used to mark the end of a sentence. Only the codes and not the text were input to the computer. A typical sentence then becomes

31 81 01 51 31 03 01 61 05 41 05 31 81 01 01 21 33 03

On the basis of these codes Milic was able to draw up tables of the frequencies of the different parts of speech in the prose works of Swift.

This method of coding was taken up by one of his pupils, Mrs Köster, in an attempt to discover the author of the *Story of St Albans Ghost*. She recoded by hand some of the texts which Milic had studied and in many cases arrived at a different total for each part of speech, showing that some subjective judgments must have been made before the material was put into the machine. The results are therefore only as reliable as the coding of the text. If this kind of hand coding is to be done, rigid rules for the coding should first be established to help to iron out inconsistencies. If a machine's parsing program is used it should at least be consistent, and inconsistencies will only be introduced at the stage of manual correction of the data.

Milic, who also worked on samples of text from other authors, including Addison, Johnson, Gibbon and Macaulay, found three tests which he considered to be the most reliable discriminators. These were high scores for the use of verbal forms, for what he calls introductory connectives, and

DETERMINER

```
FREQUENCY PER SENTENCE :    0      1      2      3      5      6
         NUMBER SUCH :      8      2      3      2      2      1
         % PROBABILITY :  100.00  55.55  44.44  27.77  16.66   5.55

         MEAN :   1.66        STANDARD DEVIATION :   1.64        POPULATION : 18

EXCLUDING NULL OCCURRENCES ...

         MEAN :   3.00        STANDARD DEVIATION :   1.76        POPULATION : 10
```

	TOTAL	SENTENCES STARTING	SENTENCES ENDING	SENTENCES LACKING
OCCURRENCES :	30	1	0	8
POPULATION :	220	18	18	18
AVERAGE :	13.63	5.55	0	44.44

NOUN

```
FREQUENCY PER SENTENCE :    0      1      2      3      4      6      7
         NUMBER SUCH :      1      6      4      2      2      1      2
         % PROBABILITY :  100.00  94.44  61.11  38.88  27.77  16.66  11.11

         MEAN :   7.66        STANDARD DEVIATION :   2.04        POPULATION : 18

EXCLUDING NULL OCCURRENCES ...

         MEAN :   2.82        STANDARD DEVIATION :   2.09        POPULATION : 17
```

	TOTAL	SENTENCES STARTING	SENTENCES ENDING	SENTENCES LACKING
OCCURRENCES :	43	6	10	1
POPULATION :	220	18	18	18
AVERAGE :	21.81	33.33	55.55	5.55

Figure 6.2. Statistics from OXEYE showing means and standard deviations.

for different patterns of three-word groups. This latter test was conducted by selecting each successive group of three words and counting how many times each possible group was found. Milic established that in these three areas Swift behaves very differently from the other prose samples he studied.

Mrs Köster took samples of known texts of two authors, Arbuthnot and Wagstaffe, and also a collection of what she calls pseudo-Wagstaffe, prose which is attributed to Wagstaffe but not signed. Very simple computer programs can be used to operate on this numeric data to obtain the counts necessary for the first two of Milic's discriminators. The third discriminator was tested by merely counting the number of three-word patterns. When these programs were run on the disputed work, it was found to have a lower score than Swift for two out of three discriminators. Three samples of Arbuthnot and Wagstaffe were each run separately and were found to be inconsistent in themselves. Mrs Koster gives absolute totals and percentages in her tables of results and states that there are differences in the results. It would have been preferable to use a χ^2 or other test of significance to determine whether these differences were noteworthy. A test of homogeneity within known works is a sound starting point, but the method of coding renders these studies somewhat suspect.

A similar approach using manual coding of data was adopted by Leighton in a study of seventeenth-century German sonnets. This was another attempt to distinguish the style of a number of sonnets, the intention being to produce a kind of literary geography, to determine whether certain towns or certain regions were distinguishable by specific stylistic traits. The syntactic structure of the sonnets was used, as it was felt that the rigidity of the rhyme scheme imposed certain limits on the type of structure possible. Contemporary evidence showed that most of the poets put their rhyme schemes together and then set about writing a sonnet to fit them. The investigation therefore looked at sentence structure in relation to rhyme structure.

A letter coding system was devised to indicate the features to be examined for each line, for example

	code
main clause	*a*
interrupted main clause	*b*
completion of main clause	*c*
elliptical main clause	*d*
extension phrase in apposition	*e*

Symbols for apostrophe and question mark and for figures of speech affecting sentence structure, such as anacolouthon and inversion, were also included, and so was a marker indicating the end of a line and a separate marker for the end of a line when it coincided with the end of a sentence. Thus there were on average three or four coded letters for each line. The data could then be input very simply, one sonnet per computer card. A short program counted the features and performed some simple calculations such as the mean number of main clauses per poem, incidences of enjambments and apostrophes, and number of sentences per poem. As each line was represented by a sequence of letters, the computer was also programmed to find the most frequently occurring patterns for each line. Even when tested on a small pilot set of data, twenty sonnets by Fleming and thirty-one by Gryphius, Leighton was able to show that each poet had his own favourite line pattern frequencies.

Leighton's approach was very simple but is worth considering for the analysis of clause structure. On a one-man project such as his, difficulties over inconsistencies in coding were less likely, and the data was reduced to a very small amount for each sonnet, much less than in Milic's coding of parts of speech. Such a process could easily be included in a vocabulary study by adding the stylistic features as an extra 'word' at the end of each line of text. In this way, both the actual words of the text and the codings could be subjected to analysis.

Oakman's study of Carlyle's syntax adopted a different procedure. In this case samples were chosen randomly from those works known to have been written by Carlyle. At total of two hundred paragraphs were chosen by using a table of random numbers, first to select the volumes and then to select the pages within the volumes. Oakman used an automatic syntactic analyser developed at the IBM San José Research Laboratory. He admits that this parser was unable to cope adequately with some of Carlyle's work, but given that it was written to analyse technical and scientific material, this is hardly surprising. Oakman does not give an error rate but merely remarks that 'glaring errors in the parsing were taken into account when the results were tabulated'. It seems clear that some kind of manual correction must be applied to machine parsing of literary text before any meaningful results can be presented. EYEBALL and OXEYE have an advantage here as they allow correction of the parsing before compiling statistics.

Much more fruitful results have been obtained in those analyses which combine the study of vocabulary with word and sentence length. One of the earliest such studies was made by Ellegard on the so-called Junius Letters, a series of letters which appeared in the *Public Advertiser* in 1769-72 under the pseudonym of Junius. There were thought to be about forty possible candidates for authorship, of whom the favourite was Sir Philip Francis. Ellegard published two books about his attempts to solve this authorship problem. The first, *Who was Junius?*, describes the background to the problem and includes one chapter on statistical methods. The second, *A*

Statistical Method for Determining Authorship, gives a full description of the methods he used. He first looked at sentence length but found considerable variability in the works of known authorship and thus concluded that the number of words per sentence could not help isolate one candidate for the Junius letters. Sentence length is of course a very easy feature to study by computer, but on many occasions it has been found to be so variable within a group of samples known to be from the same author that it is of little use in an authorship study.

Ellegard then turned to vocabulary and looked for words which occurred more or less frequently than would be expected in the Junius letters. These he called 'plus words' and 'minus words'. As he did not use a computer for counting words, but merely for performing calculations on the results, he had to rely on his own intuition as to which words occurred more or less frequently than expected. Ellegard's study was done in the early days of computing when it was not easy to handle so many words by machine. Clearly it would have been advantageous for him to have used a machine for the counting and to have counted all words, not just those he specifically noticed. Nevertheless Ellegard's work has served as a model for many later authorship studies and gives a useful introduction to the subject.

To examine the frequency of words which do not occur very often, it is obviously necessary to look at a substantial amount of text. Ellegard used very large samples of text, up to 100,000 words, far larger than is necessary for most studies. But as he was investigating words which did not occur very often, he believed that his samples had to be large enough to include at least ten occurrences of the words or words in which he was interested. He began by testing several samples from each known author against each other for homogeneity and discarded those items of vocabulary which were not uniform in occurrence. Though he was not able to reach a firm conclusion about the authorship of the Junius letters, he did find many features of their style and vocabulary which resembled closely those of Francis.

Another early computer-aided authorship study was performed by Mosteller and Wallace on the *Federalist Papers*, a series of documents written in 1787-8 to persuade the citizens of New York to ratify the Constitution. Three people were known to have written these papers, John Jay, Alexander Hamilton and James Madison. The papers eventually totalled eighty-eight in number, and they were all published first in newspapers under the pseudonym of Publius and then in book form. Of these papers, the authorship of only twelve was in dispute, and then only between Hamilton and Madison – it was known that they were not by Jay. Since there were only two known candidates and a lot of comparative material of the same nature, Mosteller and Wallace were able to test their selected criteria thoroughly in papers known to be by Hamilton and Madison before applying them to the disputed papers.

Early work on these papers by Mosteller and F. Williams consisted of a study of sentence length. After much manual counting the results produced were:

mean sentence length   Hamilton   34.55 words

Madison   34.59 words

They then considered whether there was any variability of sentence length between the two men. The standard deviations of sentence lengths for each paper were calculated and the mean of these taken. The results again were very similar:

mean standard deviation   Hamilton   19.2

Madison   20.3

Some years later Mosteller attacked the problem again, this time in collaboration with Wallace. They began a systematic and comprehensive study of the vocabulary of the papers. A computer was used to count the words and they concentrated initially on those words whose presence or absence in one or other of the authors had been noticed. They rapidly discovered that Hamilton always used 'while' when Madison preferred 'whilst' and also found that the disputed papers preferred 'whilst', as did the three papers which were considered to have been written jointly by the two. Other words such as 'upon' and 'enough' emerged as markers of Hamilton. 'Upon' was found to appear only 7 times in the 37,095 words in Madison's papers and 110 times in 34,577 words of Hamilton. It appeared twice in one of the disputed papers and not at all in the others. 'Enough' appeared 24 times in the known Hamilton papers and not at all in any other papers.

In their early work, Mosteller and Wallace calculated the percentage of nouns, adjectives and short words using manual counts. On the basis of these they constructed a statistic which they called a linear discriminant function, which was intended to separate the writings of the two authors by giving high scores to Hamilton and low scores to Madison. Though not definitive, this measure favoured Madison as the author of the disputed papers. Further evidence supported this theory more and more as they later applied more advanced statistical techniques, in particular Bayes' theorem.

It is generally accepted that this particular authorship problem has been solved conclusively, but it must be remembered that the disputed Federalist Papers were very suitable for this kind of approach. There were only two possible candidates, both of whom had written a considerable amount of undisputed material on the same subject matter. The quantity of material to be studied (some 70,000 words of known text divided equally between the two authors, and some 25,000 words of disputed text) was not too small to make the calculations meaningless, but also not too large to make them unwieldy. Sampling was used to test known works for homogeneity, but once this was found the calculations were performed on the entire texts.

A word frequency count will show which words occur frequently in a text, and comparisons can then be made to establish whether their frequent occurrence is unusual. The most frequent words in a text are almost always function words, which are largely independent of the subject matter. Cluster analysis techniques can be applied to study function words when comparisons are to be made between several texts. Ule gives an example showing a number of Elizabethan texts measured according to the distribution of three of the most common words in English, 'and', 'the' and 'to'. The vocabulary frequencies are given as percentages, such that the total number of occurrences of all three words is 100%. For example in Woodstock 'and' is 39.70%, 'the' is 36.64% and 'to' is 25.66%. The figures for fifteen texts in all are given in this form. From these a cluster analysis is performed showing which texts are most like each other on the basis of the usage of these words.

The occurrence and distribution of function words can prove fruitful in stylistic comparisons, for if the feature being considered itself occurs frequently, conclusions can be drawn from smaller amounts of text. Such function words have formed the basis of a large number of analyses of Greek prose made by Andrew Morton and his associates. Greek is a language which has many function words such as connective particles, and both the position and the frequency of these particles can also be considered.

Morton has popularised the use of computers in authorship studies and has received some criticism for his work. In a newspaper article in the early 1960s he claimed that only four of the epistles attributed to St Paul were written by him. This claim was largely based on Paul's use of the Greek word καί ('and'). Since then Morton and his collaborators have worked extensively on the New Testament and other Greek prose authors. They have recently turned their attention to English text and even to the analysis of statements given to the police, and they have been called upon to give evidence in court on the basis of these analyses. It would seem that police statements are too short to give any sound statistical basis for this work, but nevertheless Morton has been much in demand since his court appearance.

Morton's methods of stylometry are developed from those of W.C. Wake, a scientist who was interested in Aristotle. Wake's methods required the study of a frequently occurring event which is independent of subject matter. The occurrence should be examined in a wide range of texts to establish general conclusions about a writer. Wake was soon able to show that what is most characteristic of an author is not his personal idiosyncrasies but the rate at which he performs the operations shared with all his colleagues. In Greek this would be the choice and usage of particles in particular.

Collectively Morton's stylometric methods can yield a comprehensive and systematic analysis of a text. However Morton does tend to concentrate on one or two criteria. The work of A.J.P. Kenny on Aristotle will be seen to be much more comprehensive in its coverage but it was based initially on Morton's methodology.

The sort of table which Morton very frequently produces is shown in Figure 6.3. This table shows the number of sentences which have the particle γάρ as one of the first four words. Each sample is the first two hundred sentences from each book of Herodotus. Choosing a starting point by random number tables might have been preferable, but Morton very frequently takes the first two hundred sentences of a text as his sample. A χ^2 test could be used to indicate whether the high incidence of γάρ in Book 7 is significant or not. In this case it is found not to be so.

Morton has also studied the lengths of sentences in Greek. He does not delve very deeply into what constitutes a sentence, merely taking the punctuation inserted by later editors into the text to signal the ends of sentences. The question of what is a sentence in Greek prose cannot be resolved here, but clearly the same definition of a sentence must be applied to all texts. When the texts have been prepared by different editors it is as

	No. of sentences	
Book	With *gar* as one of first four words	In sample
1	25	200
2	30	200
3	22	200
4	23	200
5	18	200
6	17	200
7	30	200
8	29	200
9	19	200
Totals	213	1800

Figure 6.3. A table showing the occurrence of γάρ as one of the first four words of sentences in each of the nine books of Herodotus. (Morton and Winspear)

well to point this out. A typical Morton sentence-length distribution is shown in Figure 6.4. The sentences can vary in length up to 155 words. They are grouped in sets of five. Sentence length seems to be a more reliable discriminant for Greek than for English. Another feature studied by Morton is the last word in a sentence, whether it be a noun, a verb, an adjective or another part of speech. Word order is significant in Greek, and although many sentences frequently end with a verb, other words may be emphasised by being placed at the end of a sentence.

Morton's work should by no means be disregarded. He was a pioneer in the field of stylistic analysis of Greek and his methods could usefully be

No. of words in sentence	No. of such sentences in	
	Seventh Letter	*Apology*
1-5	17	68
6-10	41	103
11-15	51	95
16-20	44	61
21-25	36	48
26-30	34	39
31-35	25	20
36-40	20	15
41-45	12	8
46-50	10	7
51-55	8	4
56-60	5	4
61-65	4	5
66-70	3	1
71-75	4	2
76-80	—	—
81-85	6	—
86-90	3	—
96-100	—	2
116-120	1	—
121-125	—	1
151-155	1	—
Totals	326	483

Figure 6.4. Sentence length distribution in Plato's *Seventh Letter* and *Apology*. (Morton and Winspear)

followed by many. However, his work can be criticised for its failure to apply more than one or two tests to a set of data. Assumptions about the authorship of a text are made on what is statistically very questionable evidence. Morton has been criticised for his excessive use of the χ^2 test, which he also computes in a different way from other scholars. We have seen that this test is easy to calculate and can be used to indicate whether results are significant or not. For that reason it is recommended, provided the data is valid for such a test, and Morton certainly uses χ^2 only where it should be used.

Morton's methods were adopted and expanded considerably by A.J.P. Kenny in his study of the Aristotelian *Ethics*. Within the *Nicomachean* and *Eudemean Ethics* three books effectively appear twice. Kenny has made a lengthy and systematic comparison of the style of the two *Ethics* and the three disputed books. Using word frequency counts, he has established that the differences between the disputed books and the *Nicomachean Ethics* are much greater than those between the disputed books and the *Eudemean Ethics*. Kenny again concentrated on common words, dividing them into tables according to their grammatical function. In 20 cases out of 36 particles, the difference in usage between the disputed books and the *Nicomachean Ethics* is too great to be attributable to chance; but in every case but two there is no significant difference between the disputed books and the *Eudemean Ethics*. Similar results were obtained from the examination of prepositions and adverbs. A number of adverbs in particular occur much more frequently in the *Nicomachean Ethics* than in the *Eudemean Ethics*. Again these are not found so frequently in the disputed books.

Having completed an analysis of the common words in the *Ethics* which themselves totalled some 53% of words in the entire texts, Kenny then studied the disputed books, not as a whole but in small sections of about 1000 words each. As the samples had now become smaller, the words to be studied were taken in groups of words of similar meaning, not as occurrences of single words. The groups were selected so that they consisted of words which were favourites either of the *Nicomachean* or of the *Eudemean Ethics*, but not of both. Following Ellegard, a distinctiveness ratio for each group was computed. This consisted of its *Nicomachean* frequency divided by its *Eudemean* frequency. Thus a word which occurs more frequently in the *Nicomachean Ethics* will have a distinctiveness ratio greater than one, and one which occurs more frequently in the *Eudemean Ethics* will be between zero and one. Only words of high frequency were chosen for these groups, so that a frequency of not less than ten could be expected in a sample of 1000 words. By comparing the expected number of occurrences with the actual number, it was possible to determine for each sample in turn whether it resembled the *Nicomachean* or *Eudemean Ethics*. The results showed that every one of the 1000-word samples resembled the *Eudemean* much more than the *Nicomachean Ethics.*

Kenny has also studied other features such as word length, sentence length, the last word in a sentence and choice of synonyms. In every case, although the entire text was examined, block of samples were built up and each block tested with all the others from the same text before being compared with samples from another text. Those features which do not occur uniformly were noted but discarded as possible evidence for an attribution study.

Radday's work on Isaiah has used more complicated mathematical techniques, although like Kenny, Morton and others he has concentrated on function words. In collaboration with a statistician, Dieter Wickmann, he has devised a new test called an *arcsin* test which is used to distinguish between the rate of occurrence of a word in two samples of text. The method requires some knowledge of mathematics to understand. The calculation produces a value which is called z, and if z is greater than 1.96, Radday and Wickmann demonstrate that the two samples can be said to come from a different population with a 5% chance of error. The z value must be at least 2.58 for a 1% chance of error. Working entirely with relative frequencies of function words and with this z value, they have discovered a number of cases where books of the Old Testament are not homogeneous in the usage of a single word. Their study of Isaiah is based on twenty different words and divides the book into roughly four sections. Using the definite article alone, 14 books or sections of books in the Old Testament have a z value greater than 1.96 and many of these are greater than 2.58. Some of these can be explained – for example, the one section in Joshua which has a z value of 19.333 but consists of a comparison of narrative with geographical lists. It seems rather pointless to include such obvious known differences, but perhaps it does at least validate the method.

In most cases, then, these analyses of style have been based on simple calculations which are not beyond the non-mathematician. A computer can ensure that such a study is comprehensive and not based solely on isolated occurrences of words. A concordance can be a valuable start to a stylistic analysis, although unlemmatised word-frequency counts should be used with care. Words should be considered first as separate items of vocabulary and then grouped under their lemmas.

There has been considerable misuse of statistics in the published literature. It is not at all difficult to learn enough statistics to use the simple tests which have been described in this chapter. More complicated statistics should be avoided unless they are understood thoroughly. If necessary, a professional statistician should be consulted. It is foolish now to embark on any quantitative stylistic analysis without a knowledge of elementary statistics. With such a knowledge it is possible to judge whether the differences in style between two or more samples of text are significant or not. However, deductions from such evidence to conclusions on the authorship of the texts should be made with the utmost caution. One or two interesting results do not necessarily indicate that the authorship of a text is in dispute. Only in the case of the *Federalist Papers* has it been possible to provide a conclusive solution to a disputed authorship question, and as we have seen there were features of that problem which made it unusually suitable for a proof of that kind. Kenny's study of the Aristotelian *Ethics* has found what appears to be sufficient evidence to attribute the disputed books to the *Eudemean* rather than the *Nicomachean Ethics,* but nevertheless he stops short of claiming a conclusive solution to the problem. The computer will not produce an absolute solution to an authorship study, but it can be used successfully to provide sufficient evidence on which powerful conclusions can be based. It is used to best advantage in work which requires lengthy and laborious counting. Such a quantitative study using comparative tests can give sufficient significant evidence, provided it attempts to cover as many as possible of the features mentioned in this chapter. Only then can any conclusion be reached, and in many cases this may only be a negative conclusion.

REFERENCES

1. Barron Brainerd, Statistical Analysis of Lexical Data Using Chi-Squared and Related Distributions. *Computers and the Humanities* 9 (1975) 161-78

2. Fred. J. Damerau, The Use of Function Word Frequencies as Indicators of Style. *Computers and the Humanities* 9 (1975) 271-80

3. Alvar Ellegard, *Who Was Junius?* Stockholm: Almqvist and Wiksell (1962)

4. Alvar Ellegard, *A Statistical Method for Determining Authorship: The Junius Letters 1769-1772.* Gothenburg Studies in English (1962)

5. A. Kenny, The Stylometric Study of Aristotle's Ethics. *Computing in the Humanities,* 11-22 (eds Serge Lusignan and John S. North). Waterloo: University of Waterloo Press (1977)

6. Patricia Köster, Computer Stylistics: Swift and Some Contemporaries. *The Computer in Literary and Linguistic Research,* 129-47 (ed. R.A. Wisbey). Cambridge: Cambridge University Press (1971)

7. Joseph Leighton, Sonnets and Computers: An Experiment in Stylistic Analysis Using an Elliot 503 Computer. *The Computer in Literary and Linguistic Research,* 149-58 (ed. R.A. Wisbey). Cambridge: Cambridge University Press (1971)

8. T.C. Mendenhall, The Characteristic Curves of Composition. *Science* 9 (1887) 237-49

9. T.C. Mendenhall, A Mechanical Solution of a Literary Problem. *The Popular Science Monthly* 40 (1901) 97-105

10. S. Michaelson and A.Q. Morton, Things Aint What They Used To Be: A Study of

Chronological Change in a Greek Writer. *The Computer in Literary and Linguistic Studies* (*Proceedings of the Third International Symposium*), 78-84 (eds Alan Jones and R.F. Churchhouse). Cardiff: University of Wales Press (1976)

11. Louis T. Milic, *A Quantitative Approach to the Style of Jonathan Swift.* The Hague: Mouton (1967)

12. A.Q. Morton and James McLeman, *Paul, the Man and the Myth: A Study in the Authorship of Greek Prose.* London: Hodder and Stoughton (1966).

13. Andrew Q. Morton and Alban D. Winspear, *It's Greek to the Computer.* Montreal: Harvest House (1971)

14. Frederick Mosteller and David L. Wallace, *Inference and Disputed Authorship: The Federalist.* Reading, Mass: Addison-Wesley (1964)

15. R.L. Oakman, Carlyle and the Machine: A Quantitative Analysis of Syntax in Prose Style. *ALLC Bull.* 3 (1975) 211-25

16. Yehuda T. Radday, *The Unity of Isaiah in the Light of Statistical Linguistics.* Hildesheim: Gerstenberg (1973)

17. Y.T. Radday and H. Shore, The Definite Article: A Type and/or Author-Specifying Discriminant in the Hebrew Bible. *ALLC Bull.* 4 (1976) 23-31

18. D. Ross, AN EYEBALL View of Blake's *Songs of Innocence and of Experience. Computers in the Humanities*, 94-108 (ed. J.L. Mitchell). Edinburgh: Edinburgh University Press (1974)

19. L.A. Ule, Cluster Analysis. *ALLC Bull.* 2 No. 3 (1974) 16-21

Further Reading (Statistics)

Barron Brainerd, *Weighing Evidence in Language and Literature: A Statistical Approach.* Toronto University of Toronto Press (1974)

Evelyn Caulcott, *Significance Tests.* London: Routledge and Kegan Paul (1973)

Wilhelm Fucks, On Mathematical Analysis of Style. *Biometrika* 39 (1952) 122-9

W. Fucks, *Nach Allen Regeln der Kunst.* Stuttgert: Deutsche Verlags-Anstalt (1968)

Gustav Herdan, *The Advanced Theory of Language as Choice and Chance.* Berlin: Springer-Verlag (1966)

Ch. Muller, *Initiation aux Méthodes de la Statistique Linguistique.* Paris: Hachette (1973)

N.D. Thomson, Literary Statistics. Six articles in *ALLC Bull.* beginning Vol 1 No. 3 (1973)

C.B. Williams, *Style and Vocabulary: Numerical Studies.* London: Griffin (1970)

G. Udny Yule, *The Statistical Study of Literary Vocabulary.* Cambridge: Cambridge University Press (1944)

John R. Allen, Methods of Author Identification Through Stylistic Analysis. *French Review* 47 (1974) 904-16

Richard W. Bailey and Lubomír Doležel, *An Annotated Bibliography of Statistical Stylistics*. Ann Arbor: Department of Slavic Languages and Literatures; University of Michigan (1968)

W.M. Baillie, Authorship Attribution in Jacobean Dramatic Texts. *Computers in the Humanities*, 73-81 (ed. J.L. Mitchell). Edinburgh: Edinburgh University Press (1974)

Claude S. Brinegar, Mark Twain and the Quintus Curtius Snodgrass Letters: A Statistical Test of Authorship. *Journal of the American Statistical Association* 58 (1963) 85-96

Lubomír Doležel and Richard W. Bailey (eds) *Statistics and Style*. New York: Elsevier (1969)

C. English, A Computer-Assisted Analysis of Russian Prose. *ALLC Bull.* 5 (1977) 249-58

Kenneth W. Kemp. Personal Observations on the Use of Statistical Methods in Quantitative Linguistics. *The Computer in Literary and Linguistic Studies (Proceedings of the Third International Symposium)*, 59-77 (eds Alan Jones and R.F. Churchhouse). Cardiff: University of Wales Press (1976)

A.J.P. Kenny, *The Aristotelian Ethics*. Oxford: Oxford University Press (1978)

S. Michaelson and A.Q. Morton, Last Words: A Test of Authorship for Greek Writers. *New Testament Studies* 18 (1971-72) 192-208

S. Michaelson and A.Q. Morton, Positional Stylometry. *The Computer and Literary Studies*, 69-83 (eds A.J. Aitken, R.W. Bailey and N. Hamilton-Smith). Edinburgh: Edinburgh University Press (1973)

A.Q. Morton and James McLeman, *Christianity and the Computer*. London: Hodder and Stoughton (1964)

Alastair McKinnon and Rober Webster, A Method of Author Identification. *The Computer in Literary and Linguistic Research*, 65-74 (ed. R.A. Wisbey). Cambridge: Cambridge University Press (1971)

Yehuda Radday and Haim Shor, AND in Isaiah. *Revue* No. 2 (1974) 25-41

L.A. Ule, The Use of CONSTAT in Authorship Investigations. *ALLC Bull.* 3 (1975) 211-25.

7. Textual Criticism

There are several stages involved in the preparation of a critical edition of a text. Normally the text editor begins by studying all the manuscripts or editions of his text and then collates these manuscripts to find all the places where the readings differ. Variants may be anything from a misspelling or mistyping of a small and insignificant word or incorrect punctuation to the omission or insertion of whole blocks of text which may be many lines long. Once the variants have been found, the editor must decide which if any of them represents what the author wrote. This is usually done by investigating the relationships between the manuscripts. The oldest one might be considered to have the most likely reading, or alternatively the reading supported by most manuscripts may be the true one. The text can then be reconstructed using the chosen readings from the variants, and those variant readings which are considered important may be provided for the reader in the form of an apparatus criticus usually presented as a series of footnotes at the bottom of each page. The final stage is the printing of the text and apparatus.

There are therefore five stages in the preparation of a critical edition of a text:

1. Collation of manuscripts
2. Finding the relationships between manuscripts
3. Reconstruction of the text
4. Compilation of the apparatus criticus
5. Printing of the text and apparatus

The computer has been used with some success in stages one and two. Stages three and four are really a matter for human judgment, but they can be facilitated by using material already stored in the computer from stages one and two, and of course if the material is already in computer-readable form it would be sensible to use the machine for stage five – that is, the typesetting of the final edition.

Provided that there is no doubt about the readings in the manuscripts, the collation of manuscripts is a purely mechanical process, consisting of merely identifying places where two or more texts do not match. On the face of it this lends itself easily to computing and indeed the machine has been used sensibly on the kind of text which is suitable for it. Texts which differ considerably present rather more problems for computer collation, as the machine is far more likely to lose its place when comparing two manuscripts with frequent and major variants. To prevent this it may be necessary to make many comparisons between a word in the master text and successive words in the comparison text until the place is found again. These comparisons can use up a lot of computer time if care is not taken in working out a suitable method for doing them. Algorithms for computer collation of texts have therefore attracted the attention of computer scientists interested in finding the best method of collation, that is the one which uses the least number of comparisons without losing its place. Different procedures may be involved in collating verse and prose. Verse is much easier to deal with than prose provided the line format remains the same from manuscript to manuscript. Variants should also comply with the metre of the words they replace. It is therefore much easier for the computer to keep its place in verse than in prose, where the line numberings, beginnings and ends vary from manuscript to manuscript.

The format in which the text and the variants are printed out is important in computer collation. The machine is being used to simulate a series of human operations in which certain words must be noticed quickly. The computer should therefore produce output which can easily be scanned by eye for the variants. It should not be necessary always to refer back to one of the original texts when examining the variants, though this may be desirable from the editor's point of view.

Almost all of the early computer collation systems assume that the computer input from manuscripts has the same line structure. Some computer programs compare only two manuscripts at a time. Others allow a large number of manuscripts to be compared. It is usual to select one text as a base or master text and consider the others as comparison texts. The various methods developed can best be illustrated by examples to show how each system would collate the following three lines, which we shall call A, B and C. We shall assume initially that they are presented to the computer as lines which should be compared with each other without the possibility of further variants of the same line appearing on preceding or succeeding lines of text.

A. The computer can collate many of your manuscripts together
B. This computer is able to collate your manuscripts together
C. The ICL computer can collate many of our manuscripts at once.

In *La Critique des Textes et son Automatisation*, Froger includes some specifications for a collation system, although he has apparently tested his theories only on a very small amount of data. His system assigns a number to each word and to each space between words as the text is read in. One text is specified as a base against which all others are to be compared. The computer then starts at the beginning of the texts comparing corresponding words from each. When it finds a mismatch it compares a larger block of words until the texts match again. The variants are saved and the text realigned where the match was found. Froger's method of printing the variants is difficult to follow, although it corresponds in appearance to the traditional apparatus criticus. The variant is accompanied by an identification of the manuscript where it was found and a code indicating it to be deletion, addition or substitution. The place where the variant was found is indicated by the numbers assigned to each word or space as the text was read in. For our lines, Froger's program would produce:

A. The computer can collate many of your manuscripts together
B. This computer is able to collate your manuscripts together
C. The ICL computer can collate many of our manuscripts at once
2,S,this,B; 3,A,ICL,C; 6,S,is able to,B; 10,D,many of, B; 14,S,our,C; 18,S,at once,C

Here the first group indicates that position two — that is, the first word (allowing for a space before it to be numbered one) — has a substitution coded by S, the text of which is *this*, and which occurs in manuscript B. The A in the second group indicates that there is an addition, namely *ICL* in position 3 in manuscript C and so on. The chief drawback with this method, of course, is the numbering system. Even with our short example, it is not easy to see where *at once* is substituted. Finding, say, word 352 with no other identification would be impractical. However, the output does approximate to the traditional apparatus criticus. It would be vastly improved if variants were referenced by line number, or if the words in the base text of which they are variants were also given.

Dearing's collation program claims to be able to handle up to fifty manuscripts at one time. They are fed into the machine in blocks or sections, the size of each section being specified by the user. At the input stage the user must know that a block from one manuscript corresponds to the same block from another and that this correspondence applies also to each line within each block. The program then compares manuscripts line by line. It compares words at the beginning of each line of text and continues until a variant is found. It then compares words at the end of the line and works backwards. All words between two points at which the texts do not match are marked as variants. The base text is compared in this manner with each of the comparison texts. If the line is missing in one manuscript, the comparison text is searched ten lines backwards and forwards until a matching line is found. An indication is then made that the line numbers do not correspond. If no match is found, an interpolation or omission is marked. The printout contains the complete line from the base text, together with the identifiers of the manuscripts which agree with the base text. Where there is not a perfect match, the variant portion together with the identifiers or other manuscripts having this variant is printed. After all the variants have been printed, the identifiers of the manuscripts which omit the line are given. If an interpolated line is found in a comparison text, the first such text where it is found is treated as the base text and the procedure repeated. Using his system our texts would give:

A1. The computer can collate many of your manuscripts together
B1. This computer is able to collate
C1.   ICL computer can collate many of our manuscripts at once

As is rapidly apparent, many words are classified as variants which should not be so, simply because of jumping to the right of the line and working backwards from there when a variant is found. Small variations at each end of the line would generate many unnecessary variant words. This printout contrasts with Froger's, which gives many more shorter variants for the same text.

Another program by Silva and Bellamy arrives at results very similar to Dearing's, but by a method which consumes more computer time. Their system is again designed for poetry and therefore expects roughly the same words in the same line in each manuscript, thus creating a false impression of simplicity. It only operates on two texts at a time. There are two stages in their process. The first attempts to establish the alignment of the texts by comparing every fifth line from the two texts. If they do not match, the program then attempts a line-by-line search backwards and forwards for up to twenty lines in both manuscripts. When the texts are realigned, the occurrence of an interpolation or deletion is recorded. One line is assumed to be a variant of the other, if no match is found in this twenty-line search. Once the texts have been realigned in this way, a letter-by-letter search left to right and then right to left, following Dearing's method, is carried out on each line. All characters between two mismatches are considered to be variants. The printout consists of the complete line from the base text, followed by the line from the comparison text indicating where the texts do not match.

(A compared with B)
A1. The computer can collate many of your manuscripts together
B1. **is computer is able to collate *****************************

(A compared with C)

A1. The computer can collate many of your manuscripts together

C1. **** ICL computer can collate many of your manuscripts at once

Like Dearing, Silva and Bellamy's method creates apparently lengthy variants when there are two simple variants at the beginning and end of a line.

Widmann's collation of *A Midsummer Night's Dream* adopts a very different approach. The computer is not used to search back and forth for variants, but rather to print out all the editions in a format which aids eye collation. Professor Widmann is the editor of the New Variorum Edition of this play and was therefore faced with the task of collating between 80 and 100 editions. Her method is much simpler, but it clearly requires more human endeavour. It relies very heavily on the correct alignment of the editions, line by line, before any collation is attempted. Each line of text is prepared on a separate computer card, the first four columns of which are reserved for through-line numbering. The text begins in column eight, and if it is too long for one card it is then continued on to the next card. If one edition has such a long line, this is matched by a blank card in all the other editions. Therefore a line which appears as two lines in one manuscript is allocated two cards in every edition. This allows the computer to assume that the texts will always match line for line.

A sample of Widmann's output is shown in Figure 7.1. The line is given in full from the copy text q1, together with its through-line number. Only the variants are listed after this. Manuscripts which agree completely with the copy text are indicated by their identifier only. Widmann's text is coded for upper and lower case letters and differences between these are considered variants, as are differences in punctuation. The symbols >w indicate a difference in line length. The example shows one line which is in effect two lines in many editions. This is indicated by the many occurrences of >w.

For our lines, Widmann would give:

1. The computer can collate many of your manuscripts together

B   This   is able to   >w

C   ICL   our   at once >w

It is not clear from her description how an omission in one of the comparison texts is marked on the printout. The >w shows that the line length is different, but it would be convenient to know where. In other respects, Widmann's method appears to suit her needs and presents a clear readable printout. It requires more clerical effort, as the initial alignment is

2179	And this dittie after mee, Sing; and daunce it trippingly.			
q2		Ditty	me, Sing	dance
f1		Ditty	me, sing	dance	trippinglie.
f2		Ditty	me, sing	dance	trippinglye.
f3		Ditty	me, sing	dance
f4		Ditty	me, sing	dance	trippingly.>w
r1		Ditty	me, Sing	Dance
r2		Ditty	me, Sing	Dance
r3		Ditty	me>w
p1		ditty	me>w
p2		ditty	me>w
t1		ditty	me>w
t2		ditty	me>w
h1		ditty	me>w
wa	Sing, and dance it trippingly.>w			
j1		ditty	me>w
ca		ditty,	me,>w
h3		ditty,	me,>w
ma		ditty,	me,>w

2179	+1
q2	
f1	
f2	
f3	
f4	
r1	
r2	
r3	Sing, and Dance it trippingly.
p1	Sing, and dance it trippingly.
p2	Sing, and dance it trippingly.
t1	Sing, and dance it trippingly.
t2	Sing, and dance it trippingly.
h1	Sing, and dance it trippingly.
wa	
j1	Sing, and dance it trippingly.
ca	Sing, and dance it trippingly.
h3	Sing, and dance it trippingly.
ma	Sing, and dance it trippingly.

Figure 7.1. A computer collation of *A Midsummer Night's Dream*. (Widmann)

done by hand, but given that drawback it produces the most useful output we have seen so far in collating verse.

Four algorithms have been published for collating prose, although only three of them have been applied to a substantial quantity of real text. The earliest published prose program, named OCCULT, is described by George Petty and William Gibson. OCCULT is an acronym for the Ordered Computer Collation of Unprepared Literary Text. Petty and Gibson were initially interested in comparing two texts of Henry James' short novel *Daisy Miller*. The same program was later applied to Melville's *Bartleby the Scrivener*. In their method the computer compares texts in blocks of twelve words to determine whether they are similar. They consider two sets of twelve words to be matched if the sum of the number of words in the longest continuous matching sequence, plus the total number of matching sequences of two or more words, is six or more. To examine our texts by this method we need to add another sentence to bring the number of words up to twelve.

A. The computer can collate many of your manuscripts together. It works well.
B. This computer is able to collate your manuscripts together. It can work.
C. The ICL computer can collate many of our manuscripts at once. Really?

Comparisons are performed only on two texts at a time. On taking A and B we obtain the following score:

matching sequences: your manuscripts together. It

Therefore, for one matching sequence of four words, the score is five. OCCULT would say that these two lines are not variants of each other. A and C produce the following results:

matching sequences: computer can collate many of

For one matching sequence of five words the score is six. According to OCCULT criteria these lines are just variants of each other. Because of the smaller variants inserted more frequently in either A or B, these two lines appear to OCCULT to be more dissimilar than A and C. Petty and Gibson have found that about 90% of matching sequences can be established by this rule. Our one simple example implies that this may be an overestimate.

OCCULT works only on additions and deletions. A substitution is considered an addition in one text and a deletion in the other, which could be a drawback in some work. The shorter text is always taken as the base text and the longer one as the comparison text, which is again not necessarily the best methodology from the editor's point of view. If the twelve words do not match, up to three hundred words are searched forwards and backwards from the point of mismatch until matching blocks of twelve words are again found. All the intervening words are considered variants. This could well lead to a large number of spurious variants if a mismatch is found on a comparison like that between our manuscripts A and B. OCCULT's chief disadvantage is said to be the time it takes to perform all the comparisons. It was written in SNOBOL and tested before there were efficient SNOBOL compilers. The time disadvantage may be less important now, but its methods of finding a mismatch are somewhat suspect.

OCCULT produces printout in two columns. The left-hand column gives those words in the base text which have variants in the comparison text and the right-hand one gives the actual variants. One word preceding the variant is printed in both cases. The references indicate page number and line number within each text. Assuming that OCCULT was collating our original three lines and they had been found to be variants of each other, we would obtain

(A and B)	
1.1 The	1.1 This
1.1 computer can	1.1 computer is able to
1.1 collate many of	1.1 collate

(A and C)	
1.1 The	1.1 The ICL
1.1 of your	1.1 of our
1.1 manuscripts together	1.1 manuscripts at once

The printout is quite well presented. There is sufficient indication of what the variants are and where they occur, but it could perhaps be improved by saving the variants from several collation runs and printing them side by side. But, however the variants are printed, they are only useful if the methods of finding them are satisfactory.

Another algorithm for collating prose was published by Margaret Cabaniss. Her program allows the user to specify various features such as the number of words which constitute a match – that is, a return to alignment of the texts once a variant has been found. The user can also specify how many words the program is to compare, in order to find its place again after a variant. The ability to change these options adds more flexibility to the program, which also includes what is called a 'coarse scan', for finding the alignment. This would normally cause every tenth word in the master text to be compared with every word in the comparison text. Here again the user can specify how many words are to be skipped in this coarse scan. Cabaniss was the first to provide a method of dealing with function words: the user can supply a list of words which are to be ignored when looking for variants.

The chief defect of this program is again the format of the printout. It is not lined up satisfactorily as Figure 7.2 shows. Two lines which are variants of each other are not printed side by side. Collation by eye is then required to find the variants. It should not have been too difficult to modify the program so that lines which are variants of each other are printed side by side. This system again only allows two texts to be collated at once. Our example would appear as follows:

(A and B)
1. The computer can collate many   1. The computer (is able to) collate
   of your manuscripts together   ( ) your manuscripts together

(A and C)
1. The computer can collate many   1. The (ICL) computer can
   of your manuscripts together   1. many of (our) manuscripts (at
                                            once)

Cabaniss' method allows the user flexibility in determining the number of comparisons to be made, but her program is marred by poor presentation of output. The variants are too lengthy and must be collated by eye. Printing out the variants side by side is reasonable when there are only two texts to be collated. Cabaniss's program was designed to collate twenty-four texts. If each of twenty-three comparison texts is to be compared with one base text, the printouts themselves would occupy too much room side by side to be useful.

None of the programs we have considered so far are all-purpose programs and they do not entirely satisfy the needs of the textual editor. In contrast much more thought was put into the most recent program to produce results from actual text, which was devised in Manitoba by Penny Gilbert and is called COLLATE. It is part of a series of computer programs which were written to aid the production of a critical edition of Buridanus' *Quaestiones Supra Libros Metaphysicae*, of which seven manuscripts exist. The collation process is divided into a number of simple stages, at each of which manual intervention is possible. The first ten columns of the

```
      /BN16993 BIBLIOTHEQUE NATIONALE, FRANC. 16993 BOOK XV/
  0   (SENSUIT LE .XV.E LIVRE DES PROPRIETEZ DES CHOSES QUI FAIT        A15000199
 20   MENCION DES PROVINCES ET DES PARTIES DE LA TERRE , )A LAIDE       A15000199
                                                                       A15000199
 40   DIEU IL (FAULT )DIRE AUCUNE                                       A15000199
                                                                       A15000199
                                                                       A15000199
 80   MONDE EST (DIVISE )EN GENERAL                                     A15000199
                                                                       A15000199
                                                                       A15001199
                                                                       A15001199
110   TOUTES MAIS (DE (CELLES SEULEMENT DONT LA SAINCTE ESCRIPTURE      A15001199
120   FAIT MENCION , )SELON YSIDORE                                     A15001199
160   MONDE EST (DIVISE )EN TROIS                                       A15001199
180   EST APPELLEE (ASSIE )LAUTRE EUROPE                               A15001199
190   LAUTRE AFFRIQUE (, )ET CES                                       A15001199
200   NE FURENT (POINT DIVISEES EGALMENT )PAR LES                      A15001199
210   ANCIENS CAR (ASSIE )VIENT DE                                     A15001199
220   EN OCCIDENT ()A SEPTENTRION                                      A15001199
230   EST DE (SEPTENTRION IUSQUES EN OCCIDENT )ET AFFRIQUE             A15001199
```

```
  0   /BN16993 BIBLIOTHEQUE NATIONALE, FRANC. 16993 BOOK XV/
 10   A LAIDE DE DIEU IL FAUT DIRE AUCUNE
 20   CHOSE DES PARTIES DE LA TERRE ET DES
 30   PROVINCES PAR LESQUELLES LE
 40   MONDE EST DIVISIE EN GENERAL
 50   ET NE DIRONS PAS DE TOUTES MAIS SEULEMENT
 60   DE CELLES DONT LA SAINTE ESCRIPTURE FAIT SOU-
 70   VENTES FOIZ MENCION.
 80   /LE PREMIER CHAPITRE DE LA DIVISION DU MONDE/
 90   SELON YSIDORE OU .XX.E LIVRE DES E-
100   THIMOLOGIES LE MONDE EST DIVISIE
110   EN TROIS PARTIES DONT LUNE EST APPELLEE
120   ASSIE ET LAUTRE EUROPE ET LAUTRE AFFRIQUE
130   ET CES TROIS PARTIES NE FURENT PAS DIVISEES
140   EGAULMENT PAR LES ANCIENS CAR ASSIE VIENT
150   DE MIDI PAR ORIENT IUSQUES EN OCCIDENT ET
160   A SEPTEMTRION EUROPE EST DE SEPTEMTRION
170   IUSQUES EN ORIENT ET AFFRIQUE EST DOCCIDENT
180   IUSQUES A MIDI ASSIE TOUTE SEULE DE
```

Figure 7.2. Printout from Cabaniss' collation program. Note that two lines which are variants of each other (e.g. 140 and 210) are not printed side by side.

input cards were used for a reference for the line of text. The first stage of the program recreates the base text in a computer file and makes a second computer file of all the words in the text, each accompanied by its reference. The second stage performs the comparison itself. When a mismatch occurs, the computer takes the next two words in the base text and compares them to successive pairs of words in the comparison text, up to ten pairs. If this test fails, it compares the next but one, and next but two words after the mismatch from the base text to the comparison text in exactly the same manner. Then groups of four words for up to 50 words in the base text are tested against 100 words in the comparison text. The next level of search works on groups of nine words and searches 100 words in the base text and 200 in the comparison text. Finally the program adopts a different approach and searches for paragraph markers, comparing the first four words of the next ten paragraphs in an attempt to realign the texts at the beginning of a paragraph. The actual levels of search and the numbers of words to be considered in each case were chosen by Gilbert to suit the material she was collating. The program stops if it is completely unsuccessful, and the human may then realign the texts for it; but Gilbert did include a facility for control cards to be inserted to instruct the machine to ignore badly mutilated sections. As the variants are found, they are stored in another computer file. (It is surprising that none of the other collators mention the machine's obvious ability to store the variants once they are found.) As the base text is compared against more manuscripts, the variants found can be merged into a file of variants found in previous comparisons.

Gilbert's first printout attempts to simulate a traditional text with apparatus criticus. The base text is printed out in full with identification numbers pointing to the input text. Underneath there is a list of variants each accompanied by its identification number and the manuscript in which it appears. The identification numbers seem to consist of the line number followed by the position of the word in the line, although they are not described and are not easy to follow. Assuming this is so, for our lines we would obtain:

(A and B)		
The computer can collate many of your manuscripts together		10000
The	A	10010
This	B	10010
can	A	10030
is able to	B	10030
many of your	A	10050
your	B	10070

(A and C)

The computer can collate many of your manuscripts together		10000
computer	A	10020
ICL computer	C	10020
your	A	10070
our	C	10080
together	A	10090
at once	C	10011

Gilbert's system was devised after some considerable examination of the previous attempts. She appears to be unique in attempting to integrate the various stages of text editing. As we have seen, variant readings from all manuscripts can be printed underneath the text. A further stage allows variants which the editor considers insignificant to be removed. No exclusion list like that of Cabaniss is provided, because it was felt that words to be discarded were the decision of the scholar; but it would not be difficult to add this facility. The file of variants can be altered by using an editing program on the terminal, which we have seen is a very simple process. Where the same variant occurs more than once only the first example is stored together with the reference identifiers for the other examples. A final stage allows the text and variants to be printed in the traditional form.

Another collation algorithm is described by Cannon, although he does not show any examples of his algorithm working on text. He is a computer scientist concerned with efficiency of programs and has pointed out that most collation systems are slow, simply because of the number of comparisons they have to make when a mismatch occurs. He claims that the Petty/Gibson and Gilbert methods in particular perform many repeated comparisons. His method uses a table stored inside the machine to record whether a match has been found when two words are compared. He can then access this table very quickly when he needs to compare those two words again rather than do a lengthier character comparison. His algorithm does not appear to have been programmed and he does not deal with the problem of what to do when a total mismatch occurs. In fact his approach is that of the programmer whose interests may conflict with the problem which has to be solved. The text editor should always be consulted to ensure that the finished product is useful.

Computer collation is, then, much easier for verse text, although the efforts to produce suitable programs for certain prose texts have been quite successful. It is arguable whether the results can justify the work involved, especially as it is necessary to prepare all the texts in computer readable form, no mean task if there are more than a few texts involved. Widmann's Shakespeare collation was performed on a small text of something over

2000 lines, but on 100 editions and therefore 200,000 lines of input. Gilbert's seven texts filled some 80,000 cards. The human errors which inevitably creep into such large undertakings of data preparation will no doubt be discovered by the collation process, but these must all be removed before conclusions can be drawn from the results. Collating two or three editions of a short text would be suitable for a computer, particularly if there were no large variants. It is arguable whether it is worth it for much larger amounts of text. The Gilbert method was successful, but it was a relatively large undertaking. The most suitable course seems to be to follow Gilbert and to make the collation only a part of a larger computer system for preparing a critical edition.

The methods which have so far been described are not suitable for comparing texts which are markedly different. Oral texts such as folk plays have been handed down from one generation to another and can exist in many quite different versions before they are finally written down. Many scholars have shied away from the complex textual problems associated with orally transmitted material, but M.J. Preston has proposed a different method of comparing such texts in order to quantify the differences between them. He divides a text into overlapping units. Each begins at a word and continues for fifteen characters, either letters or spaces. These blocks of text are compared with similar blocks from another text and are said to have made a match when thirteen of the fifteen characters match and the first word matches or is an inflectional variant, although he does not describe how an inflectional variant is recognised. In fact several aspects of this method are not entirely clear, but he appears to have found a method which is suitable for his own material. The method could be explored further in a number of ways. It may be possible to find out how many or how few matches may be required for it to fail completely by varying the number of letters which are to be matched in each group.

The second stage of the task of preparing a critical edition, assuming that all the variants are known, is to try to deduce the relationship between the manuscripts. An attempt can be made to find the manuscripts which are more closely related to each other and those which may perhaps be considered to hold the original reading when a variant occurs. Even when there are not many manuscripts, this can involve many comparisons. When the number of manuscripts and variants becomes large, these can be handled much more easily by a computer.

Traditionally manuscript relationships have been represented as a kind of family tree, with the oldest texts at the head and those which are thought to be derived from them shown as later generations. Reconstructing such trees can be attempted by computer even when some of the manuscripts have been lost. It is frequently possible to construct several trees from the same set of variants. Only the scholar can decide which is more appropriate on the basis of his philological knowledge.

Let us suppose that we have five manuscripts now called A, B, C, D and E which read

A Jack went up the hill
B Jack climbed up the hill
C Jack went up this hill
D Jack went down this mountain
E Jill went up this mountain

We can consider what would be the relationship between these manuscripts. The variants can be represented in a tabular form.

		A	B	C	D	E	
1	Jack Jill	1	1	1	1	2	ABCD:E
2	went climbed	1	2	1	1	1	ACDE:B
3	up down	1	1	1	2	1	ABCE:D
4	the this	1	1	2	2	2	AB:CDE
5	hill mountain	1	1	1	2	2	ABC:DE

From this table we see that for variant number one *Jack* and *Jill* ABCD have reading number one, that is *Jack* and E has reading number two, that is *Jill*. In the right hand column we see how the manuscripts are grouped for each reading. Following Froger's method, based on the mathematical theory of sets, we can select one manuscript, let us say A, as an arbitrarily chosen base. The manuscripts can then be grouped in subsets of the set of all manuscripts as follows:

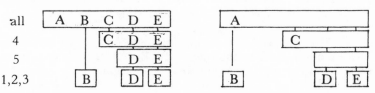

From the second drawing a stemma can be reconstructed as follows:

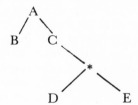

leaving the * to denote a missing manuscript which might have read

Jack went up this mountain

A computer program can construct such a diagram by examining all the variants. The computer will also provide all other possible stemmata taking each manuscript in turn as the arbitrary base. The scholar with his knowledge of the manuscripts can then select the stemma which seems most appropriate.

Poole states quite rightly that Froger's method depends on the existence of many readings which have only two variants, and that it will only produce a satisfactory stemma if there are no coincident variations, which Poole calls anomalies. If these occur, a set of manuscripts may be included in more than one higher set, thus destroying the stemmatic relationship. He demonstrates that when pairs of variants can be arranged in an endless linked sequence there is no possible stemma into which they can all fit. One of the readings at least must be anomalous. Accordingly he has devised a computer program which can detect the presence of an anomaly in the data. He can make some assumptions about which readings are anomalous and use this procedure to eliminate them, leaving the material for constructing a stemma. His program was tested on 54 lines of Piers Plowman, of which seventeen manuscripts exist. These 54 lines present profound textual problems because there are 400 readings with variants recorded. This trial showed that objective results could be obtained even from a very small sample of text showing such complicated variations; but the entire program depends on the assumptions made at the beginning, and these may not necessarily be true. Poole concludes that though the computer can only rarely produce a definitive stemma, it can be used with considerable success to provide reliable materials for the reconstruction of a stemma.

Dearing also has a set of programs which attempt to reconstruct manuscript stemmata. The first called PRELIMDI merely provides basic genealogical connections between texts. These relationships are established without consideration of which manuscript may be at the top of the tree. Two further programs, called ARCHETYP and MSFAMTRE, accept the data provided by PRELIMDI or similar input. ARCHETYP locates the position of the archetype on the basis of fully directional variations among the texts or states of the text. It gives the information necessary for drawing up a family tree. The second program, MSFAMTRE, constructs textual family trees on a theory of probability as to the general mechanics of growth. The user can specify the particular conditions for growth, such as the probable number of manuscripts copied before any were lost sight of or destroyed, rates of copying as compared to rates of loss, and the number of extant manuscripts. It is assumed that the user can reflect his knowledge of historical conditions in these instructions. The program supplies all possible family trees for the extant manuscripts, leaving the scholar to decide which is the most probable or valid.

Another approach to the reconstruction of manuscript trees was adopted by Zarri following the theories expounded by Dom Quentin in the 1920s. Zarri has constructed a number of computer algorithms to simulate and test Quentin's work. Quentin's theory of 'characteristic zeros' is adopted as follows. A set of three manuscripts A, B and C can be said to be related in a linear fashion.

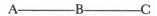

A———————B———————C

only when A and C never agree with each other against B. B is therefore intermediate between the two manuscripts. Only 'significant' variants are used, and Zarri has adopted an interactive computer program so that he can decide which variants are to be significant when the program is actually running. Three manuscripts only provide the simplest case. When four are used, they can be divided into four sets of three manuscripts.

In the case of four manuscripts A, B, C and D, we can suppose that the following triplets are characterised by zeros.

$$
\begin{array}{ccc}
C & A & B \\
 & A & B & D \\
C & & B & D
\end{array}
$$

and that ACD has no zero. This produces a linear chain CABD where the origin can be either C or D. Zarri's algorithm then goes on to examine all possible subsets of size five, split into groups each of four manuscripts using the results obtained from the previous stage to continue the linearity. It continues with larger and larger groups until either the size of the group is equal to the total number of manuscripts or until the linear construction fails.

It is apparent that this algorithm can only consider linear relationships and must discard all others which cannot create a chain. In a simple example such as if the ABD group above produces B–A–D, the chain is lost. If this relationship is discarded, it leads to a loss of information. The algorithm was therefore modified to allow non-linear structures. The analysis is now more complicated, and there are several possible groupings which may or may not allow for missing manuscripts. Zarri experimented with his algorithm on a set of real manuscripts and found that it only gave unambiguous results when the number of 'linear' and 'non-linear' elements did not exceed twenty. He does not regard the ambiguous results for higher numbers as discouraging. Further work has led him to be able to reconstruct graphs of the type

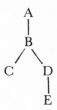

but he claims always that the scholar must use his own knowledge to decide which of these manuscripts is most likely to be the oldest. Zarri's computer model is said to have provided some appreciable results, initially on the manuscripts of the Chanson de Roland. It is not perfect, but it can provide the scholar with all possible interpretations and thus supersede purely manual reconstructions. When given all the significant variants, the computer can easily derive all the characteristic zeros and generate all possible reconstructions from these, but this method depends entirely on the acceptance of the validity of Quentin's arguments.

The reconstruction of family trees for manuscripts, or at least the attempt to find all relationships between them, lends itself to computing. The solution is rarely unambiguous; but any other solution, whether using computers or not, is unlikely to be conclusive. The advantage of using the computer is that it can be programmed to generate all possibilities. It is then for the scholar himself to consider the importance of the variants. It may be possible to develop further a system like Zarri's to allow for weighting of the important variants. The same manuscripts can also be analysed repeatedly, each time using a different subset of the variants. This is an area where more research would be useful. Zarri's method employs some mathematical methods of graph theory and matrix analysis, and anyone trying his methods would be well advised to consult a professional mathematician.

A very different method has been adopted by Griffith in studying the manuscript tradition of a number of classical texts. Griffith believes that the family tree methods are not appropriate to the study of the relationships between manuscripts. He points out that different scholars have produced totally different trees from the same variants, a view supported by the computer programs already described. The family tree method implies that the manuscripts are in a fixed set of relationships to each other. Griffith considers that the relationships between manuscripts should be considered as a whole rather than as a complicated series of linear structures.

Following methods well established in the biological sciences, he used cluster analysis to study and classify his manuscripts. This technique has already been described in Chapter Four with regard to variant words in dialectology and mentioned in Chapter Six in connection with stylistic analysis. It can be applied equally to manuscript variants. His first analyses were made manually by the method known as seriation. Under this technique the manuscripts were placed along a notional spectrum line such that those which were most like each other were placed together at one end of the line and as far as possible from those to which they bore least resemblance, which were at the other end of the line. Griffith soon discovered that a computer can compile a similarity matrix much more easily than a human. He now uses a simple program, to which is fed a list of variants, accompanied by the identifiers of the manuscripts which have those readings. The seriation method improves on the family-tree method in allowing more readings to be considered. The program has therefore been extended so that it can work in a multi-dimensional fashion, the number of dimensions being one less than the number of manuscripts. The values in the similarity matrix are transformed mathematically, and from these results only the first three dimensions are taken, as the others have become insignificantly small numbers. The computer's graph plotter is used to provide a visual representation of their spatial relations as a three-dimensional drawing. This method of visual presentation is preferred to the dendrogram, so that the distance between each pair of manuscripts can be measured more easily. Griffith claims rightly enough that such a cluster analysis only produces a classification of the documents, but this classification makes allowance for all the variants, whereas with the mechanism for constructing family trees many variants may be discarded.

Griffith can operate his program on up to 100 variants at once from about 25 manuscripts. This could and should be expanded to use many more variants to give a clearer overall picture. He has found that the clustering appears to be constant over long stretches of the same work when he has analysed it in sections. It is of course possible to weight the variants, but he has avoided this because it introduces some subjectivity. A simple experiment of weighting some variants in Juvenal by duplicating them yielded results which were only slightly different from the non-weighted ones. Griffith uses his own programs, but standard programs which perform cluster analysis can be used on manuscript data if desired. If some of the more intractable problems of textual relations are to be analysed thoroughly, mathematical methods like these are clearly useful in modern textual criticism.

We can conclude this review of computer techniques in textual criticism with an example which is characterised by the vast number of variants, so many that they can only be organised at all by computer methods. A new critical edition of the New Testament is based on some 5000 manuscripts, and there are in addition many other witnesses to the readings, such as quotations. In the compilation of this edition, Ott does not plan to use the computer to find the variants initially but only to store them all, and then to compile the apparatus criticus (which he expects to be approximately one page for each line of text). It would clearly be impossible to include all 5000 manuscripts in the apparatus criticus. All major ones will be represented and a selection of the minor ones included. The selection was made on the basis of the relationships between manuscripts and one thousand passages were selected on which these relationships could be established.

The computer is used for storing and sorting the variants according to a number of different criteria. For each variant one card was punched containing an identification number, followed by the text of the reading and the Gregory numbers of the manuscripts which have this reading. Ott's examples show 243 manuscripts at 30 selected passages in the epistles of St Peter. He is able to print out the variants in several different tabular formats.

The first printout gives the complete passage where the variant occurs, and under it is listed the first variant with the total number of manuscripts which have that variant and all their identifiers. Each variant is treated likewise in turn, so that the editor can see at a glance which is most frequent. The manuscripts which have a complete lacuna at this passage are also noted.

The next printout is a table of passages against manuscripts. Within the table each element holds the number of the variant which occurs at that passage and manuscript. A similar table shows the size of the group of manuscripts which have the same reading for the specified passage, as shown in Figure 7.3. A table like this immediately isolates the occurrence of single witnesses, and from it the reading supported by the majority of manuscripts can easily be found. A similarity matrix is then computed for the manuscripts from which a cluster analysis could be performed. The whole matrix for 30 passages in 243 manuscripts must be fairly large. Ott says that it occupied 23 pages of printout. Absolute values found in the similarity matrix must be converted to percentages for clustering, and of course they cannot make any allowances for the manuscripts which have lacunae. Ott has preferred to calculate the degrees of relationship between each manuscript and all the others rather than attempt to cluster them all together, but there are many other ways in which the relationships between these manuscripts can be expressed. The computer is being used merely as a tool for handling large amounts of data. It is enabling the compilation of the most comprehensive critical edition yet to be made. Handling such large quantities of variants would be almost impossible manually, and inaccuracies would inevitably appear. The computer can provide its classification on the basis of existing readings, thus providing the scholar with a better foundation for his judgment.

There is therefore considerable scope for using the computer in the preparation of a critical edition of a text. We have considered computer collation in some detail and found that it suffers from the major disadvantage of the need to prepare all versions of the text in computer-readable form, but it may still be worthwhile in the long run. A more straightforward application for the computer is the analysis of the relationship between manuscripts. It is preferable to input to the machine one base text together with all known variants. Providing an initial base text allows the editor to produce a concordance which may be very helpful in selecting which variants to insert, by showing their occurrences elsewhere in the text. The computer is being used to simulate those operations which have previously been performed manually. Besides speed and accuracy, its advantage is that it can handle a much larger number of variants and manuscripts. The development of a Zarri- or Griffith-type model requires some knowledge of mathematics, but procedures such as those adopted by Ott are much simpler and can provide results which are equally useful.

Once the editor of the text has selected his readings the computer can be used to create the final version of the text. If one complete version of the text is already in the machine, an editing program on a terminal or a special-purpose program can be used to produce the required text. In either case the computer can display the line with each possible variant reading, and the editor can then choose one or insert his own emendation. A computer program called CURSOR was initially developed at the University of Waterloo to perform such a task. The important variants from the file of variants can be retained for the apparatus criticus, together with the identifiers of the manuscripts which have each reading. Using the computer as an interactive text editor, the scholar can establish the final version of his text and then use a photocomposing machine to typeset his edition. There will then be no more need for proof-reading as the final version will already be accurate for printing.

		26	27	28	29	30	31	32	33	34	35	36	37	38
TESTST.														
VORH. ZEUGEN:		217	217	217	217	218	218	218	219	216	215	217	211	213
GRGNR														
1:	P72	41	213	31	1	28	200	105	45	34	13	52	110	188
2:	01	41	213	31	213	2	4	105	45	40	20	75	1	4
3:	01C	41	1	31	213	2	200	105	45	40	155	52	2	188
4:	02	41	3	31	213	10	4	105	45	40	155	52	96	188
5:	03	41	3	31	213	28	4	105	45	34	13	52	110	4
6:	04	41	213	31	213	28	200	105	45	40	13	90		
7:	04C2	41	213	31	213	28	200	105	45	40	13	90		
8:	018	175	213	170	213	111	200	100	45	40	155	90	110	188
9:	020	175	213	170	213	111	200	11	169	120	155	90	110	188
10:	025	175	213	170	213	111	200	100	169	40	155	90	96	188
11:	044	41	213	31	5	10	200	105	45	34	13	52	110	188
12:	049	175	213	170	213	111	200	100	169	40	6	90	110	188
13:	049C	175	213	170	213	111	200	100	169	40	1	90	110	188
14:	050	175	213	170	213	111	200	105	169	120	155	90	96	188
15:	0412	175	213	170	213	111	200	105	169	120	155	90	96	188
16:	4	175	213	11	213	50	200	105	169	210	155	75	110	188
17:	5	175	213	11	213	10	200	105	169	40	155	90	96	188
18:	6	175	213	170	213	50	200	100	169	120	155	90	110	188
19:	33	41	213	31	213	111	200	105	45	40			96	188
20:	36	175	213	170	213	50	3	100	169	120	155	90	96	188
21:	38	175	213	170	213	10	200	100	169	120	155	75	110	188
22:	43C	175	213	170	213	111	200	100	169	40	6	75	100	188
23:	61	175	213	170	213	111	200	105	3	3	20	75	110	188
24:	61C	175	213	170	213	111	200	105	3	3	20	90	110	188
25:	61MG	175	213	170	213	111	200	105	169	3	20	90	110	188
26:	62	41	213	170	213	111	200	100	45	120	1	52	110	188
27:	69	175	213	170	213	10	200	100	169	120	20	75	110	188
28:	31	41	213	31	213	28	4	105	45	40	155	52	96	188
29:	88	175	213	170	213	111	200	100	169	120	155	75	96	188
30:	88C	175	213	170	213	111	200	100	169	120	155	75	96	188
31:	93	175	213	170	213	111	200	100	169	40	155	75	110	188
32:	94	175	213	170	213	50	3	100	169	120	155	90	1	188
33:	102	175	213	170	213	50	200	100	169	120	155	75	96	188
34:	103	175	213	170	213	111	200	105	169	120	155	75	96	1
35:	104	175	213	5	213	111	200	105	169	120	155	75	96	188
36:	131	175	213	170	213	111	200	100	169	40	6	90	110	188
37:	133	175	213	170	213	50	200	100	169	120	155	90	110	188
38:	142	175	213	170	213	28	200	105	169	120	20	75	110	188
39:	180	175	213	170	213	50	3	100	169	120	155	90	96	188
40:	181	175	213	11	213	111	200	1	169	120	155	90	110	188
41:	189	175	213	170	213	50	200	100	169	120	155	90	96	188
42:	206	175	213	170	213	111	200	105	169	34	155	75	96	19
43:	218	41	213	170	213	50	200	105	169	40	155	52	110	188
44:	254	175	213	170	213	111	200	105	169	120	155	75	96	188
45:	254C	175	213	170	213	111	200	105	169	120	155	75	96	188
46:	255	175	213	170	213	111	200	100	169	34	155	90	110	188
47:	296	175	213	170	213	50	200	105	169	120	155	90	110	188
48:	307	175	213	170	213	111	200	100	45	120	155	75	96	188
49:	307C	175	213	170	213	111	200	105	45	120	155	75	96	188
50:	309	175	213	170	213	111	200	100	169	40	155	90	110	188
51:	312	175	213	170	213	10	200	100	45	120	155	90	100	188
52:	321	175	213	170	213	111	200	100	169	120	155	75	110	188
53:	322	41	213	31	213	111	200	105	45	120	13	52	96	4
54:	323	41	213	31	213	111	200	105	45	120	13	52	96	4
55:	326	175	213	170	213	111	200	105	45	120	155	90	110	188
56:	326C	175	213	170	213	111	200	105	45	120	155	90	96	188
57:	326MG	175	213	170	213	111	200	105	169	120	155	90	96	188
58:	330	175	213	170	213	111	200	100	169	40	6	75	110	188
59:	363	175	213	170	213	10	200	105	169	40	155	75	110	188
60:	365	41	213	170	213	111	200	100	45	120	9	52	110	188

39	40	41	42	43	44	45	46	47	48	49	50	51	52	53	54	55
215	215	214	214	218	217	218	215	215	216	216	210	217	218	215	217	217
1	1	2	2	2	11	25	8	197	26	71	26	48	19	1	14	207
18	109	113	14	209	200	162	8	1	26	71	23	48	19	158	202	207
18	109	113	14	209	200	162	207	197	26	71	23	48	19	158	202	207
18	3	5	14	209	200	10	207	197	23	71	23	48	178		14	207
18	3	20	14	2	11	25	8	3	26	113	26	48	19	25	14	10
		36	14	209	11	5	207	197	23	71	26	170	2	3	14	207
		36	14	209	200	5	207	197	23	71	26	170	2	3	14	207
180	60	113	194	209	200	162	207	197		113	141	170	19	158	202	207
180	109	113	194	209	200	162	207	197	142	7	141	170	178	158	202	207
180	109	36	14	2	200	25	8	197	3	71	26	48	19	3	202	207
1	3	2	2	209	200	162	8	197	26	71	23	48		158	14	207
180	60	113	194	209	200	162	207	197	142	113	141	170	178	158	202	207
130	60	113	194	209	200	162	207	197	142	113	141	170	178	158	202	207
180	60	113	194	209	200	162	207	197	142	71	141	170	178	10	202	207
180	60	113	194	1	200	162	207	197	142	71	141	170	178	10	202	207
180	109	113	194	209	200	162	207	197	142	18	141	170	178	158	202	207
180	37	36	194	209	200	162	207	197	26	71	23	170	13	10	14	207
180	60	2	194	209	200	162	207	197	142	4	141	170	178	158	202	207
18	37		209	11	162			1			23	48	178	158	13	207
180	109	36	194	209	200	162	207	197	26	113	26	170	178	158	202	207
180	60	113	194	209	200	162	207	197	142	4	141	170	178	158	1	207
130	60	113	194	209	200	162	207	1	142	113	141	170	178	158	202	207
180	109	113	194	200	200	162	207	197	142	113	141	170	178	158	202	207
180	109	113	194	209	200	162	207	197	142	113	141	170	178	158	202	207
180	109	113	194	209	200	162	207	197	142	113	141	170	178	158	202	207
180	60	113	194	209	200	162	207	197	142	113	141	170	178	158	202	207
130	37	36	194	209	200	162	207	197	3	113	141	170	178		202	207
18	37	36	194	209	200	2	207	197	3	71	23	170	13	2	202	207
3	109	5	194	209	200	162	207	197	2	113	141	48	178	158	202	207
3	109	5	194	209	200	162	207	3	2	113	141	48	178	158	202	207
180	60	113	194	209	200	162	207	197	142	113	141	170	178	158	202	207
180	109	113	194	209	200	10	207	197	26	18	26	170	178	158	202	207
180	60	113	194	209	200	162	207	197	142	113	141	170	178	158	202	207
180	109	113	194	209	200	162	207	197	142	71	141	170	178	10	202	207
180	109	36	194	209	200	162	207	197	3	18	23	48	178	158	202	207
180	60	3	194	209	200	3	207	197	142	113	141	170	178	158	202	207
180	60	113	194	209	200	3	207	197	142	113	141	170	178	158	202	207
180	109	113	194	209	200	162	207	197	142	113	141	170	178	158	202	207
180	60	113	194	209	200	162	207	197	142	4	141	170	178	258	202	207
180	109	113	194	209	200	162	207	197	23	113	141	48	178	158	202	207
180	60	113	194	209	200	162	207	197	142	113	141	170	178	158	202	207
180	37	20	194	209	200	25	207	197	142	71	13	170	178	3	202	207
180	109	36	194	209	200	162	207	197	142	71	141	170	178	158	202	207
180	109	20	194	209	200	3	207	197	3	71	10	170	178	25	202	207
180	109	20	194	209	200	3	207	197	5	71	10	170	178	25	202	207
180	109	113	194	209	106	162	207	197	1	113	1	170	178	158	202	207
180	109	113	194	209	200	3	207	197	142	18	23	48	178	158	202	207
180	109	36	194	209	200	162	207	197	26	113	26	170	178	158	202	207
130	109	36	194	209	200	162	207	197	26	113	26	170	178	158	202	207
130	60	113	194	209	200	162	207	9	142	4	141	170	178	158	202	207
180	60	113	194	209	200	162	207	197	142	71	141	170	178	158	202	207
130	109	113	194	209	200	162	207	9	23	113	26	170	178	158	202	207
18	37	4	14	209	200	25	207	197	23	71	26	48	19	25	202	207
18	37	4	14	209	200	25	207	197	26	71	26	170	19	25	202	207
130	100			209	200	162	207	197	142	113	141	170	178	158	202	207
180	100			209	200	162	207	197	142	113	23	170	178	158	202	207
180	100			209	200	162	207	197	142	113	23	170	178	158	202	207
180	60	113	194	209	200	162	207	197	142	18	141	170	178	158	202	207
180	100	113	104	209	200	1	207	197	142	113	141	170	178	158	202	207
180	60	113	194	209	200	162	207	197	142	113	141	170	178	158	202	207

Figure 7.3. A table showing the size of the group of manuscripts which have the same reading for the specified passage. E.g. 41 manuscripts have the same reading as P72 for passage number 26. (Ott)

REFERENCES

1. Margaret Scanlon Cabaniss, Using the Computer for Text Collation. *Computer Studies in the Humanities and Verbal Behavior* 3 (1970) 1-33

2. Robert L. Cannon, OPCOL: An Optimal Text Collation Algorithm. *Computers and the Humanities* 10 (1976) 33-40

3. L.A. Cummings, The Electronic Humanist: Computing at Waterloo in Canada. *ALLC Bull.* 3 (1975) 226-34 esp. 229-30

4. Vinton A. Dearing, Computer Aids to Editing the Text of Dryden. *Art and Error: Modern Textual Editing*, 254-78 (eds Ronald Gottesman and Scott Bennett). London: Methuen (1970)

5. Vinton A. Dearing, *Principles and Practice of Textual Analysis*. Berkeley: University of California Press (1974)

6. J. Froger, *La Critique des Textes et son Automatisation*. Paris: Dunod (1968)

7. Penny Gilbert, Automatic Collation: A Technique for Medieval Texts. *Computers and the Humanities* 7 (1973) 130-47

8. Penny Gilbert, Using the Computer to Collate Medieval Latin Manuscripts. *The Computer in Literary and Linguistic Studies (Proceedings of the Third International Symposium)*, 106-13 (eds Alan Jones and R.F. Churchhouse). Cardiff: University of Wales Press (1976)

9. J.G. Griffith, A Taxonomic Study of the Manuscript Tradition of Juvenal. *Museum Helveticum* 25 (1968) 101-38

10. John G. Griffith, Numerical Taxonomy and Some Primary Manuscripts of the Gospels. *Journal of Theological Studies* 20 (1969) 389-406

11. John G. Griffith, *An Application of Cluster Analysis to Classifying Manuscripts*. Paper read at Oxford Symposium (1976)

12. W. Ott, Computer Applications in Textual Criticism. *The Computer and Literary Studies*, 199-223 (eds A.J. Aitken, R.W. Bailey and N. Hamilton-Smith). Edinburgh: Edinburgh University Press (1973)

13. George R. Petty and William M. Gibson, *Project OCCULT: The Ordered Computer Collation of Unprepared Literary Text*. New York: New York University Press (1970)

14. Eric Poole, The Computer in Determining Stemmatic Relationships. *Computers and the Humanities* 8 (1974) 207-16

15. M.J. Preston, Solutions to Classic Problems in the Study of Oral Literature. *Computing in the Humanities,* 117-32 (eds Serge Lusignan and John S. North). Waterloo: University of Waterloo Press (1977)

16. Georgette Silva and Cliff Bellamy, *Some Procedures and Programs for Processing Language Data*, 41-5. Clayton, Australia: Monash University (1968)

17. R.L. Widmann, The Computer in Historical Collation: Use of the IBM 360/75 in Collating Multiple Editions of A Midsummer Night's Dream. *The Computer in Literary and Linguistic Research*, 57-63 (ed. R.A. Wisbey). Cambridge: Cambridge University Press (1971)

18. G.P. Zarri, Algorithms, Stemmata Codicum and the Theories of Dom H. Quentin. *The Computer and Literary Studies,* 225-37 (eds A.J. Aitken, R.W. Bailey and N. Hamilton-Smith). Edinburgh: Edinburgh University Press (1973)

19. Gian Piero Zarri, A Computer Model for Textual Criticism? *The Computer in Literary and Linguistic Studies (Proceedings of the Third International Symposium),* 133-55 (eds Alan Jones and R.F. Churchhouse). Cardiff: University of Wales Press (1976)

Further Reading

B. Fischer, The Use of Computers in New Testament Studies with Special Reference to Textual Criticism. *Journal of Theological Studies* 21 (1970) 297-308

John Haigh, The Manuscript Linkage Problem. *Mathematics in the Archaeological and Historical Sciences,* 396-400 (eds F.R. Hodson, D.G. Kendall and P. Tautu). Edinburgh: Edinburgh University Press (1971)

Jürgen Mau, Affiliation Programs, *Revue* No. 3 (1972) 63-76

Sorin Cristian Niţă, Establishing the Linkage of Different Variants of a Romanian Chronicle. *Mathematics in the Archaeological and Historical Sciences,* 400-9 (eds F.R. Hodson, D.G. Kendall and P. Tautu). Edinburgh: Edinburgh University Press (1971)

Robert L. Oakman, The Present State of Computerised Collation: A Review Article. *Proof* 2 (1972) 335-48

James M. Peavler, Analysis of Corpora of Variations. *Computers and the Humanities* 8 (1974) 153-9

D.J. Shaw, MSS – Manuscript Stemma Stimulator. *ALLC Bull.* 2 No. 2 (1974) 27-9

Gian Piero Zarri, Some Experiments on Automated Textual Criticism. *ALLC Bull* 5 (1977) 266-90

A useful bibliography of computers and textual criticism is provided by W. Ott in *ALLC Bull.* 2 No. 1 (1974) 74-7

8. Sound Patterns

The analysis of metre in poetry and rhythm in prose, and the investigation of poetic features such as alliteration and assonance, can be assisted by computer. These features are essentially incidences of regular patterns and, provided the patterns can be specified sufficiently clearly, the computer can be most useful in finding them. Once the features have been found, the computer can be used to compile tables of particular patterns or to determine where and when they are significant.

An examination of sound patterns can be very simply programmed for the computer, particularly in a language where one graphic symbol has one unique sound. A straightforward example is the investigation of sound patterns in Homer performed by David Packard, which is based on a count of letter frequencies in each line. Figure 8.1 shows a table produced by the program, from which it can be seen that 536 lines have no alphas, 1909 have one, 2840 have two, and so on, in Homer's *Odyssey*. The counts for L indicate a total for all liquids ($\lambda\rho\mu\nu$). P gives all labials ($\pi\beta\varphi$), T gives all dentals ($\tau\delta\theta$) and K all gutturals ($\kappa\gamma\chi$). Nasalised gamma is separated under the heading γK.

Many of the nineteenth-century Homeric scholars commented on lines in Homer which they thought had an unusually high proportion of one particular sound. While a high density of a sound in one particular line can be readily noted, it is not so easy without a computer to indicate the frequency of that sound in the work as a whole. Packard notes these scholars' attempts to isolate such lines. For example Stanford draws attention to a line in the *Odyssey* which has three deltas. Packard's counts show that this happens about once in every fifteen lines in the *Odyssey*. Similarly Stanford notes the 'ugly gutteral sounds' describing the Cyclops' cannibalism, citing one line with three gutturals and one with five. It can be seen from the table that these densities of gutturals are not at all infrequent.

Packard's program also records the line numbers of those lines which have a high density of a particular sound, and it is frequently useful to examine the content of the lines. The line in the *Iliad* (Book 23, line 116) which contains most alphas (11 in all) is well known for its imitation of the sound of stamping feet. Many of the lines which have five or six etas deal

	0	1	2	3	4	5	6	7	8	9	10	11	12	13	14	15	16
α	536	1909	2840	2852	1942	1239	532	190	48	17	3	2					
β	10234	1703	166	7													
γ	7310	3819	850	125	6												
δ	3372	4940	2731	872	171	23	1										
ε	235	1039	2311	2988	2573	1718	782	324	109	25	6						
ζ	11216	863	31														
η	3250	4425	2929	1101	340	59	6										
θ	6280	4252	1315	238	25												
ι	2654	4565	3053	1382	370	81	4	1									
κ	3350	4681	2686	1046	293	48	6										
λ	3996	4182	2463	1057	312	83	11	4	2								
μ	3132	4691	2936	1077	215	50	8	1									
ν	438	1659	3053	3182	2110	1125	413	104	23	2	1						
ο	1234	2714	3209	2539	1442	675	236	53	8								
π	3432	4378	2811	1161	260	60	8										
ρ	2406	4518	3369	1424	349	40	4										
σ	657	2017	2999	2918	1939	946	469	129	34	2							
τ	1232	3253	3669	2435	1115	309	77	16	4								
υ	6212	4383	1277	214	23	1											
φ	8050	3446	565	48	1												
χ	8739	2885	441	41	4												
ω	5623	4424	1627	363	66	7											
αι	6109	4301	1360	299	32	6	3										
αυ	10204	1809	97														
ει	6500	4274	1158	165	13												
ευ	9842	2134	130	4													
οι	6553	4018	1268	229	38	4											
ου	8386	2954	666	96	8												
υι	11838	269	3														
ηι	10553	1303	227	27													
ηυ	11847	263															
ωι	10742	1185	175	8													
L	2	23	143	457	1086	1778	2279	2303	1844	1124	626	278	124	35	5	3	
P	1789	3668	3528	1987	796	275	63	3	1								
T	118	702	1722	2728	2915	2230	1146	416	104	24	5						
K	1172	3396	3612	2414	1085	344	68	19									
γK	11744	360	6														

Figure 8.1. A table showing letter frequencies in each line in Homer's *Odyssey*. (Packard)

with youth and lovemaking. The verse with the highest concentration of liquid letters in the *Iliad* mentions the fair-flowing river Scamander. Packard cites many other lines as examples of high density of particular sounds. This type of study is extremely easy for a computer, but it would be almost impossible for the human brain to perform it accurately.

The occurrence of groups of letters, such as specific clusters of three or four consonants, may then be examined. Packard identified a number of Homeric lines which have unusual densities of consonant clusters. He also inspected those lines which have unusual juxtapositions of vowels, with a particular interest in the hiatus of omega and eta. Following Dionysius, he was able to calculate a 'harshness' factor for each line. Each sound was assigned a harshness number and the final harshness factor is the sum of the numbers for each sound in the lines, times ten, divided by the number of sounds. It is again easy to program a computer to apply this formula to all Homeric lines and then study the context of the lines to see whether the subject matter relates to the sound.

A similar study is reported by Kjetsaa on Russian. An eighteenth-century writer Lomonosov had attempted to classify the letters of the Russian alphabet as either *tender* or *aggressive*. The object of Kjetsaa's research was to see whether those lines of Lomonosov's own poetry which had high frequencies of either tender or aggressive sounds did in fact relate to these feelings in meaning. A high frequency of a letter was defined as the occurrence of that letter three or more times in one line. The categorising of lines into tender and aggressive was done manually, as the computer could not determine the meaning of a line satisfactorily. A first experiment on some of Lomosonov's odes showed that about 70% of lines tender in meaning were also tender in letters. The correlation was less clear for aggressive lines, but there was some indication of this. Kjetsaa also carried out further studies relating to the distribution of letters within lines, particularly investigating which letters occurred frequently in the tender and aggressive lines.

These simple frequency counts of sound patterns are based on counts of letters, but the study of alliteration and assonance presents rather more problems. Let us consider alliteration in English. The letter *c* alliterates with *s* in some cases, but with *k* in others. *c* in combination with *h* giving *ch* makes a different sound again. These distinctions could not be detected merely by letter counts. In English it would also be necessary to deal with silent letters like *k* in *knight*. Alliteration is frequently observed only as the repetition of initial letters of words, but it may also be seen in the initial letters of syllables which do not themselves begin a word. It may therefore be necessary to use some kind of phonetic transcription when studying alliteration. But whichever method of transcription is employed, the computer can be put to best use in the mechanical searching for repetition of patterns.

An investigation of alliteration in an older Scots poem, *Barbour's Bruce*, illustrates some of the ways in which alliteration may be analysed using a computer, and some of the problems which may be encountered. One program simply prints out all those lines which contain initial alliteration, which is defined as all those lines which contain more than one word beginning with the same letter. The inadequacies of this simple definition soon became apparent. Many function words were found beginning with the same letter which could not be considered to contribute to alliteration. A number of problem letters were identified, notably *q, th, c, w* and *v*, which either gave faulty alliteration (*ch* and *c*) or missed alliterations (*k* and *q*). The program was altered to print out a line of asterisks whenever it found alliteration on one of these letters. This would draw the researcher's eye to a problem which could then be solved manually. The possible missed alliterations were also dealt with by hand, once the computer had printed out those lines which contained one occurrence of a difficult phoneme. It would surely not have been difficult to program the computer to look for combinations of letters which make certain sounds. For example in English, a letter *c* is always soft when it is followed by *e i* or *y* and hard before other letters except *h*.

Once the alliterations have been found it is possible to ask such questions as how often does an alliterative letter continue into the next line. How many times is the letter repeated in the same line and then in successive lines? Is there double alliteration in one line? The number of such questions is endless, but the computer will supply rapid answers to all those which can be specific.

There have been attempts to measure the frequency of alliteration in several different ways. Wright attempted to include embedded as well as initial consonants to locate areas of high concentration of consonants and if possible to devise some means of measuring them. An experiment was conducted on two of Shakespeare's sonnets. The first stage was to count the number of times each letter occurred in each sonnet and then to calculate the probability of occurrence for each letter. Another method tried to partition a sonnet into fourteen equal segments, not necessarily consistent with line divisions. High occurrences of letters in specific segments were noted, but the very partitioning caused some information to be lost, as high clustering over a segment boundary would not be noticed. Wright could have overcome this problem by running his program again with different segment boundaries, but he does not appear to have done this, nor does he explain why he adopted this somewhat arbitrary method to begin with. He presents a table showing the percentages of occurrence of each letter in each segment. He chooses to omit five letters which occur less than four times in total, as, for example, the incidence of three *q*s in one line, and this must also have missed some noteworthy features.

A further more successful attempt used *Hildum's association measure* which calculates the relationship between each possible pair of letters from the length of the gap between their occurrences. The measure gives a value of zero if there is no association and values greater than zero for higher associations with a maximum of 0.5. Negative values indicate a high degree of disassociation. In the table shown in Figure 8.2, letters occurring less than four times have again been eliminated and values of between –0.19 and +0.19 are omitted as insignificant, except for the diagonal, which indicates the association of each letter with itself. It can be seen that t associates highly with h, which would be expected, but the central diagonal does not show much alliteration. From the inspection of his sonnets, Wright expected a higher figure for s with itself as there were two lines with six ss, but the figure given is due to the distribution of many other ss in the texts. Wright's calculations were made on letters rather than phonetic coding, but the method could equally be applied to phonetic codes. He concludes that the phenomenon of alliteration is one of domain or locale, which cannot necessarily be captured by the measurement of median gap distances alone.

Leighton measured alliteration in German sonnets by the basic criterion of three identical consonants within one line. He carried out a number of experiments before making this choice and admits that his criterion ignores alliteration which exists solely in the juxtaposition of two words with identical initial consonants. Though this latter type of alliteration is very easy to find by program, it produced too many errors to be useful. Leighton has now developed a program to break words into their syllabic components and, with a strict metrical pattern, this will allow the distribution of stresses to be taken into account in determining where there is alliteration. It will also allow medial consonants to be considered for alliteration. The bunching of function words beginning with a d or w in German can be a problem. If they are ignored completely, an unusual grouping of them would not be found. Leighton has overcome this problem by weighting them with a lower value than content words, so that they will still be found but only in higher concentrations.

Chisholm, in investigating phonological patterning in nineteenth-century German verse, follows Magnuson's concept of phonological frames, dividing texts into larger and larger units. Recurrences of consonants are only recognised if they have the same position within a syllable, i.e. if both are prevocalic or postvocalic. The text is transcribed phonologically using a dictionary look-up from the base text. Three rules were devised for identifying syllable boundaries. These were

1. between words
2. immediately before all free lexical items and derivational suffixes beginning with a consonant, e.g. *Herbst-tag*
3. after a single consonant or in the middle of consonant clusters where neither of the previous two rules apply. The cluster is divided evenly

target	base NCNT	A 40	B 5	C 9	D 20	E 61	F 10	G 10	H 31	I 28	L 23	M 23	N 33	O 44	P 4	R 29	S 42	T 40	U 13	V 5	W 5	Y 8
A		−·05	+·21	+·21			+·31		+·21						+·20	+·24						+·24
B			+·03	+·26			+·23	+·34	+·21	+·21			+·21	−·34	−·22						+·34	
C				+·27	−·21						−·20	−·22					−·22	−·21	−·34	−·39		
D					−·03	+·01						+·26			+·21							
E							+·06	−·21												+·37	−·26	
F						+·06		−·06												+·27	−·35	
G									−·06									+·30				
H		+·22	−·26							+·03												
I		−·26	−·21						−·25		−·13									+·25		−·21
L												+·03	+·00									
M		−·33	−·27	+·31										−·26	−·26					−·23	−·24	
N														+·21							+·31	+·21
O														−·02	−·13							
P																−·04	−·01				−·50	
R																			+·29	−·44		
S																		+·02		+·26		
T																			+·05			
U																	−·21			−·38		
V																						
W																				−·09	+·28	
Y		+·38												+·22						−·25		−·07

Figure 8.2. A table showing letter association measures for Shakespeare's sonnet 18. (Wright)

with any extra consonants placed to the right of the syllable boundary, e.g. *Ta-ge, fin-den*

Two SNOBOL programs then operate on the data. One counts the relative frequency of all sounds in prevocalic, vocalic and postvocalic positions in stressed and unstressed syllables. The second program identifies all repetitions of sounds in a specified number of frames and prints the results as shown in Figure 8.3. Here only the syllables which have repetitions are shown in their metrical positions within a 16-line frame of one poem. Since the number of syllable pairs varies from one frame to another, the measure of sound matching in each frame is expressed as a ratio of the number of sound repetition pairs to the total number of syllable pairs available for comparison. Chisholm is then merely investigating the repetition of sounds, albeit syllables not single phonemes, and examining their relationship with each other within specific units of the poems which vary in size from two lines upwards.

Leavitt attempts to quantify alliteration in a different manner. He used ten pieces of test data ranging from a Shakespeare sonnet to a SNOBOL manual and transcribed them in three different ways: according to the Inte·national Phonetic Alphabet, then following Chomsky and Halle, and finally following Fromkin and Rodman. He first calculated both the occurrences of high frequency consonants and the largest gaps between two occurrences of these consonants. From this he can derive what he calls a gap recurrence function which is used to represent the frequency and density of the features. Certain types of phoneme such as initial sounds can be weighted if necessary. He found that the work on the IPA transcription was in general unsatisfactory but undoubtedly an improvement on the basic text. The most satisfactory results were obtained from the Fromkin and Rodman features, using which he was able to rank his texts according to their alliteration. It is arguable whether these attempts to measure alliteration mathematically have any value in literary research. Merely finding and counting their occurrence is much simpler to perform, and the results are much easier to follow.

The computer can be programmed to select from a poem all those words which rhyme with each other, provided it has been fed the appropriate rhyme scheme. The relationship between these words can then be investigated. Joyce studied rhyming words from the standpoint of mathematical graph theory calling them networks of sound. His networks include arrows pointing in the direction of the rhyme. He makes the second of two rhyming words point to the first, not vice versa, on the grounds that the rhyme is not noticed until the second word is reached. This may not necessarily be true, but the method can be applied for whichever direction the rhyme is considered to go. Figure 8.4 shows all words linked by the

```
1.  ES IST (8N +(P2T ES VIRT (8N +KALT
2.  VAS +RAITST D7 +"AIN*Z6M DURC D2N +VALT
3.  D2R +VALT IST +LA/ D7 BIST A*+LAIN
4.  D7 +(5*N3 +BRAUT IC +F4R DIC +HAIM
 Ɛ
5.  +GR8S IST D2R +ME*N3R +TR7K UNT +LIST
6.  F8R +(MERTS MAIN +HERTS G3*+BRO*X3N IST
7.  V8L +"IRT DAS +VALT*HORN +H2R UNT +HIN
8.  8 +FL1 D7 +VAIST NICT V2R IC BIN
 Ɛ
9.  Z8 +RAIC G3*+(MYKT IST +ROS UNT +VAIP
10. Z8 +VUN*D3R*+(5N D2R +JU*/3 +LAIP
11. JETST +KEN IC DIC +GOT +(T2 M1R +BAI
12. D7 BIST D1 +HEK*S3 L8*R3*+LAI
 Ɛ
13. D7 +KENST MIC V8L FON +H8*3M +(TAIN
14. +(AUT +(TIL MAIN +(LOS +T1F IN D2N +RAIN
15. ES IST (8N +(P2T ES VIRT (8N +KALT
16. +KOMST +NI*M3R*+M2R AUS +D1*Z3M +VALT
```

GRAPHIC REPRESENTATION FOR FRAME 4

	1	2	3	4	5	6	7	8	9	10
1	ES	IST	(8N	+(P2T	ES	VIRT	(8N	+KALT		
2	VAS	+RAITST	D7				D2N	+VALT		
3	D2R	+VALT		+LA/	D7	BIST		+LAIN		
4	D7						DIC			
5			D2R		N3R		UNT	+LIST		
6	F8R		MAIN	+HERTS			Z3N	IST		
7		+"IRT		+VALT		+H2R				
8										
9		+RAIC				+ROS				
10		+VUN	D3R			+JU	/3			
11	JETST					+GOT	M1R			
12			D1							
13								+(TAIN		
14		+(TIL	MAIN	+(LOS		IN	D2N			
15	ES	IST	(8N	+(P2T	ES	VIRT	(8N	+KALT		
16	+KOMST	+NI	M3R		AUS		Z3M			

Figure 8.3. The text and one sixteen line frame of Eichendorff's poem *Waldespräche* showing those syllables which have repetitions in their metrical positions. (Chisholm)

rhyme scheme to *thee* in ten of Shakespeare's sonnets. The number 2 indicates that this particular link occurs twice. Larger and larger networks can then be built up as more text is analysed. This method of investigating rhyme words is very close to that described in Chapter Four for analysing

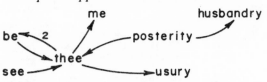

Figure 8.4. A network of sound showing all words linked by the rhyme scheme to *thee* in ten of Shakespeare's sonnets. (Joyce)

closely related vocabulary and can be applied to any text of which the rhyme scheme can be specified.

We shall now consider how the computer can be used in the study of rhythm and metre. A metrical study consist of two stages. The first scans the verse and the second investigates the frequencies of specific metrical patterns either overall or in certain positions in a line. It is possible to scan verse automatically in some languages, but it is not so easy in others. In English, for example, metre depends on the stress of a syllable and the computer has to be told the stress for every word. Normally this would be done by looking the word up in a computer dictionary of metrical forms. In some languages, such as Classical Latin and Greek, metre depends on the length of the syllable rather than the stress. There are a number of fixed rules governing syllable lengths. These can be written into a computer program which can then be used to scan the basic text automatically.

Two programs have been written to scan Latin hexameters and one for Greek. Hexameters are the easiest metre to scan. Each line consists of six feet, a foot being either two long syllables (a spondee) or a long followed by two shorts (a dactyl). The last foot of each line is always two syllables, the final syllable being either short or long. In the vast majority of hexameter lines, the fifth foot is a dactyl. Every foot begins with a long syllable and there are fixed rules for determining when a syllable is long. A vowel followed by two or more consonants which are not a mute followed by a liquid is always long. A vowel followed by another vowel is short, unless those two vowels constitute a dipthong. When a word ending with a vowel or *m* is followed by a word beginning with a vowel or *h*, the word ending syllable is ignored (elided).

On the basis of these rules, Ott was able to devise a computer program which scans Latin hexameters. His program would operate on a line of Horace as follows:

quodcumque ostendis mihi sic incredulus odi

Que is recognised as an elision, as it comes before the *o* of *ostendis*, and that syllable is thus discounted. The following syllables can be recognised as unequivocally long according to the rules described above.

quōdcūmqu(e) ōstēndis̄ mihi sic Ɪncredulus ōdi

At this stage the first two feet are established as two spondees and the two syllable final foot is also clear. The computer then attempts to fill in the rest of the line. If it made the *mi* of *mihi* long, that syllable would be the second of a foot and therefore the next syllable *hi* of *mihi*, would also have to be long as the first syllable of a foot is always long. This leads to the following scansion.

quōdcūmqu(e) ōstēndis̄ mı̄hı̄ sic iñcredulus ōdi

This scansion would force the word *sic* to be scanned as long as that is the only possible quantity for a syllable coming between two long syllables. There are then three syllables left unscanned. This scansion would result in seven feet which contradicts the rule of six feet per line. The computer then makes a second attempt taking *mi* to be short. Short syllables always occur in pairs in a dactyl and so the scansion proceeds as follows:

quōdcūmqu(e) ōstēndis̄ mĭhĭ sic Ɪncredulus ōdi

Sic must therefore be long, forming the first syllable of the fourth foot. Three syllables then remain unscanned, so the fifth foot must therefore be a dactyl. The occurrence of a dactyl in foot five is so common that a scansion program should be able to assume that this is true and only discount this if it is unable to scan the rest of the line.

Ott reports success in about 95% of scansions. In another 3-4% more than one scansion is proposed and the remaining 1-2% of lines are abandoned. In many of the cases where the computer has been unsuccessful it was later found that the Latin author had not in fact followed the rules. Greenberg reports a similar success rate to Ott but adopts a slightly different method. His program begins in the same way as Ott's by finding all the long syllables. It then attempts to match this pattern of long syllables against all the possible combinations of scansions for the hexameter lines which have previously been fed into the program. An example from his program is shown in Figure 8.5 where 1 indicates a short syllable, 2 a long syllable and & an elision. The program can either print out the text, together with its scansion, or write the scansion patterns into another computer file for further analysis.

When writing a program such as this, it is of course necessary to test the results. Ott notes that very few erroneous scansions were found and they were mostly in words like *aurea* where the final *a* is the long *a* of the ablative case and the *e* is contracted and therefore does not count as a syllable. Ott modified his program to print asterisks by the side of those lines containing

```
-ARMA-VIRUMQUE-CANO-TROIAE-QUI-PRIMUS-AB-ORIS-
-2  1- 1 2    1- 1 2-   2 2 -  2-  2 1 -1 -2 1 -
 1       2       3     4       5         6
-ITALIAM-FATO-PROFUGUS-LAVINIAQUE-VENIT-
-2 1 12 - 2 2-  1 1 2 - 1 1 21  1- 2 1 -
 1    2      3      4       5       6
-LITORA-MULTUM-ILLE-ET-TERRIS-IACTATUS-ET-ALTO-
- 2 1 1- 2    +2    &2 - 2  2 - 2   2 1 -1 -2  1-
 1     2       3      4       5       6
-VI-SUPERUM-SAEVAE-MEMOREM-IUNONIS-OB-IRAM-
- 2- 1 1 2 - 2  2 - 1 1 2 - 2 2 1 -1 -2 1 -
 1      2      3      4       5      6
-MULTA-QUOQUE-ET-BELLO-PASSUS-DUM-CONDERET-URBEM-
- 2  1- 1   &2 - 2 2- 2 2 -2 - 2  1 1 -2  1 -
 1       2      3     4     5         6
-INFERRETQUE-DEOS-LATIO-GENUS-UNDE-LATINUM-
-2  2  2    1- 12 - 1 12- 1 1 -2  1- 1 2 1 -
 1     2       3     4      5      6
-ALBANIQUE-PATRES-ATQUE-ALTAE-MOENIA-ROMAE-
-2  2 2  1- 1  2 -2    &2  2 - 2  11- 2 1 -
 1    2      3      4       5      6
-MUSA-MIHI-CAUSAS-MEMORA-QUO-NUMINE-LAESO-
- 2 1- 1 2- 2  2 - 1 1 2- 2- 2 1 1- 2  1-
 1    2      3      4      5      6
-QUIDVE-DOLENS-REGINA-DEUM-TOT-VOLVERE-CASUS-
- 2  1- 1 2  - 2 2 1- 12 - 2 -2  1 1- 2 1 -
 1       2       3     4      5       6
-INSIGNEM-PIETATE-VIRUM-TOT-ADIRE-LABORES-
-2  2  2 - 11 2 1- 1 2 - 1 -1 2 1- 1 2 1 -
 1    2      3      4      5       6
-IMPULERIT-TANTAENE-ANIMIS-CAELESTIBUS-IRAE-
-2  1 1 2 - 2  2   &1 1 2 - 2  2   1 1 -2 1 -
 1      2      3      4        5       6
-URBS-ANTIQUA-FUIT-TYRII-TENUERE-COLONI-
-2   -2  2  1- 12 - 1 12- 1 12 1- 1 2 1-
 1      2      3     4      5      6
-KARTHAGO-ITALIAM-CONTRA-TIBERINAQUE-LONGE-
- 2   2  &2 1 12 - 2   2- 1 1 2 1  1- 2  1-
 1      2      3      4       5       6
-OSTIA-DIVES-OPUM-STUDIISQUE-ASPERRIMA-BELLI-
-2  11- 2 1 -1 2 -  1 12    &2  2  1 1- 2  1-
 1     2       3      4        5       6
-QUAM-IUNO-FERTUR-TERRIS-MAGIS-OMNIBUS-UNAM-
- 2 - 2 2- 2  2 - 2  2 - 1 1 -2  1 1 -2 1 -
 1    2      3      4      5        6
```

Figure 8.5. Part of Aeneid Book I scanned by Greenberg's program. 1 indicates a short syllable, 2 a long syllable and & an elision.

an *ea* and the asterisks immediately draw his eye to those lines which may need interpretation. The same is true for the 5% of lines for which it was unable to provide an unequivocal scansion. Greenberg prints messages alongside those lines with alternative scansions as well as by those lines which are noteworthy in some respect.

On the basis of his automatic scansions, Ott has gone on to provide a vast number of tables. He has published a number of books in the series *Materialen zum Metrischen und Stylistik Analysen*, each of which deals with a separate work in Latin hexameters. In the first section of each book each line is given with its scansion for the first five feet. There is also information on word accent, word boundaries, elision, hiatus and punctuation which has been stored with the scansions. Ott makes use of the computer's most basic storage unit, the bit, in representing his material. Each line of six feet can be considered as a maximum of eighteen syllables, allowing three for each foot. These eighteen syllables are represented by eighteen bits which have 1 for presence of a feature and 0 for its absence. Therefore in our example line, word boundaries are represented as 001 000 101 100 001 001. These eighteen bits are then grouped into threes, one group for each foot and each set of three is represented by a single octal number. If the first bit is a 1, it counts as 4, the second bit counts as 2, and the third bit as a 1. The set of bits can then be added together to give an octal number, e.g. foot three has 101, giving one 4, no 2 and one 1, a total of 5. The complete octal representation of this bit pattern is 105411, which is how Ott stores the word boundary information for this particular line. 040000 gives its information for elision, as there is only a single elision at the beginning of the second foot. From the information given in the first section of his books, Ott is able to produce many different tables including frequency distributions of metrical forms at word endings, a complete metrical index and an examination of all verse and types by metre and word ending.

Packard reports 98% success with his program to scan Greek hexameters. As the Greek alphabet distinguishes long *e* and *o* as separate vowels it is easier than in Latin to produce automatic scansions. Packard claims that, although his program made eight false scansions in 440 lines of the first book of the *Odyssey*, it recognised that it may have been faulty in seven of those eight cases. He also notes that the lines which the program found difficult are those for which the rules must be relaxed. Coupled with his grammatical analysis program described in Chapter Five, it provides a powerful tool for analysing Greek hexameter poets.

A recent study in Oxford has proved that it is also possible to scan Sanskrit verse automatically as again the rules for scansion are rigid and the length of each syllable can easily be determined. It now seems clear that automatic scansion is possible and indeed practical for rigid metres in languages where the metre depends on the length of syllable. In the case of the hexameter, there are only thirty-two possible scansions for each line (or sixteen if the fifth foot is assumed always to be a dactyl). This is not the case of the iambic senarii of Plautus which have been the subject of a computer study by Stephen Waite. Plautus wrote some two hundred years earlier than the best known of the Latin hexameter poets and there is considerable doubt whether his metre is based on the length of syllable or is partially or wholly dependent on the stress of individual words. The fundamental unit of metre is an iamb (ᴗ–) of which there are six in each line. The iamb can be replaced by either a spondee (– –), an anapaest (ᴗᴗ –), a dactyl (– ᴗᴗ), a tribrach (ᴗᴗᴗ) or a proceleusmatic (ᴗᴗᴗᴗ). There are therefore 6^5 or 7776 theoretical possibilities for each line and it would be impracticable to attempt an automatic scansion similar to that for hexameters.

Waite therefore adopted the dictionary look-up method for assigning metrical values to the lines of Plautus. He began by making forward and reverse concordances of the texts. A simple word list would have been inadequate for determining the metrical form of a word because the quantity of the final syllable is frequently influenced by the next word, for example by elision. Using the concordance as a reference tool, another word list of the text was produced to which the metrical forms were added. This was done using a computer terminal interactively. The computer displayed each word in turn and its metrical form was then typed in, using the number 2 to indicate a long syllable and 1 for a short syllable. There are of course a number of written forms in Latin which do not have a unique scansion. For example the nominative and ablative singular of the first declension both end in *a*, but the *a* of the ablative is long. These forms were marked with a W in the dictionary to show that they were ambiguous. The advantage of working from a word list rather than the text itself, as in all dictionary look-up processes, is that words which occur more than once are only coded once in the dictionary.

A second interactive program was then run from a terminal to insert the scansions into the text. Each word is looked up in the dictionary and its scansion thus found. If a word is found to be marked with a W, the entire line is displayed on the terminal so that the correct scansion can be typed in. So far the text has been treated as a series of individual words which now have their scansions inserted in them. A further program then derives the scansion for each line by considering elisions and lengthening short final syllables when the next word begins with a consonant. Word endings, hiatus and elisions are marked, and the scansion is checked to see whether it conforms to an iambic senarius. Waite finally arrives at a data file consisting only of the scansions for each line. He is then in a position to ask the computer, for example, to search for all the lines which begin with each of the possible forms, or the number of times a word end coincides with a foot boundary. He can summarise his findings as shown in Figure 8.6 which indicates the iambic senarii in the *Truculentus*.

Waite's method initially requires much more work on the part of the scholar, but the computer is used to perform the counts and the calculations. The metrical dictionary he has prepared can be used for the other plays of Plautus and only the new words in these plays need be added to the dictionary as they are required. In the last century it was common practice for scholars to perform all these tasks by hand. It is much faster to do it by computer, even using Waite's method, and the results are much more likely to be accurate.

A further study by Waite investigated the interplay of verse ictus and word stress in the same texts of Plautus. It is unfortunate for our purposes that this second study does not discuss the computer methods used but rather concentrates on the results obtained. Much of the discussion centres on the position in which a number of words frequently occur. He notes particularly that forms of the possessive adjective make up a larger than expected proportion of disyllabic words at the ends of lines. Therefore a combination of metrical features and the words themselves must have been used to formulate the results.

Middle High German dactyls were the subject of a computer study of verse rhythm by Rudolph Hirschmann. His input consists of the basic text with the vowels of all stressed syllables marked and his program contains a number of rules which must be satisfied for the line to scan successfully. He managed to classify correctly all but thirty-four syllables in a text of over 16,000 syllables. He prints out each line of text with the syllabic categories and types underneath, as shown in Figure 8.7. Stressed syllables are underlined. *B* indicates that the next word begins with a consonant, and *A* that it begins with a vowel. The rhymed caesura is marked when the text is put into the machine, and *C* in the printout marks this feature. Five types of syllables are distinguished by the numerals 0, 2, 4, 6 and 8. When the vowels are stressed these numerical values are increased by one, so that all odd numbers represent stressed syllables and even numbers unstressed syllables. Once the scansion is complete the same kind of questions may be asked on the data produced.

Various features of English prosody have been investigated by Dilligan and Bender with the assistance of a computer. Their study was performed on the iambic verse of Gerard Manley Hopkins using Halle and Keyser's definition of an iambic pentameter – that is, a sequence of ten positions in which syllables receiving primary stress occupy even-numbered positions. Two optional unstressed syllables are permitted at the end of a line, and position one may be unoccupied.

The computing part of the study initially adopted similar methods to

	POSITION IN LINE											
TYPE	1		2		3		4		5		TOTAL	
·—	43	15%	105	35%	52	18%	118	40%	33	11%	351	24%
——	147	50%	122	41%	171	58%	125	42%	216	73%	781	53%
·—·	53	18%	18	6%	7	2%	7	2%	33	11%	118	8%
—··	42	14%	36	12%	54	18%	29	10%	13	4%	174	12%
···	6	2%	13	4%	12	4%	15	5%	1	0%	47	3%
····	5	2%	2	1%	0	0%	2	1%	0	0%	9	1%
TOTAL	296		296		296		296		296		1480	

POSITION 6

·—	175	59%
··	121	41%
TOTAL	296	

Figure 8.6. A table summarising the metre of iambic senarii in Plautus' *Truculentus*. (Waite)

AA 1 .WA̲-FENA-, WI̲E HAT MICH MI̲NNE GELA̲-ZEN |
    B 9̄ O 8 B 9̄ B 6 B 6 B 7̇ OB O 9 2

AA 2 ̲DIU ̲MICH BETWA̲NC DAZ ICH LI̲E MI-N GEMU̲*ETE
    B 9̄ B 6 B O 7 B 6 A6 B 9̄ B 8 B O 9̄   O

AA 3 ̲AN SOLHEN WA̲-N DER MICH WO̲L MAC VERWA̲-ZEN,
    A7̄ B 6 2 B 9̄ B 2 B 6̄ B 7̄ B 6 B 2 9 2

AA 4 ̲EZ ENSI̲- DAZ ICH MU̲*EZE GENI̲EZEN I̲R GU̲*ETE,
    A2̄ A2 9̄ B 6 A6 B 9̄ OB O 9 2 A6 B 9̄   O

AA 5 VO̲N DER ICH BI̲N / AL̲SO- DI̲CKE A-NE SI̲N.
    B 7̄ B 2 A6 B 7̄ AC 6 8 B 7̄ OA8 OB 7̄

AA 6 MICH DU̲-HTE EIN GEWIN, / UND WO̲LTE. DIU GU̲OTE
    B 6 B 9̄ OA8 B O 7 A C 6 B 7̄ OB 8 B 9̄ O

AA 7 WI̲ZZEN DIE NO̲-T DIU MIR WO̲NT IN MI-M MU̲OTE.
    B 7̄ 2 B 8 B 9̄ B 8 B 6 B 7̄ A6 B 8 B 9̄ O

AA 8 WA̲-FEN, WAZ HA̲BE ICH GETA̲-N SO- ZUNE-REN
    B 9̄ 2 B 6 B 5̄ OA6 B O 9̄ B 8 B 6 9̄ 2

AA 9 ̲DAZ MIR DIU GU̲OTE NIHT GRU̲OZES ENGU̲NDE?
    B 7̄ B 6 B 8 B 9̄ OB 6 B 9̄ 2 A2 7 O

AA10 SU̲S KAN SI MI̲R WOL DAZ. HE̲RZE VERSE̲-REN.
    B 7̄ B 6 B 4B 7̄ B 6 B 6 B 3̄ OB 2 9̄ 2

AA11 ̲DEICH IN DER WE̲RLT BEZZER WI̲-P IENDER FU̲NDE,
    B 9̄   A6 B 2 B 3̄ B 2 2 B 9̄ A8 2 B 7̄ O

AA12 SE̲HT DE-ST MI-N WA̲-N. / DA- FU̲*R SO̲- WIL ICHZ HA̲-N,
    B 3̄ B 8 B 8 B 9̄ B C 8 B 6 B 9̄ B 6 A6   B 9̄

AA13 UND DI̲ENEN NOCHDA̲N / MIT TRI̲UWEN DER GU̲OTEN,
    A6 B 9̄ 2 B 6 7̇ BC 6 B 9̄ 2 B 2 B 9̄ 2

AA14 DI̲U MICH DA- BLI̲UWET VIL SE̲-RE A-NE RU̲OTEN.
    B 9̄ B 6 B 8 B 9̄ 2 B 6 B 9̄ OA8 OB 9̄ 2

Figure 8.7. Middle High German dactyls with syllable categories and types underneath. (Hirschmann)

those of Waite on Plautus. First, a concordance was made for reference purposes from the basic text. This text was then transformed into a phonemic transcription, using a word list and dictionary look-up method. Dilligan and Bender do not seem to have had an interactive terminal at their disposal, and the entire dictionary was transferred to the machine by punched cards, making the process much slower than it would otherwise have been. The concordance was used to identify homographs and function words which need to be marked in the machine-readable text.

The scanning program operates on this transcription as its input and performs a number of functions. It determines the positions of stressed vowels and punctuation, counts the number of syllables in a line and generates lists of vowels and initial consonant clusters. The occurrences of stress and punctuation are recorded as bit strings in a similar manner to Ott. For some reason, the authors choose to use the rightmost bit to represent the leftmost syllable in the line so that scansion of a line such as

From crown to tail-fin floating, fringed the spine,

appears as

1010101010

as it has stress, represented by 1, in positions 2, 4, 6, 8 and 10. Vowels are recorded as integer numbers, each phoneme being assigned a unique integer, the first one indicating the first vowel phoneme, the second for the second vowel, and so on. This line gives a series

28 42 26 38 2 54 4 2 28 44

The initial consonants are stored as the following character codes:

FR KR T T – FL – FR) S

When the information is recorded in this way it can easily be evaluated for different patterns. Assonance patterns can be found by the repetition of a particular vowel number and then represented as another bit string. Assonance in this line would be recorded as

0010010000

Alliteration for T would become

0000001100

and for FR

0010000001

The separate bit strings can be combined using Boolean operations to find lines where certain features coincide. A Boolean OR can be performed to find all the positions in the line where there is alliteration. This operation produces a third bit string which has a 1 in all positions where either of the two originating strings have a 1.

```
0000001100
0010000001
```
```
0010001101
```

showing that alliteration occurs in positions one, three, four and eight.

A Boolean AND operation shows where assonance and alliteration coincide as it results in a 1 in those positions only which have a 1 in both the originating strings.

```
0010010000
0010001101
```
```
0010000000
```

The result indicates that assonance and alliteration coincide at position eight. Similar bit strings are used to test stress maximum and metricality. This use of bit strings is the most economical way of storing information inside the computer and combined with the use of the Boolean operations AND and OR makes very sensible use of the machine's capacities.

Though most of their information is kept as bit strings, Dilligan and Bender record the phonemes which give assonance or alliteration and the line numbers of those lines which contain some unusual metrical feature such as those without stress maximum. Their program keeps totals of thirty-eight different features automatically and many more can be requested specifically. They draw histograms showing the distribution of assonance and alliteration between the ten positions. As we have seen before, simple diagrams made on the lineprinter present results in a manner which is much easier to read than tables of numbers.

There have therefore been a number of attempts to write special-purpose programs to deal with patterns of metre. In some cases, it need not be necessary to write a special program as patterns of rhythm can be found in much the same way as patterns of words. The COCOA concordance program was used in one project to search for metrical patterns in Russian verse. The verse, Pasternak's *Volny*, was coded by hand and the machine used merely to find patterns within the coding. Five different symbols were employed to indicate metrical features and the punctuation marks and word boundaries were retained. Rhyme was also coded in letter form, there being seven different categories of rhyme which were selected by human judgment. The codings such as)*)10)1)01)010,)ADE may appear strange, but the result is that the computer can be asked to find all the lines which have a specific stress pattern such as 10101010, ignoring all the other symbols. Usage of punctuation could be inspected by making a concordance of, for example, full stops, and rhyme markers can also be investigated by concordances sorted on endings. The author of this study, Wendy Rosslyn, felt that it would take less time to do the coding manually than to attempt to automate it, but she nevertheless found it worthwhile to input the coding to the computer and search for patterns automatically.

The COCOA program was also used in a brief experiment in Oxford to study Latin prose rhythm. The rhythm of prose text has not received a great deal of scholarly attention, but it is a subject that, for classical languages, is suitable for some automation. The Oxford experiment used manual coding of the text where L represented a long syllable and S a short one. Other features such as elision and hiatus were marked and a special symbol $ used to indicate a word boundary, as it was not possible with COCOA to make a concordance of spaces. The concordance program was then used to find all occurrences of all combinations of syllables. Another program to derive the rhythm of Greek prose was recently developed in Oxford and has had some success, but Greek has the advantage of long *e* and *o* appearing as separate letters. These experiments indicate that there is much more scope for the examination of prose rhythm. A dictionary look-up similar to Waite's for Plautus may well be the best approach for larger amounts of text. Both experiments in Oxford were performed on small amounts of text within a short time scale and deserve further work. Wishart and Leach report on a study of prose rhythm in Plato which examined thirty-three samples of text. Their chief interest was in the clustering methods; and the scansion method is not described, although they do state that it was performed by a FORTRAN program and that each successive group of five syllables was classified by its scansion.

Metrical analysis can then be aided considerably by the machine. In all languages it can perform counts and statistics required of various metrical features. The scansions may have been performed entirely manually and typed into the machine, as for example in the Rosslyn study on *Volny*, or they may have been generated by a dictionary look-up system such as those described by Waite and Dilligan and Bender or they may have been generated automatically as Greenberg, Ott and Packard did for classical hexameters. Whichever method of generating scansions is adopted, it is clear that the machine can take away most of the mechanical work of counting their occurrences. Storing the scansions in a computer file, as Waite and Dilligan do, seems to be more sensible than generating lists of every possible feature as Ott does, though it could be argued that his books reach a wider audience because they are not only in computer readable form.

Alliteration and sound pattern studies are also suitable for computer analysis. Provided that sufficient thought is given to preparing the text, whether by using a phonemic transcription or by allowing for exceptions and peculiarities in a program, the study of these features can be greatly helped by the computer. There still does not appear to be an effective method of measuring alliteration. The mathematical methods which have been tried have not been universally adopted, but some of them may be considered useful. In many cases mere counts will suffice. Whichever method is chosen the advantage of using the computer is that it finds every line which satisfies certain criteria, not just those which immediately strike the eye.

REFERENCES

1. David Chisholm, Phonological Patterning in German Verse, *Computers and the Humanities* 10 (1976) 5-20

2. R.J. Dilligan and T.K. Bender, The Lapses of Time: a Computer-Assisted Investigation of English Prosody. *The Computer and Literary Studies*, 239-52 (eds A.J. Aitken, R.W. Bailey and N. Hamilton-Smith). Edinburgh: Edinburgh University Press (1973)

3. Nathan A. Greenberg, Scansion Purement Automatique de l'Hexamètre Dactylique. *Revue* No. 3 (1967) 1-25

4. Rudolph Hirschmann, A Computational Approach to the Study of Verse Rhythm; The Middle High German Dactyls. *Computer Studies in the Humanities and Verbal Behavior* 3 (1970) 173-90

5. J. Joyce, Networks of Sound: Graph Theory Applied to Studying Rhymes. *Computing in the Humanities*, 307-16 (eds Serge Lusignan and John S. North). Waterloo: University of Waterloo Press (1977)

6. Geir Kjetsaa, Sound and Meaning According to Lomonosov. *The Computer in Literary and Linguistic Studies (Proceedings of the Third International Symposium)*, 230-9 (eds Alan Jones and R.F. Churchhouse). Cardiff: University of Wales Press (1976)

7. Bernice W. Kliman, Alliteration in Barbour's Bruce: A Study Using SNAP Programming. *The Computer and Literary Studies*, 263-71 (eds A.J. Aitken, R.W. Bailey and N. Hamilton-Smith). Edinburgh: Edinburgh University Press (1973)

8. Jay A. Leavitt, On the Measurement of Alliteration in Poetry. *Computers and the Humanities* 10 (1976) 333-42

9. Joseph Leighton, Automatic Analysis of Simple Rhetorical Devices in 17th Century German Sonnets. *The Computer in Literary and Linguistic Studies (Proceedings of the Third International Symposium)*, 246-54 (eds Alan Jones and R.F. Churchhouse). Cardiff: University of Wales Press (1976)

10. Wilhelm Ott, Metrical Analysis of the Latin Hexameter: The Automation of a Philological Research Project. *Linguistica Matematica e Calcolatori (Atti del Convegno e della Prima Scuola Internazionale Pisa 1970)*, 379-90 (ed. A. Zampolli) Florence: Leo S. Olschki (1973)

11. W. Ott, *Materialen zu Metrik und Stylistik.* Tübingen: Max Niemeyer Verlag. (1973-)

12. David W. Packard, Sound Patterns in Homer. *Transactions of the American Philological Association* 104 (1974) 239-60

13. David W. Packard, Metrical and Grammatical Patterns in the Greek Hexameter. *The Computer in Literary and Linguistic Studies (Proceedings of the Third International Symposium)*, 85-91 (eds Alan Jones and R.F. Churchhouse). Cardiff; University of Wales Press (1976)

14. Wendy Rosslyn, COCOA as a Tool for the Analysis of Poetry. *ALLC Bull.* 3 (1975) 15-18

15. S.V.F. Waite, Approaches to Metrical Research in Plautus, *The Computer and Literary Studies*, 253-62 (eds A.J. Aitken, R.W. Bailey and N. Hamilton-Smith). Edinburgh: Edinburgh University Press (1973)

16. Stephen V.F. Waite, Word Positions in Plautus: Interplay of Verse Ictus and Word Stress. *The Computer in Literary and Linguistic Studies (Proceedings of the Third International Symposium)*, 92-105 (eds Alan Jones and R.F. Churchhouse). Cardiff: University of Wales Press (1976)

17. David Wishart and Stephen V. Leach, A Multivariate Analysis of Platonic Prose Rhythm. *Computer Studies in the Humanities and Verbal Behavior* 3 (1970) 90-9

18. N.B. Wright, Measuring Alliteration: A Study in Method. *Computers in the Humanities*, 82-93 (ed. J.L. Mitchell). Edinburgh: Edinburgh University Press (1974)

19. D. Wujastyk, Automatic Scansion of Sanskrit Poetry for Authorship Criteria. *ALLC Bull.* 6 (1978) 122-38

Further Reading

W. Ott, Metrical Analysis of Latin Hexameter by Computer. *Revue* 4 (1966) 7-24

S.V.F. Waite, Homer and IMPRESS: Application to Greek Metrics of a Social Science Analysis Package. *Computing in the Humanities*, 37-48 (eds Serge Lusignan and John S. North). Waterloo: University of Waterloo Press (1977)

9. Indexing, Cataloguing and Information Retrieval

The previous chapters have been concerned with the use of computers in analysing text, that is literary or linguistic text. In this chapter we shall consider the various ways in which the computer can be used to manipulate information which is structured in some way. By this we mean the sort of material which is traditionally recorded on file cards, where one card represents one particular object such as a book, a piece of pottery or biographical information about a person. In computer terms a set of file cards would be replaced by a *file* within which each object is represented by a *record*. Each record is broken down into a number of different categories of data which are normally called *fields*. Obvious examples for a book would be title, author and publisher. A computer file may consist of many thousands of such records which are all described by the same field structure. The number of fields per record may also be quite large, its limitation being more often due to the program which will manipulate the information than to the computer or information itself.

The information contained in each field may be textual or numeric or binary in nature. Most bibliographic material is textual, but a date is numeric. Historical and archaeological data can include many numeric fields, which can either be whole numbers (*integers*) or numbers containing a decimal point which are known as *real numbers* or *floating point numbers*. Binary fields indicate one of two possible states – that is, normally the presence or absence of a particular feature. All three types of information can be present in the same record although they cannot really be combined in the same field.

A distinction is also made between what are called *fixed-length fields* and *variable-length fields*. A fixed-length field occupies the same amount of room in each record, for example a four-digit date. Variable-length fields occupy amounts of space which differ from record to record. This is important in reducing the total amount of storage space on a computer tape or disc which the information occupies. If all fields in a bibliographic file were the same length, a title such as *Loot* would occupy as much room as *The Importance of Being Earnest*. If data is organised entirely in a fixed length manner, the longest title must be found first and that amount of room allowed for each title. This is clearly very wasteful of computer storage as well as not allowing for still longer titles to be added in the same format. There are two frequently used methods of storing variable length fields. One is to insert some terminating character such as * at the end of every such field, provided of course that this special character is not expected to appear anywhere else in the data. Our titles would then appear as

LOOT*
THE IMPORTANTCE OF BEING EARNEST*

The other method is to precede each title with a number indicating the count of characters in the title. Our titles would then become

4LOOT
31THE IMPORTANCE OF BEING EARNEST

A third possible method is to keep a table or directory at the beginning of every record indicating at which character position each field begins in the record. An example giving author, title and place of publication would be

THEROUX, PAULTHE GREAT RAILWAY BAZAARLONDON

When both fixed-length and variable-length fields are present in each record, the fixed-length records usually precede the variable-length ones on the storage medium, though this does not necessarily mean that the fixed-length records must be processed first in any analysis of the data.

There may be many categories of information missing, for example, in historical and archaeological data. The treatment of such missing data depends on the programs being used for the analysis, but it is usually possible to allow for it in some way and it should not be considered as an inherent difficulty.

Though the kind of data we are discussing may be very large in quantity, it is usually possible to reduce the amount of typing required to transfer it to computer readable form. The material may be repetitive and can thus be abbreviated into a form which a computer program can then expand. Let us suppose that we are compiling a catalogue of Elizabethan literature and are including all the plays of Shakespeare. It would be wasteful of time to type the name of the author for every play. Instead it could be given once with an indication that it should be taken as the author of every following record until a new author is encountered. The following could represent in a simplified form the lines of data

£SHAKESPEARE
THE TEMPEST
THE TWO GENTLEMEN OF VERONA
.
.
PERICLES
£MARLOWE
DR. FAUSTUS
etc

The £ sign is used to indicate that the information following it on the same line is a new author and not a continuation of the titles following the previous one. A program could expand the information into

SHAKESPEARE THE TEMPEST
SHAKESPEARE THE TWO GENTLEMEN OF VERONA
.
.
SHAKESPEARE PERICLES
MARLOWE DR. FAUSTUS

Another alternative is to retain the information in a computer file in the format in which it was typed ensuring that the programs which operate on the data always know that this is its format. This economy of storage can be practised if all the information is prepared for the computer at the same time. It would not be suitable for a file which is to be continually updated with more material.

Historical data allows more opportunities for reducing the amount of typing. An example from one of the computer projects at Oxford illustrates the point. The History of the University project has been using the computer to compile indexes of biographical data of students who were at Oxford. Initially the period up to 1500 was covered, but recently more information has been added to the computer files covering the years 1501-1540 for Oxford and up to 1500 for the University of Cambridge, this latter file being used for comparative purposes. In all cases the data was taken from Dr A.B. Emden's Biographical Registers and updated by some of his unpublished records. There are now almost 30,000 biographical records on the computer.

The name of each scholar is accompanied by a number of fields indicating such features as his college, hall, faculty, religious order, place of origin, whether he held any office, etc., as well as an indication of the date when he was present. A number of conventions were used for coding this data which could usefully be adopted by others. A date such as 1428-1435 consists of nine characters. The dates were reduced to two characters, by grouping them into twenty-year periods. 1428-1435 therefore becomes date code 42, by taking the middle two digits of the first date to cover the period 1420-1439. If the scholar was recorded as 1438-1445 he was allocated two date codes 42 and 44, as he comes in two twenty-year periods, 1420-1439 and 1440-1459. It will be noted that this requires two different items to be in the same field. Although some information was lost by this method of coding dates, it did reduce the amount of storage and coding considerably. Such grouping of data into bands of measurements is common practice in many computer applications in the social and biological sciences. It is usually necessary for what is called *continuous data* where the number of possible values is infinite. Such is the case for heights of people where one person may measure 5'6" and another 5'7", but where there may be many heights between these two values. *Discontinuous data* allows only a finite number of values with a fixed interval between them.

In the History's data, information for most of the other fields was compressed for typing, using two-letter codes. There is no need to use only numeric codes in modern computing. Letter codes are much easier to read and understand, and even single letters allow up to twenty-six different codes, whereas single digits allow only ten. Two letter codes allow more possibilities and are also more meaningful. There were seventeen colleges in medieval Oxford and each was represented by two letters as follows

AS	All Souls
BA	Balliol
BE	St Bernard's College
BC	Brasenose
CA	Canterbury College
CC	Corpus Christi
DU	Durham College
EX	Exeter
GL	Gloucester College
LI	Lincoln
MA	Magdalen
MC	St Mary's College
ME	Merton
NE	New College
OR	Oriel
QU	Queen's
UN	University College

Only these codes were typed in the college field. A similar set of codes were used to identify halls, orders, offices, etc. The only two fields which were typed in full were the name of each person and a four-digit identification number.

The best way of preparing such information is to rule out sheets of paper with columns for each field and enter information on these sheets as soon as it is found. This coding process can be very tedious, but it would also be necessary in some form for manual processing. In the History's project, the two letter codes, rather than the full version of the data, were stored in the computer file. This was done to save computer time in searching the file as the quantity of information would be very much larger if it was held in full. The full versions can be printed out by any program which operates on the data simply by substituting the full version for the code every time that it is encountered.

Accuracy of the data is of course essential, but structured data is easier to check, since the computer can be used to find errors which in text can only be found by proof reading. If we consider the example of the History's data again, in the college field there are only seventeen possible two-letter codes. A computer program can be written to check that each code appearing in this field is one of the seventeen possibilities. If it is not, the computer will reject the record as erroneous and it can be corrected. This kind of computer checking will not of course find as an error a valid code which is the wrong one for that record, e.g. MA for Magdalen instead of ME for Merton, but it will find common typing errors such as WU instead of QU for Queen's. A computer program can also be used to check dates to see whether they are in a valid range. This would detect for instance 2977 mistyped for 1977. Sizes, weights and classification of archaeological material can also be checked in this way.

It is more difficult to write a program for the checking of textual information, but it is possible to test some fields. Another project in Oxford, which is compiling a lexicon of Greek personal names, has structured, mainly textual, data and uses a lengthy checking program before new data is added to the computer file. Each name is accompanied by three other fields, the town of the original bearer of the name, his or her date, and a reference to the source document in which the name is preserved. The name itself is transliterated from Greek and this field is checked to ensure that it contains only those characters which exist in the transliterated Greek alphabet and those used to represent diacritics. The name of the town can also be checked in the same way. Permissible dates are in the range 1000 BC to 1000 AD. There are also a number of codings for vague dates, like Hellenistic or Imperial, and a means of denoting which dates refer to centuries rather than exact dates (e.g. a date of the third century BC is typed as 3B and a date of 3BC is typed as 3BC). The towns and names can be checked further by compiling an alphabetical list and visually searching that for any obvious spelling errors. It is not possible to perform any automatic checking on the reference field because it contains very varied information. In this project there should be no missing information, and so the checking program can also ensure that every field is present.

So far we have considered those situations where the field and record format is designed for a specific problem or program and does not conform to any recognised standard. Such a standard does exist for bibliographic material in libraries. It is called MARC, an acronym for MAchine Readable Cataloguing. MARC was devised at the Library of Congress in 1965. Its original format was based on that Library's own catalogue cards. A revised version was introduced in 1968, as a result of collaboration between the British National Bibliography and the Library of Congress, and this format is now the standard for library cataloguing records on magnetic tape. The bodies involved began distributing cataloguing information on magnetic tapes in 1969, and since 1971 the British National Bibliography has been produced by computer typesetting from MARC tapes. There have also been a number of retrospective conversion projects so that libraries could hold their entire catalogue on computer tape, not merely those items which have been added since MARC began.

The British Library Bibliographic Services Division now provides a service of current and retrospective UK and Library of Congress files for subscribers. Requests for individual records can also be met. These are matched against the various MARC files and the appropriate records sent to the library on magnetic tape. MARC records from other countries will be added to the database as they become available. The BLBSD is therefore a valuable source of bibliographic material in computer readable form and a number of computer packages for handling MARC tapes already exist.

The aim of MARC is to communicate bibliographic information between libraries who will use the information in many different ways. For this reason the format of the records is lengthy and complicated, the average size of a UK MARC record being 780 characters. National organisations have each diverged slightly from the international format known as UNIMARC, but they should be able to produce UNIMARC records for international exchange. MARC data fields are variable length. A three digit tag is used to indicate each field and there is also a directory for each record which can be divided into four parts:

1. A label which consists of twenty-four characters and contains standard information such as the length of the record, and status of the record (new, changed, deleted).

2. A directory which gives the length in characters and starting position of each field. An entry appears in the directory for each field in the record with a total of twelve characters for each field.

3. Tags 001-009 are fields which control access to the main record. For example tag 001 is the ISBN or BNB record number of the item.

4. The bibliographic information is contained within variable fields. Each begins with two numeric indicators and ends with a special marker. The information in each field is divided into subfields which are themselves tagged by subfield marker. These variable fields hold a full bibliographic description and subject information under a number of different classification schemes.

Though MARC is much more complicated in format, it should be considered for any bibliography project simply because it has become a recognised standard. Material obtained from elsewhere may easily be incorporated into the data. MARC records are also available for serials, printed music, music monographs and sound recordings, and there are computer programs which will generate MARC records on tape from a much simpler data format.

The method of organising records within a file is fundamental to the efficient access of the data. It can vary from one file to another and may depend on the hardware facilities available for storing it (tape or disc) and also the applications for which it is required. The earliest large information files or *databases* as they are now called were stored on magnetic tape as this was all that was available. Records on magnetic tape can only be accessed in sequence, which is known as *serial access*. It is not very easy to read the tape backwards once the end has been reached though it can be rewound to the beginning. Data which is stored on tape is therefore organised so that one pass, or at most two, is all that is required by one program. Winding a tape backwards and forwards several times in the same program soon wears out the tape, and it makes very inefficient use of computer resources. On tape, then, each record appears in serial order, and as in our Shakespeare example above information which occurs in many records is repeated in all the records. Such a file would usually be in alphabetic or numeric order of one or more of the fields. If more records are to be added to the file, they are first sorted into the same format and this small file then merged with the larger one. Some files are so large that they may occupy several 2400 foot tapes.

When discs first became available, they were frequently used as if they were tapes so that records were only accessed serially. This was mostly because programs were already written to operate in this way and because tapes, which are much cheaper, could easily be used instead if the data file grew too big to be held on disc. The advantages of disc-based storage soon became apparent, for the data can be accessed much faster. It is no longer stored as a very long sequence where it is necessary to read everything up to the section which is required. In *random access* files an index or directory of keys is used to point to the appropriate records in the file. The computer searches the index to find out where a particular data element is stored and then finds that place on disc immediately without having to read all the preceding records first. Records on disc may still be stored serially to facilitate operations which require a complete pass of the file, such as finding the average weight of pottery. Files organised in this way are called *indexed sequential* files.

Recently new methods of data storage have been devised and the term database technology has become increasingly used in computing. A modern database moves away from the ideas of serial or sequential files completely. Information, though conventionally viewed as records and fields, is presented to the computer as a series of sets of related information. A master item such as our Shakespeare will appear only once in the database but will 'own' a number of sub-records, those of all the titles of the plays. The items are linked by a series of pointers which indicate where the 'owned' records are stored on disc. The records can be interrelated in many different ways and a very complicated network of pointers established. The total amount of storage required is much less than for a serial file, as normally data which appears in many different fields is stored only once in the database. When new records are added to the file containing the same item, another pointer in the chain is set up. These databases can of course only be held on disc.

Modern databases therefore require very complicated programming to organise the data. Many computer manufacturers are now providing computer packages for this purpose, and the computer user is freed from any data organisational programs. He merely has to define his data in terms of the database management program and then may concentrate entirely on using the data for various applications. One such package is called IDMS (Integrated Database Management System). It allows the user to write programs in COBOL or FORTRAN, which view the data in the conventional record and field format without consideration of how it is stored on disc. IDMS has many applications in the commercial world where most computing consists of processing very large structured files such as personnel records, bank accounts and stock holdings. It is equally relevant to the needs of arts researchers and could also be used for MARC records.

Material held in a disc-based file can be updated very easily, usually by a terminal operating interactively. A file held on magnetic tape must be updated by a special program which copies it to another tape with the amendments inserted at the appropriate place. For the sake of security, the old file is usually retained, giving rise to the 'grandfather, father, son' concept of keeping old versions of the data. When new information is added to create a new 'son', the last but two version of the file, the new 'son's' 'great-grandfather' is discarded, leaving only the previous two versions to be retained.

Now that we have seen how information can be coded and stored in a file, we can examine some of the operations which can be performed on it. In brief, everything which can be done with the traditional file card system can be done using a computer, but in addition the computer allows the data to be sorted into alphabetical order according to many different criteria very rapidly. Several files of the same data may be kept sorted according to different fields. The sorting procedures are very similar to those used for concordance programs. Several fields can be considered in the sorting process and if two records are found to have the same information in one field, other fields can be compared until the records are assigned to the correct order.

Many computer packages exist which can make indexes and catalogues, and the sorting procedures required by them are some of the most widely used processes in computing. One of the commonest indexing packages in universities is called FAMULUS and it serves as a useful example for textual data. FAMULUS was developed at the South West and Forest Range Experiment Station in Berkeley, California, in the late 1960s and now runs on several kinds of computers. It is a collection of programs which are used to create, maintain, sort and print files of structured textual information. Up to ten variable-length records are allowed for each record. Each record must of course be described by the same fields, though information may be missing for some fields. Each field is assigned a four-character tag or label chosen by the user, which is typed before the information for that field when the data is first input to FAMULUS. The format of the input data requires that each field should be on a separate card and that there should be a blank card or line to separate each record. This is rather wasteful of typing time because of the repetition of the field labels, and also wasteful of cards if they are being used as the input medium. It is better to choose a more compact form of data entry and write a small program to convert it into the format required for FAMULUS. In the following example it is assumed that * and £ will never appear anywhere in the data and so * is used to separate the fields, whose labels are not typed, and £ to indicate the end of the record.

EXPLORING WALES*CONDRY, WILLIAM*FABER*LONDON*1970*0 571 09922*MAPS: WELSH PLACE N
AMES;GLOSSARY;NATURE RESERVES;INDEX;BLACK AND WHITE PHOTOS£
BRITAIN'S HERITAGE 1973**AUTOMOBILE ASSOCIATION*LONDON*1972**GAZETTEER;INDEX BY
COUNTY;BIOGRAPHIES;ATLAS;MAPS;DESIGN OF BUILDINGS£

Expanded into FAMULUS format these records would become

```
TITL    EXPLORING WALES
AUTH    CONDRY, WILLIAM
PUB     FABER
LOC     LONDON
DATE    1970
ISBN    0 571 09922
ADD     MAPS:WELSH PLACE NAMES;GLOSSARY;NATURE RESERVES;INDEX;BLACK AND WHITE PHOTO
        S

TITL    BRITAIN'S HERITAGE
PUB     AUTOMOBILE ASSOCIATION
LOC     LONDON
DATE    1972
ADD     GAZETTEER;INDEX BY COUNTY;BIOGRAPHIES;ATLAS;MAPS;DESIGN OF BUILDINGS
```

A program has added the field labels TITL, AUTH, PUB, etc, to the information which now appears as one field per line. FAMULUS expects to read data from eighty-character cards and the single S on the last line of the first record shows how it expects to find continuation cards. In the second record the fields AUTH and ISBN are missing. In the data input this was indicated by two successive asterisks. The ADD field contains a series of index terms, separated by semicolons. It will be seen that some of these terms consist of several words. These are what FAMULUS calls descriptor terms, and it is possible to make an index of them by indicating to the computer that the semi-colon is used to delimit them.

FAMULUS can deal with cross-references rather neatly. Suppose we wanted to make a cross-reference for the term BLACK AND WHITE PHOTOS in the ADD field of the first record above so that it would also appear under PHOTOS. We could create an extra record for FAMULUS consisting of

TITL   SEE BLACK AND WHITE PHOTOS
ADD   PHOTOS

An index of terms in the ADD field using the TITL field as subsidiary information would print

PHOTOS
    SEE BLACK AND WHITE PHOTOS

thus creating the appropriate cross-reference.

FAMULUS maintains its information in a serial disc file which is created by one of the programs in the package. Each record is assigned a unique number in ascending order as it is added to the file. The field labels are recorded once in a special record at the beginning of the file and not with each record. Instead a small directory is present at the beginning of each record to indicate which fields are present and where they begin and end in the record.

A file of many records can be sorted into alphabetical order of publisher, by author or date or any other field, if required. FAMULUS can print the indexes or catalogues in a catalogue-type format where the key-entry is off-set to the left and is not repeated for subsequent entries until a new key term is found. Such a simple author catalogue for a few travel books is shown in Figure 9.1. The file can be rapidly inverted to make a publisher catalogue as shown in Figure 9.2 or again by date as in figure 9.3. A simple index of the ADD terms merely indicates the number of the record in which they occur, but using another FAMULUS program called MULTIPLY the file can be expanded to hold one complete entry for each subject term and a complete subject catalogue produced. MULTIPLYing our first example on the ADD field would give us six records. The first two will suffice to indicate the results.

```
TITL    EXPLORING WALES
AUTH    CONDRY, WILLIAM
PUB     FABER
LOC     LONDON
DATE    1970
ISBN    0 571 09922
ADD     MAPS

TITL    EXPLORING WALES
AUTH    CONDRY, WILLIAM
PUB     FABER
LOC     LONDON
DATE    1970
ISBN    0 571 09922
ADD     WELSH PLACE NAMES
```

Part of a subject index of ADD terms with the author, title and publisher as subsidiary fields is shown in Figure 9.4.

FAMULUS can also produce a keyword in context (KWIC) index of any field. A KWIC index of all titles will help a reader to find a book or article if he is not sure of the exact title. The KWIC index is really a concordance as can be seen from Figure 9.5. Common words like 'and' and 'the', etc., have been omitted as they are of no use for this purpose. A KWIC index may be compiled with a *stop-list* specifying all the words not required or with a *go-*

ANDERSON, J R L

   THE UPPER THAMES   EYRE METHUEN 1974

ANDERSON, J R L AND GODWIN, FAY

   THE OLDEST ROAD: AN EXPLORATION OF THE RIDGEWAY WILDWOOD HOUSE 1975

BECKINSALE, R

   COMPANION INTO BERKSHIRE SPURBOOKS 1970

BORROW, GEORGE

   WILD WALES: ITS PEOPLE, LANGUAGE AND SCENERY JOHN MURRAY 1905

CLIFTON-TAYLOR, ALEC

   THE CATHEDRALS OF ENGLAND THAMES AND HUDSON 1967

CONDRY, WILLIAM

   EXPLORING WALES FABER 1970

DARLING, F FRASER AND BOYD, J MORTON

   THE HIGHLANDS AND ISLANDS FONTANA 1971

DYER, JAMES

   SOUTHERN ENGLAND: AN ARCHAEOLOGICAL GUIDE: THE PREHISTORIC AND ROMAN REMAINS FABER 1973

EDLIN, H (ED)

   DEAN FOREST AND WYE VALLEY HMSO 1956

JOURNEY THROUGH BRITAIN   PALADIN   1972

PHILIPSON, JOHN (ED)

  NORTHUMBERLAND NATIONAL PARK   HMSO   1969

PIEHLER, H A

  ENGLAND FOR EVERYMAN   DENT   1970

PIPER, DAVID

  THE COMPANION GUIDE TO LONDON   FONTANA   1970

RICHMOND, I A

  ROMAN BRITAIN   PENGUIN   1970

SIMMONS, I G (ED)

  YORKSHIRE DALES NATIONAL PARK   HMSO   1971

STAMP, L DUDLEY

  BRITAIN'S STRUCTURE AND SCENERY   FONTANA   1972

TRUEMAN, A F (REVISED BY WHITTOW, J B AND HARDY, J R)

  GEOLOGY AND SCENERY IN ENGLAND AND WALES   PENGUIN   1971

WILSON, ROGER J A

  A GUIDE TO THE ROMAN REMAINS IN BRITAIN   CONSTABLE   1975

Figure 9.1. An author catalogue produced by FAMULUS.

AUTOMOBILE ASSOCIATION

    BRITAIN'S HERITAGE 1973 1972

    ILLUSTRATED GUIDE TO BRITAIN 1971

    ILLUSTRATED ROAD BOOK OF SCOTLAND 1974

CONSTABLE

    WILSON, ROGER J A A GUIDE TO THE ROMAN REMAINS IN BRITAIN 1975

DARTON, LONGMAN AND TODD

    SOUTH-WEST WALES

DENT

    PIEHLER, H A ENGLAND FOR EVERYMAN 1970

EYRE METHUEN

    ANDERSON, J R L THE UPPER THAMES 1974

FABER

    CONDRY, WILLIAM EXPLORING WALES 1970

    DYER, JAMES SOUTHERN ENGLAND: AN ARCHAEOLOGICAL GUIDE: THE PREHISTORIC AND ROMAN REMAINS 1973

FONTANA

    DARLING, F FRASER AND BOYD, J MORTON THE HIGHLANDS AND ISLANDS 1971

    PIPER, DAVID THE COMPANION GUIDE TO LONDON 1970

    STAMP, L DUDLEY BRITAIN'S STRUCTURE AND SCENERY 1972

GEOGRAPHIA

DEVON: COAST, COUNTRYSIDE, FOREST AND MOORS

NORTHUMBRIA: DURHAM AND NORTHUMBERLAND

HMSO

    EDLIN, H (ED) DEAN FOREST AND WYE VALLEY 1956

    EDLIN, H (ED) NEW FOREST 1969

    PHILIPSON, JOHN (ED) NORTHUMBERLAND NATIONAL PARK 1969

    SIMMONS, I G (ED) YORKSHIRE DALES NATIONAL PARK 1971

JOHN MURRAY

    BORROW, GEORGE WILD WALES: ITS PEOPLE, LANGUAGE AND SCENERY 1905

PALADIN

    HILLABY, JOHN JOURNEY THROUGH BRITAIN 1972

PENGUIN

    RICHMOND, I A ROMAN BRITAIN 1970

    TRUEMAN, A E (REVISED BY WHITTOW, J B AND HARDY, J R) GEOLOGY AND SCENERY IN ENGLAND AND WALES 1971

SPURBOOKS

    BECKINSALE, R COMPANION INTO BERKSHIRE 1970

THAMES AND HUDSON

    CLIFTON-TAYLOR, ALEC THE CATHEDRALS OF ENGLAND 1967

WILDWOOD HOUSE

    ANDERSON, J R L AND GODWIN, FAY THE OLDEST ROAD: AN EXPLORATION OF THE RIDGEWAY 1975

Figure 9.2. A publisher catalogue produced by FAMULUS

1905

BORROW, GEORGE   WILD WALES: ITS PEOPLE, LANGUAGE AND SCENERY   JOHN MURRAY

1956

EDLIN, H (ED)   DEAN FOREST AND WYE VALLEY   HMSO

1967

CLIFTON-TAYLOR, ALEC   THE CATHEDRALS OF ENGLAND   THAMES AND HUDSON

1969

EDLIN, H (ED)   NEW FOREST   HMSO

PHILIPSON, JOHN (ED)   NORTHUMBERLAND NATIONAL PARK   HMSO

1970

BECKINSALE, R   COMPANION INTO BERKSHIRE   SPURBOOKS

CONDRY, WILLIAM   EXPLORING WALES   FABER

PIEHLER, H A   ENGLAND FOR EVERYMAN   DENT

PIPER, DAVID   THE COMPANION GUIDE TO LONDON   FONTANA

RICHMOND, I A   ROMAN BRITAIN   PENGUIN

1971

ILLUSTRATED GUIDE TO BRITAIN   AUTOMOBILE ASSOCIATION

DARLING, F FRASER AND BOYD, J MORTON   THE HIGHLANDS AND ISLANDS   FONTANA

SIMMONS, I G (ED)   YORKSHIRE DALES NATIONAL PARK   HMSO

TRUEMAN, A E (REVISED BY WHITTOW, J B AND HARDY, J R)   GEOLOGY AND SCENERY IN ENGLAND AND WALES   PENGUIN

1972

BRITAIN'S HERITAGE 1973   AUTOMOBILE ASSOCIATION

HILLABY, JOHN   JOURNEY THROUGH BRITAIN   PALADIN

STAMP, L DUDLEY   BRITAIN'S STRUCTURE AND SCENERY   FONTANA

1973

DYER, JAMES   SOUTHERN ENGLAND: AN ARCHAEOLOGICAL GUIDE: THE PREHISTORIC AND ROMAN REMAINS   FABER

1974

ILLUSTRATED ROAD BOOK OF SCOTLAND   AUTOMOBILE ASSOCIATION

ANDERSON, J R L   THE UPPER THAMES   EYRE METHUEN

1975

ANDERSON, J R L AND GODWIN, FAY   THE OLDEST ROAD: AN EXPLORATION OF THE RIDGEWAY   WILDWOOD HOUSE

WILSON, ROGER J A   A GUIDE TO THE ROMAN REMAINS IN BRITAIN   CONSTABLE

Figure 9.3. A catalogue sorted by date produced by FAMULUS

CHURCHES

THE COMPANION GUIDE TO LONDON PIPER, DAVID FONTANA

COLOUR PHOTOS

ILLUSTRATED GUIDE TO BRITAIN AUTOMOBILE ASSOCIATION

COLOUR PLATES

THE CATHEDRALS OF ENGLAND CLIFTON-TAYLOR, ALEC THAMES AND HUDSON

DESIGN OF BUILDINGS

BRITAIN'S HERITAGE 1973 AUTOMOBILE ASSOCIATION

DRAWINGS

BRITAIN'S STRUCTURE AND SCENERY STAMP, L DUDLEY FONTANA

DEAN FOREST AND WYE VALLEY EDLIN, H (ED) HMSO

ILLUSTRATED ROAD BOOK OF SCOTLAND AUTOMOBILE ASSOCIATION

NEW FOREST EDLIN, H (ED) HMSO

NORTHUMBERLAND NATIONAL PARK PHILIPSON, JOHN (ED) HMSO

ROMAN BRITAIN RICHMOND, I A PENGUIN

SOUTHERN ENGLAND: AN ARCHAEOLOGICAL GUIDE: THE PREHISTORIC AND ROMAN REMAINS DYER, JAMES FABER

WILD WALES: ITS PEOPLE, LANGUAGE AND SCENERY BORROW, GEORGE JOHN MURRAY

GAELIC PLACE NAMES

   ILLUSTRATED ROAD BOOK OF SCOTLAND   AUTOMOBILE ASSOCIATION

GAZETTEER

   BRITAIN'S HERITAGE 1973   AUTOMOBILE ASSOCIATION

   DEVON: COAST, COUNTRYSIDE, FOREST AND MOORS   GEOGRAPHIA

   A GUIDE TO THE ROMAN REMAINS IN BRITAIN   WILSON, ROGER J A   CONSTABLE

   ILLUSTRATED ROAD BOOK OF SCOTLAND   AUTOMOBILE ASSOCIATION

   NORTHUMBERLAND NATIONAL PARK   PHILIPSON, JOHN (ED)   HMSO

   NORTHUMBRIA: DURHAM AND NORTHUMBERLAND   GEOGRAPHIA

   SOUTH-WEST WALES   DARTON, LONGMAN AND TODD

   THE UPPER THAMES   ANDERSON, J R L   EYRE METHUEN

   YORKSHIRE DALES NATIONAL PARK   SIMMONS, I G (ED)   HMSO

GLOSSARY

   EXPLORING WALES   CONDRY, WILLIAM   FABER

   ILLUSTRATED ROAD BOOK OF SCOTLAND   AUTOMOBILE ASSOCIATION

   SOUTHERN ENGLAND: AN ARCHAEOLOGICAL GUIDE: THE PREHISTORIC AND ROMAN REMAINS   DYER, JAMES   FABER

Figure 9.4. Part of a subject index with author, title and publisher as subsidiary fields.

SOUTHERN ENGLAND: AN ARCHAEOLOGICAL GUIDE: THE PREHISTORIC AND ROMAN REMAINS

COMPANION INTO BERKSHIRE

ILLUSTRATED ROAD BOOK OF SCOTLAND

ILLUSTRATED GUIDE TO BRITAIN
JOURNEY THROUGH BRITAIN
ROMAN BRITAIN
A GUIDE TO THE ROMAN REMAINS IN BRITAIN

BRITAIN'S HERITAGE 1973
BRITAIN'S STRUCTURE AND SCENERY

THE CATHEDRALS OF ENGLAND

DEVON: COAST, COUNTRYSIDE, FOREST AND MOORS

THE COMPANION GUIDE TO LONDON
COMPANION INTO BERKSHIRE

DEVON: COAST, COUNTRYSIDE, FOREST AND MOORS

YORKSHIRE DALES NATIONAL PARK

DEAN FOREST AND WYE VALLEY

```
                                    DEVON: COAST, COUNTRYSIDE, FOREST AND MOORS

                       NORTHUMBRIA: DURHAM AND NORTHUMBERLAND

                  THE CATHEDRALS OF ENGLAND
             GEOLOGY AND SCENERY IN ENGLAND AND WALES
                                    ENGLAND FOR EVERYMAN
                           SOUTHERN ENGLAND: AN ARCHAEOLOGICAL GUIDE; THE PREHISTORIC AND ROMAN R

                        ENGLAND FOR EVERYMAN

                THE OLDEST ROAD: AN EXPLORATION OF THE RIDGEWAY

                                    EXPLORING WALES

                                NEW FOREST
         DEVON: COAST, COUNTRYSIDE, FOREST AND MOORS
                               DEAN FOREST AND WYE VALLEY

                                    GEOLOGY AND SCENERY IN ENGLAND AND WALES

                        ILLUSTRATED GUIDE TO BRITAIN
                      THE COMPANION GUIDE TO LONDON
                                  A GUIDE TO THE ROMAN REMAINS IN BRITAIN
SOUTHERN ENGLAND: AN ARCHAEOLOGICAL GUIDE; THE PREHISTORIC AND ROMAN REMAINS
```

Figure 9.5. Part of a KWIC index of book titles produced by FAMULUS. Common words have been omitted.

list specifying only those which are required.

Any indexes or catalogues produced by FAMULUS can be computer-typeset for publication rather than be presented in lineprinter symbols. If the output format is not appropriate, it is much easier to write a small program to change the layout of a sorted file rather than attempt to do the sorting oneself.

FAMULUS is an indexing program which creates and maintains files of sorted indexes. It does not decide which terms are to be included in the indexes. Automatic indexing and abstracting of documents is a very different matter which has attracted much interest recently. This in effect requires a parsing program, similar to those used in machine translation, to analyse the meaning of a document and abstract the most significant information from it. It must then generate an intelligible abstract which faithfully represents the meaning of the original document. One such system called LOUISA is an indexing system which deals only with abstracts. It uses a comprehensive dictionary, together with rules for concatenation, disambiguation and amalgamation, in an attempt to produce index terms and paraphrases of abstracts. It is arguable whether this is yet economic, but the volume of material now being published makes such research inevitable, particularly for indexing and abstracting technical material.

The computer can only be of marginal help in compiling an index to a book for publication. If the whole work is in machine readable form, the computer can produce an index of all the words, but even if the list is reduced to a manageable size by a comprehensive stop-list, the human must decide which entries are useful. A better method of using a computer in compiling a book index is one which was adopted for this book. The text was read, and, as items for inclusion in the index were found, they were typed into the computer together with the page number and any other subsidiary information. The computer was only used to sort and file the entries.

For compiling cumulative indexes it is necessary to use a thesaurus of known terms or controlled vocabulary. The computer then keeps a record of the allowable index terms, possibly including synonyms. All the different forms of one lemma can thus be reduced to one term, e.g. EXPLORE could stand for EXPLORATION, EXPLORING, etc. Most indexes which are made for cumulative publication keep such thesauri, updating them as new terms are encountered. It must not be forgotten that the computer only does the mechanical part of such an indexing process. It cannot decide what to put in the index. Some such indexing projects have been known to go astray because too much was being expected of the computer and not enough of the human.

Many recent bibliographies have been compiled with the help of a computer. Packard and Meyer's Homer bibliography is one example. Two advantages in using a computer in this way are that information which is already in computer readable form can be updated much more easily and that the material is then ready for computer typesetting. Such bibliographies are now so commonplace that they rarely warrant publication of the method used. One exception is a bibliography of Scottish poetry being compiled at South Carolina, which expects to include over 15,000 entries. As the aim of the project was to compile a good literary bibliography which required a detailed description of each book, fourteen fields were used, and these differed from those in a library information system. The fourteen fields consisted of two main categories. In the first were those concerned with the author such as his epithet and dates, as well as biographical and bibliographic references. The book itself can occupy up to ten fields. Apart from the usual title-page information, the editor's name is added if appropriate; also the number of pages or volumes and the name of at least one library which holds a copy of the book. One additional field is reserved for any other useful information, such as the format of books printed before 1800. In the final printout the author's name will appear only once, followed by the author fields and then by all the references attributed to him.

Another indexing project at the Oxford Centre for Postgraduate Hebrew Studies uses FAMULUS to compile subject indexes to a collection of Hebrew periodicals dating between the French Revolution and the First World War. These periodicals cover a period of upheaval in the Jewish world and for that reason are important to students of Jewish history and Hebrew language and literature. The indexes are intended to serve as guides to the contents of the periodicals. For this reason articles may be listed under many headings ranging from the vague such as 'Hebrew literature' to detailed descriptions of the contents. For each periodical it is planned to make a table of contents on the lines of the Wellesley Index to Victorian Periodicals. In the table each article is assigned an identification number which is used to refer to that article in the indexes rather than using the complete bibliographic reference.

For each article up to eight categories were allowed. Apart from the identification number, author and title, a second more specific title was assigned if the main title was vague or gave little indication of the subject matter. Four types of keywords were used. The first keyword field holds keywords associated with the main title. These keywords then appeared in the main subject index with the main title as subsidiary information underneath. The second title if present also has a series of keywords associated with it. A third category of keywords was also allowed which contain much wider terms such as 'poetry' or 'biography'. Three separate keyword indexes are first compiled of all three categories of keywords.

These three indexes can then be merged to form a master subject index. A final category is reserved for keywords which are in Latin characters. This is used to make a supplementary index for such items as European books reviewed and discussed in Hebrew journals.

This project illustrates how several different kinds of indexes can be made using a simple package like FAMULUS. It was felt initially that the limitation of only ten fields would prove insurmountable if all the bibliographical reference for the article was to be included in the index. The Table of Contents with its reference number proved to be a neat solution to this problem. The indexes are not cluttered with long bibliographical details and the table can be used to browse through the contents of a journal. If a user is only interested in a particular period, he need only inspect that part.

In many applications both inside and outside the academic world, the computer can also be used to search files of information to find all those records which satisfy specific search criteria. This process is known as *information retrieval* and it is usual to specify which field or fields are to be inspected. The computer will then pass through the whole file and print out only those records which have the required information in that field or fields. A simple search will specify only one request but it is however usually possible to combine requests to make them more specific using Boolean operators AND, OR and NOT with the following connotations:

AND A record will be retrieved if it contains all of the terms linked by AND
OR A record will be retrieved if it contains any of the terms linked by OR
NOT A record will be retrieved if it does not contain the term following NOT

It is often possible to link many terms together with a combination of Boolean operators. Sometimes brackets are needed so that the request is not ambiguous. Consider the following search request:

LOUVRE AND MONET OR MANET

As it stands this request is ambiguous. It is not clear whether the first term is LOUVRE and the second MONET OR MANET or whether the first is LOUVRE AND MONET and the second just MANET. A computer would interpret it as the latter. To ensure that it is correctly understood, brackets should be inserted as follows

LOUVRE AND (MONET OR MANET)

This would ensure that both terms within the brackets are connected to LOUVRE by logical AND.

Most computers have a standard package to perform retrievals on structured files. Some may be oriented towards textual data, while others provide for both textual and numerical data. One such package called FIND2 operates in ICL 1900 computers and is used for the History of the University's project in Oxford which was described earlier in this chapter. This package allows several fields to be specified in the search request. The computer may be asked such questions as 'Who were all the scholars who read theology at Merton between 1400 and 1460?' It will search the entire file and print out indexes of all the records which satisfy the request. In this case three fields, faculty, college and date would be inspected and the record only retrieved if it satisfied all the request. Not all of each 'hit' record need be printed out. The user may specify which fields are to be printed for those records found and the others will be omitted. Figure 9.6 shows an example of FIND2 printout showing scholars at Magdalen in the period 1440-1459, that is, at the time of its foundation.

By extracting data from the raw material in this way the History of the University project has been able to analyse comprehensively the distribution of scholars among the colleges of the University, which colleges attracted the students of particular subjects, and (so far as the raw material allows) the geographical origins of scholars. By varying the dates specified in the search requests it has been a relatively simple matter to repeat these studies on different periods of the University history, so that a picture of the changes in the scholarly population of medieval Oxford has been built up. The volume of the raw material is such that it would have been totally impractical to produce such analyses without the assistance of the computer.

The computer can also be asked to transfer those records which have been found to another file, for example if further searches are to be performed on that part of the data. This saves computer time as a smaller number of records is then searched. It can also merely count how many records satisfy a search request and not print them out. If the number is too large, the search can be modified using Boolean operators in the hope that fewer records will be found the next time. For numerical data all those records which have a value greater or less than a specific value in one field can be retrieved. There are six different relationships between numerical values. They are usually (but not in FIND2) abbreviated as follows:

EQ   equal to
NE   not equal to
LT   less than
LE   less than or equal to
GT   greater than
GE   greater than or equal to

Note the difference between LT and LE and between GT and GE. These relationships can also be combined with the logical operators to find values within or outside a particular range.

Information retrieval is a very common use of computers for all kinds of data, and there are many archeological and historical examples to illustrate its use in the humanities. In the simplest case, the record is retrieved if the search term matches the whole of the field inspected. Sometimes when there are several fixed-length entries in one field the computer is instructed to move along the field in steps of so many characters until it has either found a 'hit' or exhausted the field. Such a request is performed on the History of the University's file to look for colleges, faculties and dates as there can be several entries in these fields. For example, since all the colleges are entered as two-character codes in the same field, the computer is instructed to move on two characters at a time through this field as it searches for the one or ones required.

The retrieval of textual information is more complicated. It is usual for search terms to consist of complete words and for them to be found anywhere within a field or fields. Some programs permit a search for all the words which begin with a series of letters by specifying a truncation character. E.g. RESID* would find all the words which begin with the letters RESID. This may be intended to find all records concerned with *reside* and *residence*, but it could also produce unwanted material like *residue*. Synonyms must also be considered when searching text, which is one reason why a database of textual material usually has a thesaurus associated with it. This contains the terms which are to be included in the search request and the user may spend some time studying it before formulating a request.

Even so, a search may produce some information which is not relevant and it may miss some which is relevant. These two factors are known as precision and recall and can be measured as percentages as follows:

$$\text{precision} = \frac{\text{number of relevant references retrieved}}{\text{total number of references retrieved}} \times 100$$

$$\text{recall} = \frac{\text{number of relevant references retrieved}}{\text{total number of relevant references in database}} \times 100$$

SCHOLARS AT MAGDALEN COLLEGE 1440-1459

NAME	DATECODE	FACULTY	COLLEGE
BERNYS, RICHARD	444648		MA
CALTHORPE, ROBERT	44		MA
COLLYS, JOHN	4446	TH	LIMA
FISHER, HENRY	44		MA
FORMAN, JOHN	44		MA
LAUGHARNE, RICHARD	4446		MA
LAUGHTON, WILLIAM	42444648	TH	MALI
LUPTON, EDWARD	4446	TH	MA
MAYEW, RICHARD	44464850	TH	NEMA
NEFLE, JOHN	4446	TH	MA
PASLEW, THOMAS	44	CN	MA
PRESTON, JAMES	4446	TH	MA
ROWSE, ROBERT	4446	TH	MALI
SALTER, RICHARD	44464850	AJ	ASMA
TIBARD, WILLIAM	424446	TH	MA
TULLY, ROBERT	4446	TH	GLMA
UNDERWOOD, EDWARD	4446	TH	MA
WAYNFLETE, WILLIAM	4244	TH	MA

Figure 9.6. Printout from FIND2 which has retrieved all scholars at Magdalen College in the period 1440-1459.

The two measures are inversely related to each other. The only way to measure recall is to check the database and count the number of relevant references manually. Experiments to compare computer and human information retrievals have shown that the computer is much more successful than the human at finding information, but its precision is not so good.

In the early days of computing, retrieval was performed as a batch process. A number of requests were prepared and submitted as a job to the computer, and the results were printed out later. Nowadays it is common to search a database interactively from a terminal. The advantage of immediate response enables the user to redefine the search many times before he is finally satisfied. He may ask for some of the retrieved records to be printed at the terminal. If these are satisfactory all of them can then be printed on the lineprinter.

A number of commercial organisations provide bibliographical services for searching abstracts and indexes on a computer file. Most of these databases are designed for scientists and social scientists. The best known one is MEDLINE, the database of medical publications operated from the National Library of Medicine, Washington D.C., which was originally called MEDLARS. Lockheed of California also offer over thirty databases of mostly scientific publications on their DIALOG® service. Recently three historical databases have become available for computer searching, and it is anticipated that these services will be expanded to cover more arts-based subjects. Access to the database is provided to all libraries and other information services, who pay a subscription in addition to the cost of individual searches. The response time is very quick, some seven seconds to find over 4000 articles. Though technically these databases can be searched by a novice, it is usual to have an operator who is trained in their use. The search terms are first found from a printed thesaurus before any contact is made with the computer. The operator knows roughly how many references are likely to be found and can help a user to construct a fruitful set of terms which find a manageable number of references.

There are a number of computer packages which can search textual material on-line, and these usually include programs which set up and update the database. When the database is changed, an alphabetical list of meaningful words is created which contains references indicating where the words occur in the documents. When the user makes an initial query on-line, the computer will use this index, which can be searched rapidly as it is in alphabetical order, to give a count of the occurrences of the term. The user may then need to refine the request several times before he is satisfied, and then the document references or the entire documents may be printed at the terminal. Some retrieval programs may help the user by retaining a list of common synonyms or by providing a facility for building up files of frequently used requests. The programs may also contain messages to assist the user if he cannot remember which instruction to issue next.

Among the earliest users of such computer packages were lawyers who need to search through vast amounts of statute and case law to find information relevant to a particular case. Subsequent programs have been designed with their needs in mind, though there is no reason why they should not be used for historical or other documents. STATUS, written at the Atomic Energy Research Establishment, Harwell, is one example. It was originally designed to search those statutes relevant to atomic energy but has subsequently been used for a number of different applications, including Council of Europe legislation in both English and French. Another similar program was written at Queen's University, Belfast. The original version of it was called BIRD, but it is now marketed by ICL's software company Dataskil as QUOBIRD. An experimental version of it called QUILL exists for research purposes in universities.

The most recent attempts at on-line retrieval systems allow complete freedom of input from the user. Since the user's request is formulated as the user wishes, not as the computer is programmed to expect, the program must incorporate a natural language parser, which must be quite complex even for simple requests. Such a system is being developed at the Institut für Deutsche Sprache, Mannheim, initially in connection with a project for the Stuttgart Water Board. The parser is however intended to be used with other databases and is therefore sufficiently comprehensive. An approach of this kind enables anyone to use the computer system at a cost of the extra time spent in parsing the request, but it is debatable whether it is worth the extra effort.

In this chapter I have attempted to show how the computer can be used in the manipulation of structured material. These operations are performed very frequently in computing in the commercial world. A file of personnel records and a file of bibliographical data are very similar in nature, and similar operations will be performed on them. Both will be sorted into alphabetical or numerical order according to various fields and both will be searched for records which satisfy certain criteria. There exist very many programs which can sort and search these files. Though they may not satisfy your needs exactly, every computer manufacturer produces software for commercial applications, as that is where most of their customers are. As in the case of FIND2, it may be found to be just as useful for the arts user.

218 *Computer Applications in the Humanities*

REFERENCES

1. T.H. Aston, Oxford's Medieval Alumni. *Past and Present* 74 (1977) 3-40

2. G.L.M. Berry-Rogghe and M. Kolvenbach, *The Automatic Generation of Lexicon Entries for a Natural Language Analyser.* Paper presented at the Third International Conference on Computing in the Humanities, Waterloo (1977)

3. John Bing and Trygve Harvold, *Legal Decisions and Information Systems.* Oslo: Universitetsforlaget (1977)

4. Eric H. Boehm, The Data Bank of the American Bibliographical Center-Clio Press. *Computers and the Humanities* 9 (1975) 299-302

5. I.F. Croall, R.P.L. Jones and J.P. Scanlon, *Status II Full Text Information Retrieval System User Guide.* Harwell: AERE (1976)

6. Susan M. Hockey, *FAMULUS on the 1906A.* Chilton: Atlas Computer Laboratory (1975)

7. Susan M. Hockey, Alan Jones and George Mandel, Indexing Hebrew Periodicals with the Aid of the FAMULUS Documentation System. *The Computer in Literary and Linguistic Studies (Proceedings of the Third International Symposium),* 38-46 (eds Alan Jones and R.F. Churchhouse). Cardiff: University of Wales Press (1976)

8. International Computers Ltd., *FIND2 Multiple Enquiry System TP 4187.* London: ICL Technical Publications Service (1969)

9. International Computers Ltd., *MARC TP4268.* London: ICL Technical Publications Service (1972)

10. A. Michiels, J. Mullenders and J. Noel, Automatic Skimming: The LOUISA System. *ALLC Bull.* 5 (1977) 2-14

11. B. Niblett and N.H. Price, Mechanised Searching of Acts of Parliament. *Information Storage and Retrieval* 6 (1970) 289-97

12. C.D. Paice, *Information Retrieval and the Computer.* London: Macdonald and Janes (1977)

13. N.H. Price, C. Bye and B. Niblett, *On-Line Searching of Council of Europe Conventions and Agreements: A Study in Bilingual Document Retrieval.* Harwell: UKAEA Report No. AERE R7663 (1974)

14. G.R. Roy, R.L. Oakman and A.C. Gillon, A Computerised Bibliography of Scottish Poetry. *Computers in the Humanities,* 168-74. (ed. J.L. Mitchell). Edinburgh: Edinburgh University Press (1974)

15. Colin Tapper, *Computers and the Law.* London: Weidenfeld and Nicholson (1973)

16. L.A. Tedd, *An Introduction to Computer-Based Library Systems.* London: Heyden (1977)

Further Reading

J.E. Doran and F.R. Hodson, *Mathematics and Computers in Archaeology*. Edinburgh: Edinburgh University Press (1975)

F.R. Hodson, D.G. Kendall and P. Tautu (eds), *Mathematics in the Archaeological and Historical Sciences*. Edinburgh: Edinburgh University Press (1971)

James H. Levitt and Claude E. Labarre, Building a Data File from Historical Archives. *Computers and the Humanities* 9 (1975) 77-82

B.R. Schneider, Jr., Analysis of a Database for Information Retrieval: The London Stage 1660-1800. *The Computer and Literary Studies*, 275-82 (eds A.J. Aitken, R.W. Bailey and N. Hamilton-Smith). Edinburgh: Edinburgh University Press (1973)

Edward Shorter, *The Historian and the Computer*. Englewood Cliffs: Prentice-Hall (1971)

G.P. Zarri, Sur le Traitement Automatique de Données Biographiques Médiévales: Le Project RESEDA. *Computing in the Humanities*, 151-61 (eds Serge Lusignan and John S. North). Waterloo: University of Waterloo Press (1977)

Periodicals

Aslib Proceedings
Information Storage and Retrieval
Journal of Documentation
Program
VINE (Very Informal Newsletter on Library Automation)

10. How to Start a Project

We have now covered the major areas of computer usage in the humanities and it should be possible for the reader to decide whether the computer can be of any use in a research project. If so, some advice on how to start will be found in this chapter. This advice is inevitably given in general terms, as there will be differences between one computer centre and another, and should therefore only serve as a guide.

University computer centres in the UK are funded largely by the Computer Board, a government body, which was set up to provide computing facilities initially for research and later also for teaching. At the time of writing there is no charge for approved research workers in the UK who wish to use their university computer centre. The methods of organising computer users vary from country to country, but in most cases it is not necessary for the user himself to pay. Often each university department has an allocation of time or 'money' units on the computer. Although you will probably not have to pay to use the computer, the computer centre will not do your computing for you. You will have to learn how to use the computer and organise your work for it or else pay somebody else to do it for you. The centre merely provides the machinery and back-up services.

You will first need to register as a computer user at your local computer centre. The computer will have been programmed to accept only valid user identifiers and you will be issued with one of these if your department does not already hold one. On different computers they are called account numbers, job numbers or usernames and are used by the computer centre to record the amount of computer time each user has. They will also be used for charging if real or notional money is involved. Each account number will have a certain amount of computer time allocated to it as well as units of file space on disc, perhaps magnetic tapes and even paper for printing. These budgetary categories vary from centre to centre, but an explanatory leaflet on them will be provided. In some centres the time units are updated weekly, in others monthly. Others again operate a different system of allocating time which is divided into shares of daily usage. You will probably be allocated only small computer resources to begin with to encourage you to use them economically. Your budgets can be increased by the centre if you find you need more time.

The computer centre will have a number of card punches, tape punches and terminals for users to use. Some large users of the computer will also have a terminal for themselves. These are usually allocated by the centre to the people they feel need them most and they may have to pay for the terminal itself. Working in the centre itself is often easier, as all the other equipment is also there and you will not have to walk far to collect printout.

It will also be necessary to find out what facilities, if any, the centre offers for arts computing. If you are lucky they may already have several people from arts departments already using the computer and a specialist in the computer centre to help them. If not, you may have to find out much more for yourself. All university centres provide some kind of advisory service for users – that is, staff whose job it is to hold a 'surgery' to help users. The level of assistance varies from centre to centre, but it is there to help you rather than to do the computing for you. A number of centres now have specialist advisers for computing in the humanities or what the computer specialists prefer to call 'non-numeric' computing. These people may well have had previous experience of problems similar to yours. If there is no such person you will have to explain your project to a computer specialist who may never have heard of terms like textual criticism or iambic pentameters. You may find that the scientists regard your work as somewhat amusing and certainly esoteric. Try to ignore this attitude and explain as clearly as you can exactly what you want the computer to do for you.

The computer centre will tell you whether they have any standard packages to suit your requirements. Most centres now have access to a concordance package such as COCOA either on their own machine or at a remote site over a network. When working on a text it is often useful to make a concordance first. From it you will be able to decide which features of your text to study further. Even without a standard program for concordances much useful information can be obtained from the data by manipulating it from a terminal. If the computer has a good editing program and allows a reasonable amount of terminal usage, you will be able to use that method to search the text for instances of particular words or phrases. The usages found may be transferred to another file and manipulated again. The main advantage of searching a text file interactively is the virtually instant response, but it can be more expensive of computer time. A concordance selecting only a few words as keywords can also provide much useful information and even a small concordance done on just a few pages of text may help you to plan your future computing.

The computer centre may have other information retrieval or database programs which you could use. They will probably recommend you to read a users' manual for any package which they think suitable for your project. Many computer manuals are written by the programmers who wrote the package, and although they may be very useful once you have started to use the computer you may find them a little difficult at first. Most computer manuals, at least those for packages, have plenty of examples. Look at these carefully before you read all of the text, for a good manual should show what comes out of the machine as well as what goes in. It is often easier to see what the package does from examples rather than from a detailed explanation. In some cases the examples may be on data which is different from yours, perhaps scientific or commercially-oriented. Do not be put off by this but look at the method used. The procedures which have been applied to the data may be exactly the ones you want to use on your data even if its nature appears to be very different.

Some packages require data to be in a particular format. If your data is already in computer readable form, but in a different format, this does not mean that you cannot use it. A simple computer program can be written to transfer the data to another computer file or tape in the required format. If this is the only program you need which is not already written, it may be possible to persuade someone at the computer centre to do it for you.

If there are no packages to suit your requirements and the terminal editor cannot be used for your purpose, you will have to learn to write programs yourself. Learning to program may be frustrating in the early stages but very rewarding when everything finally works. It is not at all difficult to write simple programs and these can be used as a basis for more complicated work as the project grows. The choice of computer language depends on what is available at the computer centre. The most commonly used computer language in the academic world is FORTRAN. FORTRAN was originally written for scientific purposes and is not ideal for handling textual information, but as it was one of the earliest computer languages it has become so well established that its use is self-perpetuating. Most programs are written in FORTRAN because everybody knows FORTRAN and everybody knows FORTRAN because most programs are written in it. All computers except the very small ones support compilers for FORTRAN and this could be a suitable choice of language if you know that you want to start your project on one computer and then move it to another. Another advantage of using FORTRAN is that all the program advisers at the computer centre will know it and there will therefore be more help available to you.

If the computer centre already does some arts computing, it will probably also support other computer languages which are more suitable, such as SNOBOL (or SPITBOL as it is sometimes called) or ALGOL68 or PASCAL. Any of these would be easier to apply to an arts project than FORTRAN or ALGOL60. SNOBOL in particular is very easy to learn. It is the language usually taught in specialised courses for arts computing, and is particularly recommended for the non-mathematician. The business language COBOL is also suitable for some arts computing but it is rarely used in the academic world and an academic computer centre may be unable to give assistance for COBOL programs.

Many computer centres provide courses for their computer users to learn programming. These are frequently 'crash courses' of the kind that require attendance on every day for a week and for this reason are often held during the vacation. This is the best way to learn, as you can concentrate entirely on computing to the exclusion of other work. The courses should include some opportunity for you to try out some small programs on the computer. Do make the most of this opportunity, as trying it for yourself is by far the best way to learn. These courses are sometimes presented on videotape, but there should be somebody available to answer questions.

Computing courses are, however, often directed at scientists, and the arts user may not be able to understand the examples. He will understand the logic of the programming language but find that many examples are mathematical. The same is true of many computer programming manuals. They explain the logic and syntax of the languages well, but illustrate it by mathematical examples. It is possible to learn to program from such courses or manuals provided you ignore all those examples which you cannot understand. We have seen throughout this book that very little mathematical knowledge is required to use a computer. However, most people who write computer manuals are mathematicians and scientists and do not realise that their approach is not suitable for non-scientists.

Those universities which are now enlightened about arts computing sometimes put on special courses for arts users. These will contain non-mathematical examples and should be much easier to understand. If these courses are planned by computer scientists, they may include non-mathematical examples which are not particularly useful to the arts user. Try the examples during the programming course in order to learn the language and then later you can program yourself the procedures which are useful to you. On the other hand, some computer courses for arts people which have been planned by computer scientists are very simple and do not give a full enough coverage of what the computer can do. The arts user is no less intelligent than the scientist and is no less capable of handling complex problems on a computer, but a different approach is required. If you attend an arts computing course which appears to be very elementary and without any useful substance, do try and find out more about the subject by reading or asking people. A very simple course will give you enough information to read some manuals and find out what else is possible.

You will also have to learn some basic instructions for the computer's operating system. Large computers run many programs at the same time and so they have to be told who you are – that is, your account number, and what you want to do – that is, which compiler or package you want to use. They also schedule or organise their work depending on information supplied by the user. Programs are not processed in the order in which they are fed into the machine. Instead the user specifies the amount of time he thinks his job might take and possibly also a priority – that is, how soon he wants it to be done. Some computer centres now link their budgeting of notional money against priority so that more units are used up if the job is to be run very quickly. Work is also normally scheduled according to the number of magnetic tapes required by a job, as the computer will only have a limited number of tape decks on which tapes can be mounted. This particularly affects the arts user who often has amounts of data which are too large for one user's allocation of disc space and therefore must be kept on tape.

Many large academic computer centres also provide a fast turn-round service, called a 'cafeteria' or 'debug' system for very small jobs such as testing programs. Usually several different compilers are provided as well as one or two simple packages. Programs should always be tested thoroughly on small quantities of data before they are put into large production runs, and such a service is very useful for this. Once the program works, large jobs can then be run as normal and can very probably be left to be done overnight. The computer will store up all the large jobs which have been submitted during the day and schedule them to be run during the night, when it has no urgent work to be done.

The methods of organising work vary from one computer centre to another but are usually on these lines. The amount of work which users are allowed to do at a terminal may also vary. Though this is the easiest way for a user to operate, it is also the most expensive in terms of machine usage. A centre whose computer is heavily overloaded may not allow more than a limited number of terminals to be operational at one time. The actual instructions to the operating system also vary from one kind of computer to another. You will certainly have to learn them again if you move to work on a different kind of machine. The basic principles are much the same, but the details vary.

Arts users inevitably have a lot of data to be processed. If it is archaeological or historical it is unlikely to be already in computer-readable form. Much of the researcher's time will be spent in collecting and verifying the material. It will then have to be typed on punched cards or through a terminal directly into computer files. Many computer centres provide data preparation operators to do this for you, but some do not, in which case you will either have to do it yourself or pay someone to do it. There are a number of commercial bureaux which provide a data preparation service, at the time of writing for a charge of around £30 for 1000 cards. If you need to use one of these, it is advisable to shop around. Asking other users at the computer centre may bring to light some cheap way of doing it. Remember that accuracy is more important than cost. You will not want to spend many months correcting data which has been badly punched, and it may be worth some extra money to have the data verified as well. The data preparation service will prefer to receive your information written out neatly, probably on computer coding sheets, and certainly not on untidy pieces of paper. Coding sheets are ruled out in eighty columns, and their use will ensure that your data is more accurate. It is not quite so necessary to write out literary text on to coding sheets, but you will need to give some instructions for typing special characters and for continuation symbols for long lines of text. It is not very likely that you will find a data preparation service which can transliterate from a non-Roman alphabet, and in this case you may well have to write it all out for them in transliteration.

For those working on literary texts, the situation is becoming much brighter. Once a text has been prepared for the computer it can be kept in computer-readable form permanently and can therefore be made available for other people to use. Indeed it is common practice for such texts to be made available for others to use at little or no charge.

There are several ways of finding out if a text is already available. There are now two archives of texts in computer readable form which are kept specifically to act as a clearing house for that material. One organised by Professor S.V.F. Waite, at the Kiewit Computation Center, Dartmouth College, keeps Classical texts, both Greek and Latin, and now has a large library including most of the well-known classical authors. Recently another has been established at Oxford University, which specialises in English literature. Both these archives will supply copies of the texts they hold for a very small charge. (Their full address may be found on p. 241.)

The texts they supply are on magnetic tapes and it is important to find out about the technical characteristics of these tapes first. Information can be written on to magnetic tapes in several different formats and it is unlikely that your local computer can read all of them. You may not understand the technicalities, but do ask someone at the computer centre about these before you order any texts. They will probably give you a small document describing the tape formats which they can read. Both archives have accepted formats in which they supply tapes, but they may be able to write you a tape in a different format if your computer cannot read their normal one. This information about magnetic tapes applies in all cases where material is being transferred from one computer centre to another. You do not need to understand the technicalities, but make sure that the people at each computer centre have them.

There are other possible sources of text if the one you require is not held at Dartmouth or Oxford. There now exists in California a very large archive of ancient Greek literary texts, consisting of all extant literary material written up to the fourth century AD. This archive is called the Thesaurus Linguae Graecae and is located at the University of California at Irvine under the direction of Professor T. Brunner. They supply tapes of any texts from the archive but make a higher charge than Dartmouth or Oxford and will only provide one magnetic tape format, which is only compatible with IBM computers, and no others. For linguistic analysis there is the Brown University Corpus of a million words of present-day American English, made up of 500 samples each of 2000 words and covering about fifteen different kinds of material such as literature, newspapers, and church sermons. All the texts in it were first published in 1961. There is also a manual which identifies each sample of text and describes the coding system used. At the University of Toronto, the entire body of Old English texts has been put into computer-readable form for the *Dictionary of Old English* and it is possible to purchase texts from them. The Trésor de la Langue Française at Nancy also makes available French texts for a charge.

For other languages in which there is no less activity but perhaps less cooperation, a little more research may be necessary to find out if a text has already been prepared. There are two main sources of information. The periodical *Computers and the Humanities* began in 1966 and covers all computer applications in the humanities. Twice a year it publishes a *Directory of Scholars Active*, which is in effect a catalogue of projects. They rely on scholars filling in questionnaires to keep the directory up to date and so it is inevitably not comprehensive. Recently a cumulative edition of the first seven years of the *Directory of Scholars Active* was published, which includes author and subject indexes to the material. The same periodical occasionally produces lists of texts in machine-readable form, again relying on information sent in by their readers. It is always worth looking through these lists to see if anybody else is working on the same text and writing to them about it.

In 1973 an Association for Literary and Linguistic Computing (ALLC) was formed in London. It is now an international association and publishes a Bulletin three times a year. It has a number of specialist groups, some of which are oriented to particular languages. The names of the chairmen of these groups may be found in the Bulletin and they should be aware of who holds texts in their language. You may also be able to find out from these journals if anyone else has written a program which meets your needs. It may be worth approaching them for a copy of the program rather than spending a long time trying to write one yourself. The general bibliography in this book gives a list of references, most of which are conference proceedings. You may also discover an article in one of these books about your text. Again it may be worth following up the author to enquire about the computer version of the text.

If all else fails, the text will have to be prepared somehow. If your computer centre does not have a data-preparation service, it could be a long job for you or your assistants. It will also be an exacting task, which will compel you to make some decisions about your text that you may have been putting off for a long time. You should always start with a number of tests to ensure that your coding will work out as you want. You will have to devise a coding scheme to suit your text. If it is a non-standard alphabet it is advisable to use a transliteration scheme already in use, such as the one at Dartmouth or Irvine for Greek. Whatever scheme you choose for coding, it is important to use a unique code for each character or symbol in the text. These can always be changed to another symbol later on if you wish by a simple computer program, but ambiguous codes cannot be resolved automatically. If you are planning to use a package like COCOA, you can use more than one computer character for each character in your text but be aware that this makes programming more difficult if you want to write some of your own programs as well. It is always worth finding out what other people have done in similar circumstances.

Once you have begun your project, or even before you start, it is useful to meet other people who have similar interests. There are now two major series of conferences on computing in the himanities. The delegates to the meetings are from a variety of disciplines, but they all have an interest in computing. Some are programmers who work on packages for arts users, others are computer users from the humanities, many of whom write their own programs. The first such meeting on computers in literary and linguistic research was held in Cambridge in 1970. This has now become a biennial event at Easter and has so far been held at Edinburgh, Cardiff, Oxford and Aston (Birmingham). In 1973 a series of conferences was begun in North America, covering all computer applications in the humanities, not just in literary and linguistic research. These have been held so far in Minnesota, Los Angeles and Waterloo, Ontario. The published proceedings of these meetings have formed valuable sources of material for this book. The conferences are open to all. Though the UK ones are now sponsored by the ALLC, it is not necessary to be a member of the association to attend the meetings. The ALLC now holds a one-day meeting in December each year which is held either in London or on the continent of Europe. It also organises a number of smaller local gatherings, details of which may be found in its *Bulletin*. There are also specialist conferences on computers in archaeology and on information retrieval, details of which may be found in *Computers and the Humanities*.

This final chapter should have given you some ideas on the best way to start a computer project. It will not be very easy at first, particularly if there is not much local expertise in humanities computing. You will see the word 'error' appearing very frequently during your first few weeks of computing. With a little experience you will gradually begin to be more amused than depressed at your mistakes. Remember that it is very rare for a program to work first time and very surprising if it works the second time. It may take several attempts to get it right, but once it is correct it can be run many times on different data and the results will come out very quickly. If you cannot see what is wrong, you must ask for help. The advisory service is there for just this purpose and you will often learn more by talking to others than by reading manuals. Many beginners at computing do not like to feel that a machine knows better than they do, but if there is something wrong it is almost always your fault and if you cannot see the mistake you must ask for help. Once the project gets going, the results will appear rapidly. You will be able to extract much more information from your data than ever you could manually. The computer will give you a much more comprehensive view of your material and your research will be that much more thorough. Finally, it will also give you a taste of another discipline which is both exacting and rewarding for the arts user as well as for the scientist.

REFERENCES

1. G.L.M. Berry-Rogghe, The Activities of the Institut für Deutsche Sprache Mannheim in the Field of Literary and Linguistic Computing. *ALLC Bull.* 3 (1975) 97-9

2. Roberto Busa, S.J., Computer Processing of Over Ten Million Words: Retrospective Criticism. *The Computer in Literary and Linguistic Studies (Proceedings of the Third International Symposium)*, 114-17 (eds Alan Jones and R.F. Churchhouse). Cardiff: University of Wales Press (1976)

3. Computers and the Humanities (ed.), *Computer-Oriented Humanistic Research: A Directory of Scholars Active* 1966-1972. New York: Pegamon Press (1976)

4. L.A. Cummings, The Electronic Humanist: Computing at Waterloo in Canada. *ALLC Bull.* 3 (1975) 226-34

5. A. Colin Day, FORTRAN as a Language for Linguists. *The Computer in Literary and Linguistic Research*, 245-57 (ed. R.A. Wisbey). Cambridge: Cambridge University Press (1971)

6. M.G. Farringdon, Natural Language Data Processing with ALGOL68. *The Computer in Literary and Linguistic Studies (Proceedings of the Third International Symposium)*, 1-7 (eds Alan Jones and R.F. Churchhouse). Cardiff: University of Wales Press (1976)

7. Susan M. Hockey, *Computing in the Arts at Oxford University*. Oxford University Computing Service (1976 and 1977)

8. Rosemary Leonard, Some Possible Uses of the Computer Archive of Modern English Texts. *ALLC Bull.* 2 No. 2 (1974) 13-18

9. Robert L. Oakman, A Videotape Course for Computer Education in the Humanities. *Computers and the Humanities* 9 (1975) 123-6

10. N.F. Palmer, The Computer and Medieval German Studies. *ALLC Bull.* 1 No. 3 (1973) 20-1

11. D. Sherman, A Computer Archive of Language Materials. *Computing in the Humanities,* 283-94 (eds Serge Lusignan and John S. North). Waterloo: University of Waterloo Press (1977)

BIBLIOGRAPHY

(1) *Books – principal sources* (all conference proceedings)
1. A.J. Aitken, R.W. Bailey and N. Hamilton-Smith (eds), *The Computer and Literary Studies*. Edinburgh: Edinburgh University Press (1973)
2. Alan Jones and R.F. Churchhouse (eds), *The Computer in Literary and Linguistic Studies (Proceedings of the Third International Symposium)*. Cardiff: University of Wales Press (1976)
3. Serge Lusignan and John S. North (eds) *Computing in the Humanities – Proceedings of the Third International Conference on Computing in the Humanities*. Waterloo: University of Waterloo Press (1977)
4. J.L. Mitchell (ed.) *Computers in the Humanities*. Edinburgh: Edinburgh University Press (1974)
5. R.A. Wisbey (ed.) *The Computer in Literary and Linguistic Research*. Cambridge: Cambridge University Press (1971)
6. A. Zampolli (ed.) *Linguistica Matematica e Calcolatori: (Atti del Convegno e della Prima Scuola Internazionale Pisa 1970)*. Florence: Leo S. Olschki (1973)

(2) *Books – other sources*
1. Edmund A. Bowles (ed.) *Computers in Humanistic Research: Readings and Perspectives*. Englewood Cliffs: Prentice-Hall (1967)
2. Jacob Leed (ed.) *The Computer and Literary Style: Introductory Essays and Studies*. Kent, Ohio: Kent State University Press (1966)
3. Jitka Štindlová and Zdena Skoumalová, *Les Machines dans la Linguistique*. Prague: Academia Editions d'l'Académie Tchécoslovaque des Sciences (1968)
4. A. Zampolli and N. Calzolari (eds) *Computational and Mathematical Linguistics: Proceedings of the International Conference on Computational Linguistics*. Florence: Leo S. Olschki (1977)

(3) *Periodicals – principal sources*
1. *Bulletin of the Association for Literary and Linguistic Computing* (1973 –)
Published by the ALLC whose current secretary is Dr J.L. Dawson, Literary and Linguistic Computing Centre, Sidgwick Avenue, Cambridge. Three issues per year – covers language and literature.
2. *Computers and the Humanities* (1966 –)
Published by Queen's College, Flushing, New York until 1974. Now

published by North Holland. Six issues per year. Covers language, literature, history, archaeology, music and education
3. *Computer Studies in the Humanities and Verbal Behavior* (1968-1972)
   Was published by Mouton. Four volumes only. Covers literature, history, psychology and music.
4. *Revue* (1966 –)
   Revue of the International Organisation for Ancient Languages by Computer (LASLA), 110 Boulevard de la Sauvenière, Liège, Belgium. Four issues per year. Originally covered only Latin and Greek but now carries articles on other languages as well.

(4) *Periodicals – other sources*
1. *American Journal of Computational Linguistics*
   Published by Association for Computational Linguistics, 1611 North Kent Street, Arlington, Virginia 22209 USA
2. *CIRPHO*
   Journal of the International Society for Computer Research in Philosophy. Obtainable from Professor A. McKinnon, Department of Philosophy. McGill University, Montreal, Canada.
3. *Siglash Newsletter*
   Association for Computing Machinery Special Interest Group on Language Analysis and Studies in the Humanities. Obtainable from SIGLASH c/o Association for Computing Machinery, P.O. Box 12105, Church Street Station, New York, NY 10249, USA.
4. *Sprache und Datenverarbeitung*
   Published by Max Niemeyer Verlag, Tübingen, Pfrondorferstrasse 4, Germany.

(5) *Free newsletters*
1. *CALCULI*
   Deals with classical studies and some archaeology. Obtainable from Professor S.V.F. Waite, Kiewit Computation Centre, Dartmouth College, Hanover, New Hampshire 03755, USA.
2. *CAMDAP*
   Deals with medieval studies. Obtainable from Professor S. Lusignan, Institut d'études mediévales, Université de Montréal, CP 6128, Montréal, Canada.
3. *ARITHMOI*
   Deals with biblical and related studies. Does not appear as regularly as *CALCULI* and *CAMDAP*. Obtainable from Professor R.E. Whitaker, Central College, Pella, Iowa 50219, USA.

GLOSSARY OF COMPUTER TERMS

This glossary includes many terms besides those mentioned in this book in the hope that it may be useful to the uninitiated entering the world of computers.

Account number A user's identification code.

Algorithm The procedural steps for the solution of a specific problem.

Applications The problems to which computing techniques are applied.

Arithmetic and logic unit The part of a central processor which performs arithmetic and logical operations.

Assembler A programming language representing the computer's machine code.

Background job A job which is not run interactively.

Backing store A store of larger capacity but slower access time than the main memory (eg magnetic tapes or discs).

Backup A facility or resource which may be used in the event of breakdown or loss of information.

Batch processing A method of working where programs are processed one after another and not interactively.

Binary (1) The basic format in which information is represented inside the computer consisting of a pattern of bits. (2) Pertaining to a number system with a base of 2 (as opposed to the 'decimal' system with a base of 10).

Binary variable A variable which can be represented by one of only two possible states.

Bit (binary digit) The smallest unit of computer storage. Each bit can have two possible states conventionally represented by 0 or 1.

Bit pattern A group of bits representing data.

Bits per inch (bpi) A means of measuring the density at which information is written on to magnetic tape.

Block A conceptual unit of storage usually consisting of several records.

Boolean operations The logical relationships between concepts indicated by the connectors AND, OR and NOT.

Budget The amount of time, notional money, file space etc. which a user is allocated on the computer.

Bug An error in a program.

Byte A set of bits, frequently eight, considered as a unit.

Cafeteria One name used for part of a computer centre's system which gives a very fast turnround for small jobs.

Card code   The patterns of holes used to represent characters on punched cards.

Card image format   Information which is held in 80-character records, in which each character is equivalent to a column on a punched card.

Card punch   (1) A machine for typing information on to punched cards. (2) A device attached to the computer which produces output on punched cards.

Card reader   A device for reading information into the computer from punched cards.

Card reproducer   A machine which makes copies of punched cards.

Case   A term used in the social sciences to represent one record or major unit in structured information.

Cathode ray tube   A device similar to a television screen on which data can be displayed.

Central processor   The part of the computer where all programs are executed.

Character   A graphic symbol, e.g. a letter, a number or punctuation mark, represented by a fixed number of bits.

Character code   The specific combination of bits used to represent characters.

Character set   The group of symbols which any computer or device recognises.

Coding sheet   A sheet which is ruled in 80 columns on to which information is first written to facilitate keypunching on cards.

Communications   The transfer of information between remote locations and the main computer and the equipment necessary for this.

Compiler   A program which translates a high level language program into machine code.

Computer readable form   A means of storing information so that it can be input directly to the computer.

Configuration   A collection of hardware which together makes one computer.

Console   (1) The device, either teletype or VDU, by which an operator communicates with the computer. (2) Any terminal equipped with a keyboard.

Control card   A card or line of instructions to a package specifying the user's exact requirements from the package.

Core store   The main memory of the computer.

Data   Information to be processed by the computer.

Data preparation   Transferring data into computer readable form.

Database   A collection of data stored in the computer.

Debug   To eliminate errors from a program. It can also be used to describe that part of a computer system which allows fast turnround for small jobs.

Deck   (1) A collection of punched cards which are to be input together. (2) An abbreviation for tape deck.

Delete character   A character which is used to delete the previous character typed on a terminal.

Delimiter   A character used to mark the beginning and end of a sequence of characters.

Density   The rate at which information is written on to magnetic tape measured in bits per inch.

Descriptor term   An indexing term consisting of more than one word.

Device   A piece of computing machinery.

Direct access   Backing store on disc or drum, to which access is not necessarily serial.

Directory   Information written at the beginning of each file and/or record to indicate where each record and/or field begins.

Disc   A fast access storage device which looks somewhat like gramophone records stacked one above the other.

Disc drive   A device on which a disc or disc pack is mounted.

Disc pack   A term sometimes used instead of disc.

Down   Any piece of equipment, including the whole computer, which is not working.

Drum   A fast access cylindrical storage device.

Dump   (1) To write an area of memory to a peripheral. (2) To copy files from e.g. disc to tape for backup copies.

Editor   A program for amending the contents of a computer file.

Exchangeable disc   A disc pack which can be removed easily from the disc drive and replaced by another.

Field   A category or sub-division of structured information within a record.

File   A collection of related records or information forming one unit.

Filmsetter   A computer typesetting device.

Fixed disc   A disc which is not exchangeable.

Fixed length field   A field which contains the same number of characters in each record.

Fixed length record   A record which contains a fixed number of words or bytes.

Flexowriter   A machine for punching paper tape.

Floating point number   A number containing a decimal point with a variable number of digits after the decimal point. Otherwise called real number.

Flowchart   A diagram representing the procedural steps for a program or algorithm.

Go list   A list of words which are to be included in an index to the exclusion of all others.

Graphics   The process of drawing pictures by a computer.

Hard copy   Output in a form suitable for the human eye to read.

Hardware   The computing machinery.

Hashing   A method of computing the storage location by applying an algorithm to the record key.

Header label   A computer readable record at the beginning of a file or tape containing data identifying the file.

Hexadecimal   Pertaining to a number system with a base of 16.

High-level language   A programming language which has been designed to make program writing easier and can often be run on many different computers. Each instruction is the equivalent of several machine code instructions.

Implementation   The setting up of a program or programs on a particular computer.

Indexed sequential   A means of organising structured information in which the location of a record is found by reference to an index containing the record key.

Information retrieval   Searching a computer file for those records which satisfy certain criteria defined by the user.

Input   What is put into the computer.

Installation   A computer centre.

Integer   A whole number.

Interactive   A mode of working from a terminal where the computer responds immediately to each instruction issued.

Interpreter   (1) A machine which reads the holes in a punched card and prints the corresponding characters along the top of the card. (2) A program which translates a high level language into machine code as the program is executed, not before as with a compiler.

Job   A unit of work for the computer.

Job control language   The language used to give commands to the operating system of a computer.

Job number   A user's identification code.

K   The number 1024 which is often used in measuring a computer's memory.

Key   The symbols used to identify a record.

Keypunch   To type on a card punch or paper tape punch.

Lineprinter   A machine for printing information produced by the computer one line at a time.

Low-level language   A programming language in which each instruction is the equivalent of one machine code instruction.

Machine   What computer people call the computer.

Machine code   The computer's basic set of instructions.

Machine independent   Used to describe a program which will run on many kinds of computers.

Macro   A single instruction to the computer which generates several instructions when executed.

Magnetic disc   A fuller name for disc.

Magnetic tape   A storage device which looks like tape recorder tape.

Mainframe   A large computer to which other computers may be attached.

Manual   (1) A document or book describing the operation of a program. (2) Done by humans.

Mark sensing   A means of computer input by reading pencil marks on preprinted paper.

Master file   A file containing data which may be processed by several programs.

Memory   Usually the main core store of a computer but it can be used also for some types of backing store.

Merge   To combine two files which have been sorted into the same order.

Microfiche   A piece of film about the size of a postcard which contains many pages of printed information.

Microfilm   A roll of film usually 35 mm wide containing printed material.

Microprocessor   A very tiny computer.

Minicomputer   A small computer.

Modem   A device which is used to link a terminal to a computer over a telephone line.

Network   A number of computers linked together over telephone lines.

Object program   A program which is already compiled.

Octal   Pertaining to a number system with a base of 8.

Off-Line   A device which is not directly connected to the central processor.

On-Line   A device which is directly connected to the central processor.

Operating system   A large program permanently running which organises the work of the computer.

Operator   A person who operates the computer.

Optical character reader   A device which reads printed characters directly into the computer.

Optical character recognition   The identification of printed characters.

Output   What comes out of the computer.

Package   A large program which performs a number of tasks which many users may require.

Paper tape   A means of inputting and storing data which consists of a one inch wide, long strip of paper perforated with holes across the width of the tape, each row of holes representing one character.

Paper tape code   The patterns of holes representing characters on paper tape.

Paper tape punch   (1) A machine for typing information on to paper tape. (2) A device attached to the computer for producing output on paper tape.

Paper tape reader   A device for reading information into the computer from paper tape.

Parameter   A term much favoured by computer people, usually meaning information supplied to a program to control its running and which can change each time that it is run.

Parity   A means of checking data by adding a bit if necessary so that the sum of bits for each character is always even or always odd.

Peripheral   Any device which is connected to the central processor.

Photocomposer   A computer typesetting device.

Plotter   A device which draws pictures generated by the computer.

Production run   A run of a program which is intended to produce genuine results as opposed to a test run.

Program   A complete sequence of instructions to the computer.

Punched card   A means of holding computer readable data consisting of a piece of card 7⅜″ x 3¼″ perforated with holes which can hold up to eighty characters.

Random access   A means of accessing any record in a file without having to read all the preceding records.

Real number   A number containing a decimal point.

Record   All the information for one unit of data.

Remote job entry   Submitting work to a computer from a terminal which is not sited at the computer centre.

Run   The execution of one program.

Runout   A blank area of paper tape at the beginning and end of each piece.

Scheduling   The control of the flow of work through the computer.

Sequential access   Access to data only in the sequence in which it is stored.

Serial access   Access to records in the order in which they occur.

Software   Programs.

Sort   To rearrange into alphabetical or numerical order according to one or more keys.

Source program   A program which is not compiled.

Stop list A list of words which are to be excluded from an index

System A general term for almost everything connected with the computer.

Tape An abbreviation for paper tape or magnetic tape, usually the latter.

Tape deck A device on which a magnetic tape is loaded when it is required by the computer.

Teletype A computer terminal which resembles a typewriter.

Terminal A remote device used to transmit and receive data from the computer.

Throughput The volume of work processed by a computer.

Thesaurus An index of controlled terms used by many information retrieval services.

Track (1) The number of bits held crosswise on magnetic or paper tape. On magnetic tape it can be 7-track or 9-track, on paper tape it is usually 5-track, 7-track or 8-track. (2) An area of disc.

Turnround The length of time to wait for a job to be run on the computer.

Up Any piece of equipment including the whole computer which is working.

User A person who uses a computer.

Username A user's identification code.

Utility A program which performs some housekeeping function such as making a copy of a magnetic tape.

Variable In the social sciences, the term used for a field.

Variable length field A field whose length can vary from record to record.

Variable length record A record which contains a variable number of fields or bytes.

Verify To check data already punched on to cards or tape, by feeding the cards or tape through a verifying device.

Visual display unit A terminal which resembles a television screen.

Volume A unit of magnetic storage e.g. a magnetic tape or disc.

Word A unit of computer memory which consists of a number of bits. The number of bits per word varies between 8 and 60 from one computer to another.

Write permit ring A plastic ring held in the back of a magnetic tape reel without which the tape can only be read from and not written to.

ACRONYMS, ABBREVIATIONS AND PROGRAM NAMES

This list includes all the acronyms, abbreviations and program names mentioned in this book and a few other very common ones.

ALGOL	*Al*gorithmic *L*anguage. A programming language.
ALGOL68	*Al*gorithmic *L*anguage 68. A programming language.
ALLC	*A*ssociation for *L*iterary and *L*inguistic *C*omputing.
ARCHETYP	A program written by Dearing for locating archetypes in family trees of manuscripts.
ASCII	*A*merican *S*tandard *C*ode for *I*nformation *I*nterchange. A character code.
BALCON	*B*ilingual *A*nalytical *L*iterary and Linguistic *Con*cordance. A method devised at Cardiff for making a concordance of a bilingual text.
BABEL	The Cardiff machine translation program.
BCD	*B*inary *C*oded *D*ecimal. A character code.
BIRD	*B*ibliographic *I*nformation *R*etrieval and *D*issemination. A package for information retrieval.
BPI	*B*its *p*er *I*nch. A means of measuring the density at which information is recorded on magnetic tape.
CARLEX	*C*omputerised *A*nalytical *R*ussian *Lex*icon. A program written at Cardiff to generate morphological endings for Russian words.
CDC	*C*ontrol *D*ata *C*orporation. Computer manufacturers.
CLUSTAN	A package for cluster analysis.
COBOL	*Co*mmon *B*usiness *O*riented *L*anguage. A programming language.
COCOA	Word *C*ount and *C*oncordance Generation on *A*tlas. A package written at the Atlas Computer Laboratory for producing concordances.
COLLATE	A group of programs written at the University of Manitoba for computer collation.
COM	*C*omputer *O*utput *M*icroform.
CPU	*C*entral *P*rocessor *U*nit.
CRT	*C*athode *R*ay *T*ube.
CURSOR	A program written at the University of Waterloo for comparing texts.

DIALOG®	The information service of the Lockheed Missiles Corporation of Palo Alto, California.
EBCDIC	*E*xtended *B*inary *C*oded *D*ecimal *I*nterchange *C*ode. A character code.
EYEBALL	A package written at the University of Minnesota for syntactic and stylistic analysis of English text.
FAMULUS	A package for cataloguing and indexing.
FIND2	*F*ile *I*nterrogation of *N*ineteen hundred *D*ata. A package for information retrieval written by ICL.
FORTRAN	*For*mula *Tran*slation. A programming language.
GRAPH	The graphical output part of the THEME package.
HAWKEYE	A version of the EYEBALL package written at the University of Southern California.
IBM	*I*nternational *B*usiness *M*achines. Computer manufacturers.
ICL	*I*nternational *C*omputers *L*td. Computer manufacturers.
IDMS	*I*ntegrated *D*atabase *M*anagement *S*ystem. A package for organising data.
IMPRESS	A statistics package used at Dartmouth College.
INFOL	*I*n*fo*rmation *O*riented *L*anguage. A package for handling documentary or survey type data.
I/O	*I*nput/*O*utput.
KWIC	*K*eyword *i*n *C*ontext.
LOUISA	*L*inguistically *O*riented *U*nderstanding and *I*ndexing *S*ystem for *A*bstracts. A program written at the University of Liège for indexing abstracts.
MARC	*Ma*chine *R*eadable *C*ataloguing. The standard format for bibliographical data on magnetic tape.
MEDLARS	*Med*ical *L*iterature *A*nalysis and *R*etrieval *S*ystem. A large database of medical literature.
MEDLINE	*MED*LARS on-*line*
MSFAMTRE	A program written by Dearing for constructing textual family trees.
MSS	*M*anuscript *S*temma *S*imulator. A program written at the University of Kent to simulate manuscript stemmata.
OCCULT	The *O*rdered *C*omputer *C*ollation of *U*nprepared *L*iterary *T*ext. A program to collate prose text.
OCR	*O*ptical *C*haracter *R*ecognition.
OPCOL	*Op*timal *Col*lation. An algorithm for collation.
OXEYE	Oxford University's version of the EYEBALL package.
PL/1	*P*rogramming *L*anguage *1*. A programming language.
PRELIMDI	A program written by Dearing for making preliminary diagrams of the relationships between manuscripts.
QUILL	*Q*ueen's *U*niversity *I*nterrogation of *L*egal *L*anguage. An information retrieval package written at Queen's University Belfast.
QUOBIRD	*Q*ueen's *U*niversity *o*n-line *B*ibliographic *I*nformation *R*etrieval

	and *Dissemination.* An on-line information retrieval package written at Queen's University, Belfast.
RJE	*Remote Job Entry.*
SNOBOL	*String Oriented Symbolic Language.* A programming language.
SPITBOL	*Speedy Implementation of SNOBOL.*
STATUS	*Statute Search.* A package written at the Atomic Energy Research Establishment, Harwell for searching documents.
THEME	A package written at the University of Manitoba for thematic analysis.
UNIMARC	The format of MARC used for international exchange.
VDU	*Visual Display Unit.*
VINE	A *very informal newsletter* on library automation.

USEFUL ADDRESSES

1. *Association for Literary and Linguistic Computing*
   Current secretary of the ALLC is

   Dr J.L. Dawson
   Literary and Linguistic Computing Centre
   Sidgwick Avenue
   Cambridge
   England

2. *Text Archives*
   1. English for linguistic studies

      (a) Brown Corpus

          Department of Linguistics
          Brown University
          Providence
          Rhode Island 02912
          USA

      (b) International Computer Archive of Modern English
          (Lancaster Corpus and Survey of English
          Usage material)

          Dr Stig Johansson
          Co-ordinating Secretary
          International Computer Archive of Modern English
          University of Oslo
          Norway

   2. English literature

          Oxford Archive of English Literature
          Oxford University Computing Service
          13 Banbury Road
          Oxford
          England

3. Greek

Thesaurus Linguae Graecae
University of California
Irvine
California 92717
USA

4. Latin and Greek

LIBRI Archive
Kiewit Computation Centre
Dartmouth College
Hanover
New Hampshire 03755
USA

Index

abstracting, 210
accents: coding of in French, 18; coding of in Greek, 20; treatment of in a concordance, 64
account number, 220
Addison, 130
addition of records, 195
adverbs in stylistic analysis of Greek prose, 139
advisory service, 221
agglutinative languages, lemmatisation of, 101
air-conditioned environment, 14
ALGOL, 11
ALGOL60, 222
ALGOL68, 11, 222
algorithm, 9
ALLC *see* Association for Literary and Linguistic Computing
Allén, Sture, 81
alliteration, 170-2, 184-5; measurement of, 171-2
allocation, of resources, 221
alphabetical order, in a concordance, 64-5
American English, 226; corpus of, 88
American Regional English, dictionary of, 93
Ammianus Marcellinus, concordance to, 49
anacoluthon, 132
anapaest, 180
anomalies, in manuscript variants, 158
apostrophe, treatment of in a concordance, 64
Apparatus criticus, 144, 162, 163
Aquinas, Thomas, 15
Arabic: coding of, 20-1; lemmatisation of, 103; words in Turkish, 82
Arbuthnot, 132
archaeological data; input methods, 33; preparation of, 189-94
archaeology, 16
ARCHETYP, 158
archive of texts, 71, 225-6
Arcsin test, 140

Aristotelian Ethics, 139-40, 141
Aristotle, 136, 137
arithmetic mean, 124
Armstrong, Christine, 91
artificial intelligence, 120
Association, of words, 90-1
Association for Literary and Linguistic Computing, 226
associative thesaurus, 90-1
assonance, 184-5
Aston, 227
ATLAS, 15
Atomic Energy Research Establishment, 217
authorship, analysis of, 122-41
authorship study, excellent example, 134-5
automatic indexing, 210

BABEL, 114, 117
backup copies, of magnetic tape, 28
Bacon, 122
Balder, 83
bar codes, use in OCR work, 33
Barbour's Bruce, 170
base text, 163
batch processing, 216
Bathurst, R.D., 103
Bayes's theorem, 135
B.B.C., *see* British Broadcasting Corporation
BCD, card code, 22
Beckett, 85
Bellamy, Cliff, 147-8
Bender, T.K., 181-5
Berkeley, California, 197
Berry-Rogghe, Lieve, 85-8
Bible, Gothic, 15
bibliographic data, 194-5
bibliographic services, 216
bibliographies, 210-11
bilingual concordances, 65
binary, format for storing packages, 12
binary data, 189
binary digits, 13
binary field, 189
binary search, 74
biographical indexes, 191
Biographical Registers, 191
BIRD, 217
bit, 13; representation of on magnetic tape, 28; use in

metrical analysis, 184; use in storing scansions, 179
bits per inch, 28
Blake, 114
BLBSD, *see* British Library Bibliographic Services Division
block, on magnetic tape, 28
Bodleian Library, 16
book, compiling index for, 210
Boolean AND, 185, 212
Boolean NOT, 212
Boolean operations, 184-5
Boolean operators, 212
Boolean OR, 184, 212
Bpi, 28
breathings, coding of in Greek, 20
British Broadcasting Corporation, 81
British English, corpus of, 89
British Library Bibliographic Services Division, 194
British National Bibliography, 194
Brown Corpus, 88-90, 226
Brown University, 88
Brunner, T., 226
Buck, C.D., 90
budget, 220
Buridanus, 152
Burley, 93
Burnett-Hall, D.G., 81
Busa, Roberto, 15, 41, 63, 68-9
business correspondence, machine translation of, 118
byte, 13; on magnetic tape, 28

Cabaniss, Margaret, 151-2
caesura, 181
cafeteria, 224
California, University of, 226
Cambridge, 15, 33, 103, 191, 227
Cannon, Robert L., 155
canonised form, 84
capital letter, coding of, 19
card image, 28
card interpreter, 22
card punch, 22
card reader, 25
card reproducer, 22
card verifier, 22

Cardiff, 96, 114, 227
cards, punched, 22-4
CARLEX, 105
Carlyle, 133
case, coding of upper and lower, 19
catalogues, 16, 197-212
cathode ray tube, 34
CDC 6600, 18
CDC 7600, 18
Céline, 85
centrally-aligned, concordance, 41
Centre de Recherche de Lexicologie Politique, 90
Chanson de Roland, 160
character set, of lineprinters, 25, 27
characteristic zeros, 159-60
characters, representation of in bits, 13
checking of data, 193-4
chemists, German course for, 79
chi-square, 126-8; computed by Morton, 139
Chinese: coding of, 21; machine translation of, 114, 117; output of, 34; Standard Telegraphic Codes, 21
Chisholm, David, 172-4
choice of edition, for a concordance, 65
Chomsky, 174
classical text, 225
clause analysis, 108-9
CLUSTAN, 93
cluster analysis, 91-3; for manuscript relationships, 161; in stylistic analysis, 136; of lexical items, 93
co-occurrences, 85-91
COBOL, 11, 12, 14, 196, 223
COCOA, 11, 14, 16, 41, 79, 108, 185, 186, 221
coding, of text, 18-22, 227
Coleridge, 114
COLLATE, 152-5
collation, 144-56; advantages, 155-6
collocations, 85-91
column, on punched cards, 22
COM, 36
commercial applications, 217
compilation, 11
compilers, 11
computational semantics, 120
computer, description of, 12-13
Computer Board, 220
computer centres, use of, 220-1
computer output microform, 36
computer paper, format of, 25-6
computer typesetting, advantages of, 36
Computers and the Humanities, 226

concordances, 15, 41-9; bilingual, 65; in dialectology, 96; in metrical analysis, 183; left sorted, 49; reverse, 49; right-sorted, 49; use in metrical analysis, 180; use in stylistic analysis, 140; use to find metrical patterns, 185
condition code, in suffix removal, 103
conferences, 227
consonant clusters, 170
context: in a concordance, 42, 48; in lexicography, 71
continuous data, 192
cooking recipe, 10
Cooper, Giles, 88
Cornell, 15
correcting, use of terminal for, 31-2
corrections, of OCR input, 33
Council of Europe, 217
counting machine, of Mendenhall, 122-3
Courses for programming, 223
Crawford, T.D., 114
critical edition: all-purpose program for, 152-5; preparation of, 144
cross-references, 198
CRT, 34
Curling round, of context, 48
CURSOR, 163
Cyclops, 168

dactyl, 176, 180, 181
Dartmouth College, 225
data preparation, 224-5, 227
database technology, 196
Dataskil, 217
dates, coding of, 192-3
Dawson, John, 103, 104
Dearing, Vinton A., 146-7, 158-9
debug service, 224
deck, for magnetic tape, 27
degrees of freedom, 128
delimiter, use of in an editor, 31
dendrogram, 160
density, on magnetic tape, 28
Devanagari, coding of, 21
Diacritics, treatment of in a concordance, 64
dialect maps, 93-6
dialectology, 91-7
DIALOG, 216
Dickens, Charles, 88
dictionary, compilation of, 69; machine-readable, 73-4
Dictionary of American Regional English, 93
Dictionary of Old English, 71
Dictionary of the Older Scottish Tongue, 71

dictionary slips, printing of, 71
Dilligan, R.J., 181-5
Dionysius, 170
directory, to a file, 196
Directory of Scholars Active, 226
disc, 29, 195-6; exchangeable, 29; fixed, 29; magnetic, 27
discontinuous data, 192
discriminators, used by Milic, 130
distinctiveness ratio, 139
Dom Quentin, 159-60
Dowsing, Anita, 106
drum, 29-30
Dudrap, C., 81
Dutch, thesaurus of, 83; vocabulary, 83

EBCDIC, card code, 22
economy of storage, 191
Edinburgh, 227
editing, of quotations for a dictionary, 74-5
editor: for correcting data, 31-2; on terminal, 106-7, 163, 221
editorial emendation, in text for concordance, 65
EDSAC, 15
elision, 179
Elizabethan literature, 190-1
Elizabethan texts, 135
Ellegard, Alvar, 16, 126, 133-4
Emden, A.B., 191
Emery, G., 81
endings, alphabetical order of, 49
engineers, computer, 13
English: alliteration in, 170; Cornell concordances, 15; loan words in French, 82; metrical analysis of, 176; Old, 106; Old – text archive, 226; prosody, 181-5; suffix removal for, 103; text archive, 225; words in Turkish, 82
English Dialects, Survey of, 93
ENIAC, 15
Epistles of Paul, 16, 136
equipment, at computer centre, 221
Ethics, Aristotelian, 139-40
Eudemean Ethics, 139-40
exchangeable disc, 29
expansion of fields, 199
experimental psychologists, 90-1
EYEBALL, 108-14, 130, 133

family tree, 156-60
FAMULUS, 11, 197-212, 211
Federalist Papers, 16, 134, 141
field, 189

field labels, in FAMULUS, 197-9
Fielding, Henry, 88, 114
file, 29, 189
file card, 197
File cards, 9, 11, 189
FIND2, 212-13, 217
First World War, 211
Firth, J.R., 85
fixed disc, 29
fixed-length field, 189
Fleming, 133
Flexowriter, 24; for specialised output, 33-4
floating point numbers, 189
folk plays, 156
foreign words: coding of, 21; treatment of in a concordance, 62
format of data, 222
formulas, in Old English, 107
Fortier, Paul, 84
FORTRAN, 11, 12, 14, 108, 186, 196, 222
France, 16
Francis, Sir Philip, 133
French: coding of accents, 18; lemmatisation of, 102; recognition of finite verbs, 105; study of nominal genders, 81; words in Turkish, 82
French Revolution, 211
frequency count, of words, 79
frequency profile, 79
Froger, J., 145-6, 157
Fromkin, 174
function words, in stylistic analysis, 136

gap: interblock gap, 28
gap recurrence function, 174
Gaskell, Mrs, 114
German, 105; alliteration in, 172; coding of umlaut, 18; course for chemists, 79; output of, 33; phonological patterning in, 172-4; preparation of a language course, 81
German sonnets: stylistic analysis of, 132
German, Early Middle High, concordances of, 15; scansion of, 181
Gibbon, 130
Gibson, William, 149
Gilbert, Penny, 152-5, 156
go list, 199
Gothic Bible, word index of, 15
GRAPH, 85
graph plotter, 161
graph theory, 174
graphs, of word length, 123
Greek: characters on VDU, 30;

coding of, 20; concordances, 64-5; hexameters, 179; lemmatisation of, 102-3; lexicon of personal names, 193; prose rhythm, 186; sound patterns in, 168-70; texts, 225, 226
Greek prose, stylistic analysis of, 135-40
Green, Donald C., 107
Greenberg, Nathan A., 177-9
Gregory, 162
grids, metal grids in smaller typesetters, 34
Griffith, J.G., 160-1, 163
grouping of data, 192
Gryphius, 133

Halle, 174, 181
Hamilton, Alexander, 134
Hampshire, 93
Hanon, Suzanne, 82
hardware, 13
harshness factor, 170
Harwell, 217
hashing, method of search, 74
Haskel, Peggy, 89-90
HAWKEYE, 108
Hebrew: algorithm for generating forms, 105; coding of, 20-1
Hebrew periodicals, indexes to, 211-12
Hellberg, Staffan, 101
Herodotus, 137
hexameters, 176-9
hiatus, 179
hieroglyphs, Minoan, 69
high frequency words, in a concordance, 48-9
high-level language, 10
Hildum's association measure, 171
Hirschmann, Rudolph, 181
histogram, 84
historical data: input methods, 33; preparation of, 189-93
History of the University (of Oxford), 191-3, 213
Holland, 15
Homer, 170, 211; sound patterns, 168-70
homographs, in a concordance, 62-3
Hong Kong, 114, 117
Hopkins, Gerald Manley, 181
Horace, 176
Howard-Hill, T.H., 66, 68
hyphenated words, treatment of in a concordance, 63-4

iamb, 180
iambic pentameter, 181
iambic senarii, 180
IBM, 226

IBM San Jose Research Laboratory, 133
IBM 360, 13, 18
IBM 370, 12, 13, 18
I.C.A.M.E., *see* International Archive of Modern English
ICL, 217
ICL 1900, 212
ICL 2900, 12, 13, 18
Identifiers, coding of for text references, 22
IDMS, 196
Iliad, 168-9; example coding, 20
image, card image, 28
Index Thomisticus, 41; description of, 68-9
indexed sequential, 196
indexes, 197-212; to Hebrew periodicals, 211-12
indexing: a book, 210; automatic, 210; on microfiche, 36
Indus Valley inscriptions, 69
INFOL, 11
information retrieval, 212-17; natural language analysis in, 119
input, 13, 14; best method, 36; devices, 18; methods for archaeological data, 33; methods for historical data, 33
input format, for FAMULUS, 197-9
Institut für Deutsche Sprache, 217
integers, 189
interactive program, in metrical analysis, 180-81
interactive working, 30, 216
interblock gap, on magnetic tape, 28
International Archive of Modern English, 89
International Phonetic Alphabet, 96, 174
interpreter, for punched cards, 22
Isaiah, 140
ISBN, 195
isogloss, 91, 93

James, Henry, 149
Japanese, coding of, 21
jargon, 14
Jay, John, 134
Jewish history and language, 211
job number, 220
Johnson, 130
Jones, Alan, 81-2
Jonson, 122
Joyce, J., author of *Ulysses*, 114
Joyce, James, 174

Junius Letters, 16, 133
justification, in typesetting
    program, 35
Juvenal, 161

K, unit of computer storage, 13
K characteristic, 79
Kanocz, Stephen, 81
Katakana, 21
Keats, 114
Kenny, A.J.P., 137, 139-40, 141
keyboard, with special format,
    30
Keyser, 181
Kiewit Computation Center,
    225
King's College, London, 15
Kiss, G., 91
Kjetsaa, Geir, 170
Koskenniemi, S., 69
Koster, Patricia, 130
KWIC format, 41
KWIC index, 199

lacunae, coding of, 20
Lancaster, University of, 89
Lance, Donald M., 93
language teaching, 79
last word: in a sentence as
    stylistic discriminator, 138;
    in Greek prose style, 140
Latin, 105; concordances, 65;
    hexameters, 176-9; scansion
    of, 176-9; texts, 225
Latin prose rhythm, 186
Lawrence, D.H., 88
lawyers, 16, 217
Leach, Stephen V., 186
Leavitt, Jay A., 174
left-aligned, concordance, 41
left-sorted, concordance, 49
Leighton, Joseph, 132, 172
lemmatisation, 101-105; in a
    concordance, 63; in
    lexicography, 73; in
    vocabulary counts, 80
length of syllable, use of in
    metre, 176
Lessing, Doris, 88
letter coding, in stylistic
    analysis, 132
letter combinations, in loan
    words, 82
letter frequencies, 168
lexicograph, 90
lexicography, 69-75
Lexicon of Greek personal
    names, 193
Library of Congress, 194
Linear A, 69
Linear B, 69
linear discriminant function,
    135
linear relationships, between
    manuscripts, 159-60

lineprinter, 25-7
Literary and Linguistic
    Computing Centre, 103
Literary geography, 132
Livy, concordance to, 41
loan words, 82-3
Lockheed, 216
Lomonosov, 170
London, King's College, 15
look-up, of machine dictionary,
    73-4
Los Angeles, 227
LOUISA, 210
Lovins, Julie Beth, 103
lower case, coding of, 19

Macauley, 130
machine translation, 114-18,
    210
Madison, James, 134
Maegaard, Bente, 105
magnetic disc, 27, 29, 195-6
magnetic tape, 27-9, 195;
    backup copies, 28; care of,
    28; serial numbers, 29
Magnuson, 172
Manitoba, 84, 152
Mannheim, 217
manuals, 222
manuscript relationships,
    156-63
maps, 93-6
MARC, 194-5
mark sensing, use in OCR
    work, 33
Marlowe, 114, 122
Martin, Willy, 83
McConnell, J. Colin, 84
mean, arithmetic, 124
Medieval Oxford, 213
MEDLARS, 216
MEDLINE, 216
Melville, 149
Mendenhall, T.C., 79, 122-3
MERCURY, 15
metre, 176-84
metrical dictionary, 181
metrical patterns, 185
Meunier, Jean G., 102
Meyer, Tania, 211
microfiche, 36
microfilm, 36
microfilm recorder, 96
microprocessor, 12
Midlands, East, 93
Milic, Louis, T., 130
Mill, John Stuart, 122
Milroy, R., 91
Milton, influence of on Shelley,
    83-4
minicomputer, 12
Minnesota, 108, 227
Minoan hieroglyphs, 69
minus words, 134
missing data, 190

modem, 30
morphological analysis, of
    Greek, 102-3
morphology, using a
    concordance for, 49
Morton, Andrew Q., 16, 136-9
Mosteller, Frederick, 16, 134
MSFAMTRE, 158
Muller, C., 124
Multistorey lexicograph, 90

National Library of Medicine,
    216
network database, 196
networks, for linking
    computers, 31
networks of sound, 174
New Testament, 136; new
    critical edition of, 162
New York, 134
newspapers, use in frequency
    counts, 81-2
Nichomachean Ethics, 139-40,
    141
node: in associative thesaurus,
    90-1; in collocations, 85-6
non-Roman alphabets, coding
    of, 19-21
non-standard characters, on
    VDU, 30
North Sea, 14, 15
Nottingham University of, 79
Nouveau Petit Larousse, 81
number: serial number for
    magnetic tape, 29
numeric coding, in stylistic
    analysis, 130
numeric data, 189
numeric relationships, 213-14

Oakman, R.L., 133
OCCULT, 149-51
OCR A, 32
OCR B, 32
octal number, use in storing
    scansions, 179
Odyssey, 168, 179
Ohio, 108
Old English, 106, 226;
    Dictionary of, 71
Old Testament, 140
Older Scots, alliteration in,
    170-1
Older Scottish Tongue,
    Dictionary of, 71
on-line working, 30
Open University, 33
operating system, 12, 224
optical character readers, 32-3
optical character recognition,
    32-3; errors, 33
oral texts, 156
order of occurrences, in a
    concordance, 49
organisation of data, 195

ORION, 15
Oslo, 89
Ott, W. 162-3, 176-9, 184
output, 13, 14; best method, 38; high quality, 35-6
OXEYE, 108, 130, 133
Oxford, 81, 108, 179, 186, 193, 227; Bodleian Library, 16; History of the University of, 191-3, 213; medieval, 192
Oxford Centre for Postgraduate Hebrew Studies, 211
Oxford Classical Texts, 65
Oxford English Dictionary, 73
Oxford Shakespeare Concordances, 66-8
Oxford text archive, 226

packages, 11, 221; use of, 16
Packard, David, 41, 102, 168-9, 179, 211
paper, 25-6
paper-tape, 24-5; advantages, 24; as output, 27; disadvantages, 25; for output of German, 33
paper tape reader, 25
Paris, 90
parity, 24-5; on magnetic tape, 28
parity track, on paper tape, 24-5
Parpola, A. and S., 69
parsing, 109, 133, 210; of search requests, 217
particles, used in stylistic analysis of Greek prose, 136-40
parts of speech, 109
PASCAL, 222
past participle, in Old English, 106
Pasternak, 185
patterns, in SNOBOL, 114
Paul, epistles of, 16
Pecheux, M., 90
Persian, words in Turkish, 82
Peter, epistles of, 162
Petty, George, 149
phonetic transcription, 184
Phonetic Alphabet, International, 96
phonetics, of Welsh dialects, 96
phonological frames, 172
phonological patterning, 172
photocomposer, 34-6; design of characters for, 34
phrasal verbs, 88
phrase structure, grammar, 117
phrases, syntactic analysis of, 108-9
Piers Plowman, 158
Piper, J., 91
Pisa, 16
PL/1, 11, 14

Plato, 186
Plautus, 180-1, 183, 186
plus words, 133; in stylistic analysis, 133
pocket calculators, dangers of using for variance, 129
police statements, 136
political documents, 90
Poole, Eric, 156
population, 125
Postgraduate Hebrew Studies, Oxford Centre for, 211
precision, 214
PRELIMDI, 158
Preston, M.J., 156
Price, James D., 105
probability, 128
proceleusmatic, 180
program, example of, 11
programming courses, 223
programming language, 10; choice of, 222
pronunciation, in dialectology, 93-6
proper names: coding of, 19; treatment of in a concordance, 62
prose, collation of, 149-56
prose rhythm, 186
psychologists, 90-1
public advertiser, 133
publication: by computer methods, 36; cost of, 36; of a concordance, 66
Publius, 134
punched cards, 22-4; as output, 27

Queen's University, Belfast, 217
Quemada, Bernard, 15
Quentin, Dom, 159-60
QUILL, 217
QUOBIRD, 217
Quotations: coding of, 21; treatment of in a concordance, 49-50

Raben, Joseph, 83-4
Radday, Yehuda, T., 140
random access, 196; on magnetic disc, 29
random sampling, 125
Rasche, Robert, 108
reading machines, 32
real numbers, 189
recall, 214
recipe, 10
record, 189
reduction of typing, 190-2, 198-9
references: coding of, 22; in a concordance, 48
rejection, error in OCR work, 33

relationship, between manuscripts, 156-63
remote job entry, 30-1
representation, of text, 18-22
reproducer, for punched cards, 22
retrieval of textual information, 214-17
reverse concordance, 49
rhyme: analysis of, 174; coding for, 185
rhyme schemes, using a concordance for, 49
right-sorted, concordance, 49
ring: write permit ring, 27-8
Riverside edition of Shakespeare, 66
RJE, 30-1
Rodman, 174
Roland, Chanson de, 160
Roman alphabet, coding of, 18
Romanisation, of Turkish, 82
Ross, Donald, 108
Rosslyn, Wendy, 186
Rubin, Gerald M., 93
runout, 25
Russian, 105; characters on a terminal, 106; characters on VDU, 30; coding of, 20; concordances, 64-5; machine translation of, 114, 117; preparation of a language course, 81; sound patterns in, 170; teaching of, 105

samples: how to choose, 125-6; of text, 134
Sanskrit, scansion of, 179
Scamander, 169
scansion, 176-84
Scots, alliteration in Older Scots, 170-1
Scottish poetry, 211
Scottish Tongue, Dictionary of the Older, 71
search requests, analysis of, 119
searching, of machine dictionary, 73-4
searching files of data, 212-17
security of files, 197
semantics, 117
Semitic languages, concordances of, 64-5
sentence length: in Greek prose style, 137-8, 140; in stylistic analsysis, 133-4
serial access, 195; on magnetic tape, 29
serial number, for magnetic tape, 29
seriation, 161
set theory, 157
sets, in databases, 196
Shakespeare, 27, 122, 155, 174,

190-1; Oxford Shakespeare Concordances, 66-8
Shakespeare's sonnets, 171-2, 175
Shaw, David, 91
Shelley, influenced by Milton, 83-4
Shibayev, V., 105, 106
Silva, Georgette, 147-8
similarity matrix, 161, 162
size of samples, 125-6
Slemons, Stephen V., 93
slips, printing of for a dictionary, 71
SNOBOL, 11, 14, 108, 150, 174, 222; patterns, 114; tables, 74
software, 13
Somerset, 96
Songs of Innocence and Experience, 114
sound patterns, 168-87
South Carolina, 211
South West and Forest Range Experiment Station, 197
Southern California, University of, 108
span, in collocations, 85-8
Spanish, 105; coding of tilde, 18
Spevack, Marvin, 66, 68
SPITBOL, 222
spondee, 176, 180
spread, measure of, 124-5
sprocket holes, on paper tape, 24
St. Cloud, 90
St. Paul, 136
St. Peter, 162
stage directions, treatment of in a concordance, 62
Standard Chinese Telegraph Codes, 21
standard deviation, 124-5
Stanford, 168
starting a project, 220-8
stationery, 26-7
Statistics: calculation of, 123-8; misuse of, 140; produced by OXEYE, 114
STATUS, 217
stemmata, 156-60
step search, 213
stop list, 199
storage of data, 195
stress, use of in metre, 176
Stupples, P., 81
Stuttgart Water Board, 217
style: analysis of, 122-41; definitions of, 122
stylistic analysis, general hints, 129-30
substitution, error in OCR work, 33
sum of squares, 125
Survey of English Dialects, 93

Swedish: frequency count of, 81; lemmatisation of, 101-2
Swift, 130
syntactic analysis, 106-8; for style, 130
syntax: analysis of, 106-8; in Old English, 107; using a concordance for, 49

tape, magnetic, 27-9
tape deck, 27
tape reader, 25
teaching: of languages, 79; of Russian, 105
technical characteristics, of magnetic tapes, 225
technical specifications, of magnetic tape, 28
technical text, 79; machine translation of, 117
telephone, use of for linking computers, 30
teletype, 30
Tennyson, 114
terminating character, 190
text archives, 225-6
texts, oral, 156
thematic analysis, 84-5
THEME, 85
thesaurus, 210, 214
Thesaurus Linguae Graecae, 226
T.L.F., *see* Trésor de la Langue Française
tokens, 79
Tollenaere, Felicien de, 15, 71
Toronto, 71, 226
track; on magnetic tape, 28; 7-track, 28; 9-track, 28
tracks, on paper tape, 24
Trésor de la Langue Française, 15, 69, 226
tribrach, 180
Truculentus, 181
truncation, of search terms, 214
Turkish, frequency counts of, 81-2
type/token ratio, 83
types, 79
typesetting, 118, 163
typesetting, 210; by computer, 34-6; of a dictionary, 75; program, 35
typing, reduction of, 190-2

UK MARC, 194
Ule, L. A., 135
undeciphered scripts, 69
UNIMARC, 194
University College, Cardiff, 96
updating of files, 195-7
upper case, 19
user identifier, 220
username, 220

variable length field, 189-90
variance, 125; calculation of, 129
variant readings, 144; problems of large numbers, 161-2
variation, measure of, 124-5
VDU, 30
Ventris, Michael, 69
verifier, for punched cards, 22
verse, collation of, 144-9
verse ictus, 181
Victorian Periodicals, Wellesley Index to, 211
visual display unit, 30
vocabulary distribution, 129
vocabulary study, in stylistic analysis, 133
Volny, 185

Wagstaffe, 132
Waite, Stephen V.F., 180-1, 183, 186, 225
Wake, W.C., 136
Wallace, David L., 16, 134
Waterloo, 227; University of, 163
Webster, 73
Wellesley Index to Victorian Periodicals, 211
Welsh, phonetics of dialects, 96
Welsh Language Research Unit, 96
Wesselius, Jacqueline, 90
Weston, 96
Wickmann, Dieter, 140
Widmann, R.L., 148-9, 155
Williams, F., 135
Wisbey, R.A., 15, 33, 63
Wishart, David, 186
Wolff, Al, 81
word, unit of computer storage, 13
word accent, 179
word association, 90-1
word boundary, 179
word conflation, 104
word endings, generation of, 105
word frequency count, 79
word frequency profile, 79
word index, 15
word length, 122; in Greek prose style, 140
word stress, 181
Wordsworth, 114
Wright N.B., 171, 172
write permit ring, 27-8

Yule, George Udny, 79
Yule's K, 79

Z-score, 86-8
Zarri, G.P., 159-60, 163